The Best American Spiritual Writing 2007

The Best American
Spiritual Writing™ 2007

EDITED BY *Philip Zaleski*

INTRODUCTION BY *Harvey Cox*

HOUGHTON MIFFLIN COMPANY

BOSTON • NEW YORK 2007

www.houghtonmifflinbooks.com

ISSN 1555-7820
ISBN-13: 978-0-618-83333-7   ISBN-10: 0-618-83333-1
ISBN-13: 978-0-618-83346-7 (pbk.)   ISBN-10: 0-618-83346-3 (pbk.)

Printed in the United States of America

MP 10 9 8 7 6 5 4 3 2 1

Contents

Foreword

Is ANY DREAM more enticing than that of the magic book, the hidden parchment, the cryptic message charged with seraphic fire, discovered through chance or providence, in a forgotten library corridor or a cobwebbed attic, a treasure compacted of word and spirit that will, when one succumbs to its incantatory power, transform life for good or ill? Variants of this myth haunt the history of literature. Consider the fourteenth-century legend of Nicolas Flamel, bookseller and alchemist, whose metamorphosis from clerk to mage began when he stumbled across a volume of mysterious equations and coded phrases, authored by "Abraham the Jew, Prince, Priest, Levite, Astrologer, and Philosopher." For twenty-one years Flamel and his wife, Perenelle, labored to decipher the text and carry to fruition its cryptic recipes. Success, the story tells us, came on April 25, 1382, when the long-suffering couple transmuted half a pound of mercury into gold, thereby affirming the existence of the philosopher's stone. With the wealth thus accrued they endowed churches, hospitals, and poorhouses throughout Paris and became, five centuries later, literary fodder for the creator of Harry Potter (both Mr. and Mrs. Flamel make brief appearances in J. K. Rowling's first book). Nicolas's tombstone, retailing his hermetic triumphs, rests today in the Musée de Cluny on Paris's Left Bank, where it invites the skepticism of tourists and the adulation of acolytes.

The story of Nicolas Flamel strikes us now — as it did many of his contemporaries — as an engaging fable with just enough verisimilitude (grave marker, charitable foundations) to give it a whiff of reality. The dream of the magical text, as this tale demonstrates, straddles both fact and fiction. We find it in the lucid nightmares of Borges, the theosophical visions of Balzac, the mythic voyages of Verne, the otherworldly fantasies of Lewis (whose *Voyage of the Dawn Treader* offers not only a magical text but a magical painting), and, if we sat through the entire series, perhaps half a dozen *Twilight Zone* episodes. But like most potent archetypes, that of the magical book has its counterparts — sometimes a wan simulacrum, sometimes a version brighter and more intense than the original — in real life as well. How often has a sinner made a volte-face toward sanctity after hearing a passage that conveyed, through its very syntax, grammar, and vocabulary, the elixir of transformation? Thus St. Anthony entered the desert to do battle with demons after overhearing verses from Matthew's gospel, while a text from St. Paul sent the anonymous protagonist of *The Way of the Pilgrim* on an epic trek across Russia to unearth the secret of constant prayer. C. S. Lewis's life forked when on a whim he purchased from a railroad bookrack a worn copy of George MacDonald's *Phantastes* and encountered for the first time that literary quality he later defined as "holiness." I know a man who spent seventeen years in an esoteric religious movement after chancing upon a stained, well-thumbed book during an overnight visit to Boston. A parallel event led the young Stanley Kunitz to become a poet and, in time, United States poet laureate. As a Harvard undergraduate, wandering in the stacks of Harvard's Widener Library, Kunitz reached up for a now-forgotten volume and knocked down instead Robert Bridges's pioneering edition of the poems of Gerard Manley Hopkins. He opened the book, which had just been released, and Hopkins's sprung rhythms opened to him the world of poetry.

These Aladdin's lamps come in a rainbow of forms: a cheap paperback bought at Goodwill, a treasure map, a message in a bottle, an illuminated manuscript, a last will and testament, an inscription in a ring, a love letter found in the snow. They possess, too, multiple aims: to delight, scold, instruct, titillate, amuse, frighten, or inspire. What sets them apart is their unexpected advent and their magical influence. Paolo and Francesca fly forever through the black tempests of *Inferno*'s second circle as punishment for adultery occasioned by reading a chance passage in a romance about Lancelot. Mysterious words on a shard of pottery (beautifully depicted in a fold-out illustration in my well-read copy of the first edition) that fall into the possession of the narrator of H. Rider Haggard's *She* lead to the most grandiose mythic adventure in Victorian fiction. In like manner — the late nineteenth century loved such breaches in its well-corseted ways — an encoded message on a plumb bob found in a hunk of Icelandic lava points, in Verne's dreamlike fable, to the center of the earth.

What characteristics do these magical texts share? First, they must be obscure. A well-known book is rarely a surprise, if one assumes a well-rounded education (perhaps one assumption too many in this era of infinite distraction). An essential aspect of the kind of text under discussion is its mystery, its residue of terra incognita, the dust on its ancient binding an echo of the dust raised by every trek into the unknown. There may be great reward in one's first look at *Hamlet* or *The Cloud of Unknowing*, but this is not the sort of discovery I mean. The books I have in mind rarely or never appear in a university syllabus or, for that matter, in the paperback racks at the local supermarket. As Flamel's tale suggests, there is something mysterious — a hint of enchantment or kismet — about these treasures. When one finds one, no matter how mundane the circumstances, suddenly one's room becomes seventeenth-century Prague, the text itself an athanor, and the received message the philosopher's stone.

This hint of the marvelous points to another quality shared by almost all of our examples. They deal in the spirit, directly or glancingly; they offer an unexpected word that opens an unforeseen pathway in the soul. What responsibilities and joys this places upon us, as parents, lovers, friends! Lucky the child who finds under his pillow his first book by L. M. Boston or BB; lucky the spouse who receives on Valentine's Day some verse by Arnaut Daniel or Basavanna. Lucky anyone who dredges up, from the primordial depths of the public library's discard bin, an unknown book that communicates insight and joy. All discoveries like these mark us in some way, and in some way they remake the world. Precisely at this moment, reading becomes a spiritual discipline, a way inward and upward.

Below is a list of twenty books, arranged by publication date, that have offered me the kind of serendipitous delight I have just described. It is my sincere wish that one or two of these titles may confer upon you a similar reward. In keeping with the strictures mentioned above, all these texts qualify as spiritual writing, most are obscure, and many are out of print.

Thomas Traherne, *Centuries of Meditation*, 166?. Seventeenth-century prose poems, miraculously discovered in a London bookstall in 1896 and first published in 1908, describing the author's rhapsodic early years, when heaven kissed earth with every breath.

Novalis, *Henry von Ofterdingen*, 1802. A romance, unfinished at Novalis's death, recounting the search for a blue flower glimpsed in a dream. A work of impeccable purity and beauty.

Alexander Carmichael, *Carmina Gadelica*, 1900–1971. A noble, mad production, a six-volume work displaying the fruit of Carmichael's decades of tramping in the Scottish Highlands and islands, where he collected aboriginal blessings, hymns, chants, incantations, and runes. Rumor has it that Carmichael polished the raw material, which lessens its value as folklore but helped to elevate it into a glory of Gaelic literature.

Amy Murray, *Father Allen's Island*, 1920. A specialist in Celtic harp travels to the Outer Hebrides, where she falls in love with the austere landscape and befriends Allen MacDonald, the saintly Catholic priest, poet, and folklorist. Nonfiction with "elemental music," as Padraic Colum describes it, in every sentence.

Mrs. Sinclair Stevenson, *The Rites of the Twice-Born*, 1920. Meticulous and comprehensive description of Brahmanical rituals, observed in situ by a sympathetic outsider with an eye for beauty.

David Lindsay, *The Haunted Woman*, 1922. Fantasy, by the author of *A Voyage to Arcturus,* about a house that confers higher consciousness upon its visitors. An exquisite presentation of the dangers and rewards of the interior life.

Roger Pater, *Mystic Voices*, 1923. Sweet, sometimes profound tales about the peculiar psychic gift of clairaudience, or prophetic hearing, written under a pseudonym by Benedictine monk Dom Roger Huddleston. *My Cousin Philip* (1924), Huddleston's fictional biography of the protagonist of *Mystic Voices,* is even rarer and equally appealing.

Greville MacDonald, *George MacDonald and His Wife*, 1924. A long, loving biography of the creator of modern mythic fantasy and his wife, written by their devoted son.

T. F. Powys, *Mr. Weston's Good Wine*, 1927. Mystical fable about how God comes to earth to distribute his good wine of death to the inhabitants of the small British village of Folly Dawn.

Friedrich von Hügel, *Letters from Baron Friedrich von Hügel to a Niece,*

1928. Tender, passionate letters about the Christian faith from a prominent Catholic philosopher and scholar of mysticism to his young niece. Published posthumously.

George Seaver, *The Faith of Edward Wilson,* 1948. The inner world of Edward Wilson, naturalist and explorer, who perished with Sir Robert Scott on the doomed 1910–12 Terra Nova expedition to the South Pole. A vivid portrait of a Christian mystic who found the signature of God in icebergs and penguin's eggs.

René Daumal, *Mount Analogue,* 1952. Novel by a young French surrealist about the ascent of a mythical mountain that joins heaven and earth. Unfinished at the time of Daumal's death in 1944 and perhaps the more provocative for it. Thrilling and comic.

Jacques Lusseyran, *And There Was Light,* 1953. Deeply moving autobiography of a blind Frenchman who became a resistance leader during World War II, survived a concentration camp, and made of his blindness a heavenly gift.

Eleanor Cameron, Mushroom Planet series, 1954–67. *The Wonderful Flight to the Mushroom Planet, Stowaway to the Mushroom Planet, Mr. Bass's Planetoid, A Mystery for Mr. Bass,* and *Time and Mr. Bass.* Children's books drenched with a sense of wonder both mystical and scientific, about an invisible planetoid, swirling with green mists and ruled by the splendidly robed and serenely semi-divine Ta, that circles Earth inside the orbit of the moon. Only the first two books in the series remain in print.

Dame Felicitas Corrigan, *In a Great Tradition,* 1956. Elegant account of the friendship between playwright George Bernard Shaw, museum curator Sir Sydney Cockerell, and Benedictine abbess Dame Laurentia McLachlan. A beautiful exposition of the unifying power of the contemplative life.

Agehananda Bharati, *The Ochre Robe,* 1962. Autobiography of an Austrian who traveled to India to become a Hindu monk. Brilliant, colorful, and idiosyncratic.

François de Sainte-Marie, *The Photo Album of St. Thérèse of Lisieux,* 1962. Haunting images of the great French saint laundering, cooking, praying, dying. How often do we see photographs of sanctity in action?

Leslie C. Peltier, *Starlight Nights,* 1965. Autobiography of America's greatest amateur astronomer, a lovely evocation of rural Ohio in the early decades of the twentieth century, and a plea for the purity and beauty of the heavens.

Tom Neale, *An Island to Oneself,* 1966. Firsthand account of how and why a thoughtful, good-humored New Zealander spent more than twenty years by himself on a South Pacific desert island. A delightful exploration of the mystery of the mundane.

Valentin Tomberg, *Meditations on the Tarot,* 1985. Introduction by Hans Urs von Balthasar. A magisterial study of Christian esotericism, in the guise of ruminations on the twenty-two major arcana of the Tarot. A book like no other; strange, profound, often inspiring.

Happy hunting!

As always, submissions are encouraged for future volumes of this series. Only essays and poems previously published in an American periodical are eligible. Please send submissions, with a self-addressed stamped envelope, to Philip Zaleski, 138 Elm Street, Smith College, Northampton, MA 01063. The best way for a magazine or journal to ensure that its contents will be read and considered for future volumes is to add the Best American Spiritual Writing series, at the above address, to its subscription list.

I would like to thank all who contributed to this year's volume, especially Professor Harvey Cox; all the great folks at Houghton Mifflin, including Anton Mueller, Susanna Brougham, and Nicole Angeloro; my terrific agents, Kim Witherspoon and David Forrer of Inkwell Management; and, as always, my beloved Carol, John, and Andy, who have imbued the text of my life with magic beyond measure.

PHILIP ZALESKI

Introduction

THERE IT IS, right before me: sometimes inviting, sometimes mystifying, sometimes terrifying. Sometimes I dive into it with gusto, and things seem to blossom and flow. Sometimes it baffles and resists my most heroic exertions. Most often, however, it is just a matter of plodding ahead, pausing, going back, trying again.

But what is "it"?

That blank page! Be it a yellow legal pad of the kind on which I used to do all my writing, or the light blue tinted screen of the word processor now before me, or the back of a crumpled envelope I pull out on the subway so I can scratch out a fleeting thought: there it is, inescapable, featureless, refusing to divulge any of its secrets.

Well, is writing more like prayer, or more like life itself, or a little like both? I am not sure. They all seem remarkably akin to me. They all *exact* something from us, but it is hard — maybe impossible — to know in advance what that something is. My wife, Nina, an eloquent writer, has a little sign on her desk. It says: "Writing is easy. You just sit and stare at the blank page until the drops of blood form on your brow." Those who remember the gospel account of Jesus in the Garden of Gethsemane, however, know that when the drops of blood formed on his brow, he was not writing. He was trying to pray. He was facing the biggest crisis of his life, and he was trying, if at all possible, not to go ahead with what seemed to lie before him.

Writing, prayer, life: they meld and fuse for me, although if I had to choose, I would surely dispense with the writing before the other two. But so far I have not been required to make that choice, so it is hard to think of any one of them without the other two peeping in from the wings. Consequently, I have come to think of writing as a kind of spiritual discipline. Linger with me awhile as I try to explain why.

A spiritual discipline is something you engage in on a regular basis, and you do it whether you feel like it or not. Of course, prayer can be spontaneous, and some of the most heartfelt prayers are: "God, please get me out of this!" "Please make it stop hurting!" "Thank you for this dazzling day." Some prayers may be traditional ones, even written in books. These were the ones my very low church Baptist parents disdained ("*Pray?* Out of a *book?*"). But I no longer share their disdain since gradually, and to my surprise, some of these oldies but goodies, like the ones in the Book of Common Prayer, now speak for me, despite centuries of repetition. After all, does *Hamlet* or Mozart's Requiem become less powerful because it has been around awhile? Besides, when we pray a prayer that has been around a long time, we sense that we are praying with a lot of company, past and present, and often that company feels very good.

But the *discipline* in spiritual discipline kicks in, I have learned, when spontaneity slumbers, and traditional prayers begin to sound like what my parents, and many like them, said they were: "vain repetitions." You need discipline when the skies turn leaden, when God is absent, when no desire for communion with the great mystery claws inside, when no birds sing. You need it when what St. John of the Cross called "the dark night of the soul" smothers you and when you have begun to wonder whether the light will ever again appear.

I have never written a book without suffering through the writer's equivalent of the "dark night of the soul," that ghastly moment — or hour, day, week, or more — when *nothing comes to mind.* This paralysis has crept over me during the writing of every book from *The Secular City* to *When Jesus Came to Harvard.* What to do? Good writers I know tell me that when they feel stalled (as we all do sometimes), they just start writing, anything, even "Well here I sit and can't get started writing." I find that a good tactic. Usually something then begins to come to mind. But not always. Then what?

When St. Jerome tried to write in the desert, he was assailed by demonic visions, sometimes — it is reported — of beautiful, scant-ily clad women. When Martin Luther was trying to translate the Bi-ble in his cold chamber in Wartburg castle, the devil reviled him from across the room, so he hurled an inkpot at Old Harry. I think what these wonderful stories tell us is that when we are treading wa-ter in the dark night of writer's block, the biggest danger we face is distractions. I know that is true with me. Mine are — alas — not as colorful as Luther's or St. Jerome's, but when I am in such a state it is terribly easy to get distracted. What to do?

I don't think the inkwell strategy is a good one. It just isn't useful to try to drive the distractions away. That just empowers them. One of the most valuable things I learned from Trungpa Rinpoche at Naropa was that when I am meditating and stray thoughts pop in, as they always do, *notice* them. Do not follow them or try to expel them. Just watch them with the aloof attitude of a detached ob-server watching flotsam float by under a bridge. It took me a while to develop this skill, but eventually it helped me to be less dis-tracted by the distractions. Treated gently, they lose their power to befuddle us. On a more terrestrial level, it also helps sometimes to take a trip to the bathroom, drink a glass of water, do a couple of stretches. Sometimes, when I've done that, then return to my desk, the stream of flotsam has moved on.

This is a point at which prayer and writing almost exactly coin-cide. Maybe I am too verbal, but if I mumble something similar to the blocked writer's mantra, it often helps. "Well, God, if you are really out there or in there, here I sit with nothing much to say." It sounds vacuous, and it undoubtedly is, but if God hears the prayers of both the verbose and the stammering, I am sure God also hears the prayers of the vacuous.

I use "prayer" here in a broad sense. It includes speaking; the "groaning" that St. Paul speaks about, in his Epistle to the Romans; sitting in (sometimes sullen) silence; raging; listening; and much more. Let's start with the speaking. My first rule is this: it does not have to be eloquent, or even coherent. Martin Buber some-where tells the story of a Hasidic rebbe who was becoming discour-aged because the prayers of his congregation seemed flat. They sprawled, inert and bloodless, just over the heads of his people and never rose to the heavens. Then one day he noticed a poor shep-herd who always stood in the back of the synagogue and never joined in the prayers. Was he the problem? Eventually the rebbe asked him why he never said the prayers. Shifting from one foot to the other, the shepherd confessed that he could not read and could say only the first few letters of the Hebrew alphabet. The rabbi's heart was touched. He said, "Then just pray those letters, and God will understand." So the shepherd prayed, "Aleph, beth, gimmel . . ." Suddenly, the prayers of the whole congregation began to soar up to the divine throne. The point of this story, and of St. Paul's words about "groaning," is that God does not require good grammar or even comprehensibility. The Pentecostals know this; so do the Quakers.

Did I also say "raging"? Yes, I did. But is that an appropriate thing to do in prayer? Well, just read the Psalms. They are mostly prayers, and they include literally hundreds of curses and imprecations, some of them quite imaginative, aimed at the enemies of Israel. The Hebrews seemed amused at the idea, for example, that their enemies would "fall into their own traps." Sometimes, in a less sardonic mood, they called upon God simply to destroy their adversaries, including the women, the children, and the livestock. Spiritualize the Psalms as we do, nonetheless they brim and seethe with volcanic anger. What is going on here?

Anger is a part of being human. It is also a part of being God, although scripture assures us that God's wrath does not last forever. It was also part of the repertory of Jesus' emotions. Remember that unfortunate fig tree, and the sharpies selling pigeons in the Temple courtyard? But why bother God with our anger?

It is true that we say God is one from whom "no secrets are hid," so presumably God already knows when we are at a slow boil. But I think God wants us to know about our anger too because often we do not, at least consciously. Does God want us to share all our thoughts and feelings with him, even the nasty, questionable, and socially improper ones? I think the answer is yes. He is the one who "maketh the wrath of man to praise him." Women too. Some years ago a friend of mine found herself suddenly abandoned by her husband of many years. At first, good Christian that she was, she tried nobly to "understand" him, to put herself in his place. But she still woke up in the middle of the night with a pounding headache, grinding her teeth. After a while she talked candidly with her spiritual counselor. He urged her to spend a few minutes each day reading the most rancorous, hard-edged Psalms. She did, and little by little it helped her get through the jungle and avoid expensive dental work. She has since told me she now believes that tidying up prayers so as to censor our rage and resentment really amounts to a kind of distrust of God. I think she is right.

Only in recent years have I learned that prayer can be simply listening, and that listening itself can be a spiritual discipline. I learned this from the Buddhists when I spent a couple of summers teaching (and learning) at the Naropa Institute in Boulder, Colorado. It was headed by Chögyam Trungpa Rinpoche, who had acquired a reputation as both an inspired teacher and something of a rogue. He was indeed both, but what was critical at Naropa was "the practice," as they called it, which involved hours and hours of sitting, watching your breath, and paying attention to what was going on inside. One of the great ironies of my life, incidentally, was that the fellow faculty member who gave me my first instruction in this Vajrayana (Tibetan) style of "sitting" was Allen Ginsberg, who at that time was head of the poetry department. Maybe I should write an article someday on how the author of "Howl" taught me to meditate.

At first I found the silent sitting practice — awkwardly perched cross-legged on a cushion — virtually unendurable. But gradually I learned to watch and listen — without judgment — to what was galloping through my mind. The next step was to listen more carefully to everything around me, even when I was not on the cushion, to "tune in," in Timothy Leary's phrase, but in a very different way. After that I discovered something I should have known before, that there is a long tradition of listening prayer in Christian spirituality. Nowadays I find I often listen more than I speak. "Be still," the Bible says, "and know that I am God," or more colloquially, "Shut up and listen; let your creator get a word in."

Writing demands an awful lot of listening. If you are trying to learn something from people, you have to listen to them and stifle the impulse to think about what you are going to say next. If you are writing fiction, something I would love to do but so far cannot, you have to listen carefully to how people say things, to their pace and tone. If you are writing poetry, you learn to listen to the music of words. Whatever you are writing, some form of disciplined listening is utterly essential.

I invite the reader to peruse the following pages not just as fine writing, which much of it surely is, but also as a series of examples of spiritual discipline. The writers represented in this volume are a varied lot. Their approaches to spirituality differ greatly, but they have one thing in common. They all write, or they would not be included in these pages. Some may have pondered the relationship between writing and spirituality, and some perhaps have not. It really doesn't matter that much. There is a danger that we can sometimes take either our writing or our spiritual disciplines too seriously. We can distort and even smother them if we become too self-conscious about them. Like dancing or swimming or riding a bike, both are at their best when they become habitual. Still, even then, there will inevitably be times when we will sweat blood. If Jesus himself did not avoid it, why should we?

HARVEY COX

The Best American
Spiritual Writing 2007

DICK ALLEN

"And All Shall Be Well; And All Shall Be Well; And All Manner of Thing Shall Be Well"

FROM *The Hudson Review*

And you shall be lost in Tinker Toys and spices.
And alongside the garden walls of old computers,
women will walk in long pale dresses, scattering roses,
men shall lie down beside their work,
arms thrown across it.
And all shall be well. And the sins of our fathers
shall be as boulders and fruit flies on an Idaho morning.
You shall read Yeats's poems
in lieu of prayer, whispering the lines
as quietly as you might paint each raindrop
in a landscape of cedars or a watercolor of plum blossoms.
And all shall be well. And evil
will blow itself up a thousand miles from Dakar
with no one to pronounce "Ginnie Mae" or "Rumpelstiltskin"
or "Martyr, Martyr, ring around the martyr."
You shall not fear, you shall confound the world
with absolute kindness and forgiveness,
and with the right ear of a turkey in the straw,
and one of those 120-count boxes of Crayola crayons:
Bittersweet, Cornflower, Maize,
Periwinkle, Prussian Blue,
Thistle, Sunglow, Denim,

Timberwolf, Tumbleweed, Fern,
Outer Space, Shadow.
And as did the Harmoniums in the Caves of Mercury,
you shall recite, *"Here I am. Here I am. Here I am,"*
and you shall be answered,
"So glad you are. So glad you are. So glad you are."
And you shall gaze upon a hazelnut
and know that in the palm of your hand
is all that is made
and you are created, you are loved, you are sustained
by iambs and anapests, by Julian of Norwich,
by the black-and-white chickadee that just now came to my
    window.
And despite insult and spittle and disfiguring and bruising
    and lingering pain,
all shall be well;
and all manner of thing shall be well.

DORE ASHTON

On Constantin Brancusi

FROM *Raritan*

I BEGIN WITH a fable, curiously tided "The Story of Brigands," written by Brancusi sometime before 1925, when it was published in *This Quarter* magazine:

> Long ago — very, very, very long ago, when men didn't know how animals come into the world . . . One day in those days, a man found a chicken incubating her eggs. And since in those days animals and men understood each other, he asked her what she was doing. And since the chicken was nice — because in those days animals had a lot of respect for men — Ah! much, much, much more than now — she got up in order not to leave a man standing, and went to him to explain. And she explained for a long time, a long time, so that when she returned to her eggs, they were already spoiled.
>
> That is why in our time chickens who are sitting on their eggs are angry enough to spit in our eye!

The moral of this story is obvious: it is that artists take a dim view of explanations, and often have to defend themselves from the stupidities of their commentators. Picasso, for example, when pestered by critics about the influence of African sculpture on his work, answered, *"L'art nègre? Connais pas"* (African art? Never heard of it).

By the time Brancusi jotted down his fable, he had had ample experience with pests wanting explanations, and some experience with interpretations that enraged him. I think that his profound respect for intuition and his conviction that, as he wrote on one of his scribbled notes, "When one is in the sphere of the beautiful, no explanations are needed," are fundamental to our understanding of his work. What is more, all explanations seem gratuitous when in the presence of his best works.

Yet even Brancusi had recourse to words, which are, after all, necessary for explanation. Far from being the unlettered, divinely inspired peasant he was imagined to be by some of his critics, he listened attentively to the words of his early friends such as Guillaume Apollinaire, and read the works of others. When, for instance, his sculpture *Princess X* was attacked for obscenity, he angrily explained — yes, explained — that his endeavor could be compared to Goethe's principle of the Eternal Feminine. Not, certainly, an unsophisticated remark.

Just as Brancusi's oeuvre is complex, varied, and far more experimental than is usually granted, he himself had a complicated temperament. In the often oversimplified history of post–World War I artistic trends, two quite opposing strands of thought and feeling are usually discerned: a new preoccupation with classicism, and a new preoccupation with all that is not classic — all that is explosive, antirational, and even corrosive. Brancusi was already a prominent personage, and was seen by many, such as the British aesthetician Clive Bell in 1926, to be "as pure an artist as Bach or Poussin." But there was a powerful impulse toward iconoclasm in Brancusi. He was a vigorous contestant in a fateful game, and he knew the value of what the French call *drôle de type* (strange type) — eccentric challengers of just about all received ideas. His closest friends comprised a procession of outspoken droll types. When the Dada movement arrived in Paris in the person of Tristan Tzara, who was a fellow Romanian, Brancusi was quick to respond, even saying in one of his fragments of writing underneath a drawing on the Socrates theme, "Dada will bring us the things of our time." Tzara was a frequent visitor, and sent little notes to Brancusi's address in the Impasse Ronsin, signing himself "Tzara with open eyes." Brancusi was also friendly with Blaise Cendrars, another rollicking writer, full of tall tales, and, of course, with the arch-exception, Marcel Duchamp. One of his oddest friendships was with the very young iconoclast, Cocteau's protégé Raymond Radiguet, whose rebelliousness was paradoxical: he attacked what he called *"le conformisme anti-conformiste"* (the conformism of anticonformists). Brancusi was himself no stranger to paradox. In one of his notes he referred to forms that were "relatively absolute."

Brancusi's attraction to these *drôles de type* does not cancel his own proclivity for idealism, or principle. An anecdote related by Mlle. Pogany, who had posed for Brancusi for almost two months during the winter of 1910, illustrates this point. There were occasions when Brancusi created a clay bust so admirable that she implored him to keep it. But, she wrote, "he only laughed and threw it back into the boxful of clay that stood in the corner of the studio." Eventually, Brancusi completed Mlle. Pogany's portrait in several variations and materials spanning twenty years of meditation, beginning perhaps with *Muse* (1912). I take it he was seeking not the likeness of her face but the principle — the idea at the very origin of identity. Principle is finally a mysterious combination of faith and reason.

One of Brancusi's most fruitful associations with a notable eccentric was his close friendship with composer Erik Satie, also, finally, a man of principle, a faithful adherent to Plato's theory of ideal forms. Brancusi enjoyed his conversations with Satie, a unique man whose everyday banter was always amusing. Brancusi used to quote him laughingly, as when he disparaged snobbism and officialdom in the art world: "Getting the Légion d'Honneur means nothing in itself. The main thing is not to deserve it."

But that was only one side of their relationship. The other, and far more significant, was the meeting of similar spirits. Satie, beneath his banter, was a profoundly searching spirit who had taken upon himself the task of purging music of all but its innermost form. His admirer, Jean Cocteau, in his 1918 essay on modern music, "Le Coq et l'Arlequin," wrote that Satie "cleans, simplifies, and strips rhythm naked." The following year, Brancusi and Satie were introduced and saw a great deal of each other, as each was working around the figure of Socrates. Satie's Platonism can be found in his remark to himself: "Do not forget that melody is the Idea, the contour, just as much as it is the form and content of the work." In his comments on Satie's *Socrate*, Roger Shattuck says: "The aesthetic of *Socrate* is one of chaste, unembellished subordination of music to text . . . one note to each syllable." He sees it as Satie's "approach to immobility and repetitiousness." *Socrate*, I imagine, is Satie's expression of the principle of infinity, just as the various Mlle. Pogany portraits can be seen formally as infinity signs. Amid jokes and banter, both Satie and Brancusi were seriously engaged in symbolizing the figure of Socrates. As early as 1917, Brancusi had carved a symbolic cup and placed it atop one of his endless columns and, with the

Child sculpture, called it a "mobile group." By 1922, he had photo-
graphed his sculpture *Socrate* surmounted by his cup, presumably
of poison. Brancusi's cup, like all of his works, can be perceived
from many points of view, and can serve as a vessel of his concerns.
It is a fundamental form derived from the geometric imagination
at work in many of his pieces: a half sphere, in which the challenge
to a sculptor resides in its equilibrium as it touches the ground only
at a single point. At the same time, since it is carved in wood, it is
Brancusi's acknowledgment of an organic essence with its own
weight and grain. It also suggests something of the normal func-
tion of the cup, as we know from Brancusi's letter to John Quinn,
inviting him to accept the cup as a gift to keep in his dining room.
For Brancusi, the cup metamorphosed from a homely adornment
for a rich man's dining room to a grave philosophic metaphor.

Socrate is hewn rather roughly from wood, and we know from
Isamu Noguchi that Brancusi knew wood intimately, and that when
he wielded his ax he could "come down heavily, exposing with its
sharpness the grain as though polished." We can see the gesture in
Socrate, where Brancusi cuts deep and sure, and in which the circular hollow is visibly hewn to reveal the grain. In one of his notes to
himself, Brancusi characterized *Socrate,* saying "The whole universe
flows through. Nothing escapes the great thinker." The notion of
flowing is caught in the circular void, but also in the grain of the
wood.

Brancusi had a long history with wood, since he came from a
place where wood was abundant and where carving was a rural pastime. But he had also begun his training in an Arts and Crafts
school where handling wood, for furniture and decorative purposes, was part of the curriculum. After that, he had a perfectly academic training, where he learned how to model clay for bronze
casting, and, probably even before he arrived in Paris in 1904, was
familiar with Rodin's ideas, by that time widely broadcast in Europe. It is often said that from the beginning he rejected Rodin
(even though he spent an entire month as Rodin's assistant in
Meudon before he struck out on his own). But Rodin, looking back
to Michelangelo, spoke of form emerging. That is, drawn by the
artist from the rough block, exposing the duality of art and craft,
nature and culture. Brancusi tried his hand at this method in *Sleep*
(1908), said to be his first direct carving in marble. He had clearly

derived an important lesson from Rodin: the form is within the block and the artist must reveal it. Brancusi's aesthetic was not, in fact, so far from Rodin's. It was Rodin, after all, who said, "Each profile is actually the outer evidence of the interior mass; each is the perceptible surface of a deep section from which the final surface emanated."

Naturally, since Brancusi had his own point of view, his search for the inner structure in each piece of wood or marble would arrive at a very different place. If you look at many statements by both painters and sculptors from around 1905 to World War II, you will find in the French a certain word constantly repeated: the word *dépouillier,* which means "to strip, to lay bare." Brancusi obviously set about stripping bare, stripping down to essential forms, soon after he arrived in Paris. He early expressed his contempt for certain nineteenth-century habits of modeling, especially in clay, and reserved great disdain for Michelangelo, and, at times, Rodin, calling their works *biftek.* For instance, in an interview in London, in 1925, he said, "Michelangelo's sculpture is nothing but muscle, beefsteak; beefsteak run amok." According to Noguchi, Brancusi used the word *biftek* frequently to refer to sculptors he didn't like and their work. We can assume, then, that hardness — a fundamental characteristic of wood and stone — was, as a matter of principle, something with which he could contend. And he was contentious.

Brancusi liked to begin at the beginning — as he said, he placed himself within nature and sought to experience, through nature's creations such as wood and stone, the metamorphosis within each material. We know from his many photographs of his studios that he treasured great timbers and great blocks of stone. What commentators tend to forget is that the process of creating an image, a sculpture, begins with the quest outside of the studio. Both Brancusi and his admirer Noguchi visited quarries and timber yards. The initial act is not the cut, but the choosing. The divining. A stone sculptor, for example, tries to divine the inner crystals and veins as he gazes at a block of stone or a quarry wall. A wood sculptor does the same, divining the direction of the wood grain and its irregular patterns. And all this, they never forget, has been wrought by nature — by winds and waters and climate. Time. Furthermore, they think with their hands, that is, their tools. The heft of a tool and the sharpness of a blade are always with them. As they

gaze at the virgin block of timber, they bring an almost visceral cal-
culation with them. Brancusi made his own tools for good reason.
The point for him was that these substances — limestone, marble,
cherry, oak — have a past. For artists as for writers the past is essential and, above all, alive. As Hannah Arendt so often said, quoting
William Faulkner: "The past is never dead. It is not even past." So
for Brancusi the process was to reveal, and in so doing, make visually poetic metaphors. The question became for him: how much
could be condensed to create a vital image?

The partial answer can be visually assessed in the sequence of
torsos in marble, revealing in every sense. Each torso is a summary,
a distillation. The earliest suggests Rodin's adaptation of ancient
Greek fragments in marble about which the poet Rilke was so eloquent. Meditating on Rodin's achievement, Rilke wrote: "The object is definite, the art object must be even more definite: with-
drawn from all chance, removed from all obscurity, lifted out of
time and given to space, it has become lasting, capable of eternity.
The model *seems,* the art object *is.* " Rilke exhorted himself, "Somehow I too must manage to make things . . . realities that proceed
from handwork. Somehow I, too, must discover the smallest basic
element, the cell of my art." Later, he would say of Cézanne and his
idea of realization: "The convincing quality, the becoming a thing;
the reality heightened into the indestructible through his own experience of the object." I cite these lines by a consummate poet because I think Brancusi's way of creating is closely related. Like
the poet, he was searching for the ideal form that is definitively
removed from all chance and, in its infinite reduction, or what
Matisse used to call distillation, becomes a new metaphor. A very
difficult idea, I'm afraid, and not given to easy explanation. When
Samuel Beckett wrote about his master, James Joyce, he said that
Joyce's writing "is not about something. It is the thing itself."

The earliest stone torsos were somewhat about something, but
his *Torso of a Young Girl,* carved a decade later, *is* something, something complete within itself. For this wonderful sculpture, Brancusi
chose a kind of stone with special properties. Onyx is a crystalline
stone, whose inner facets of light — the light that the crystal ema-
nates — glimmer and, when polished judiciously, have the glow of
life itself as exemplified by the elements — skin and curves — perceived in the persona of a young girl. Brancusi has succeeded in re-

ducing her features to the quality of roundness, the Idea of roundness — breasts, buttocks, and belly subsumed in a perfection of
curvingness, and skin itself becoming light from within, and without. His accomplice is matter, the stone itself, which is why, I sup-
pose, sculptors often refer to *living* stone.

The decision to elicit both the life and the Idea of life can be en-
acted only by perseverance, a signal quality in Brancusi. In the
same period as the torsos of the young girl, he carved from veined
marble *Young Bird,* again conflating several essential characteristics
of his subject to reveal its fundamental character. (The word *character* comes from the ancient act of incising, or cutting a figure in a
clay tablet — cutting *into* to make a sign.) There is the sound quality: *Young Bird* has a sheared plane symbolizing a cry — as we know
from earlier marble characterizations of the newborn human in-
fant — and it has the general form of birdness, that is, the rounded
breast that the nineteenth-century writer Michelet admired, saying
that the bird is the only creature that creates its environment — its
curved nest — with the action of its breast. A hollow echo, or an
echoing hollow, in fact; or, a metaphor. To accent the bird's smallness, its infancy, Brancusi builds a complicated and bulky base so
that we are presented with the fragile creature at eye level, but
peripherally we are aware of the concreteness, even the earth-
boundness, of the bird's environment. Another good example of
Brancusi's diligent search for the most telling characteristic is his
carving *Torso of a Young Boy,* which is an admirable abstraction from
a fact of nature — a piece of wood with its branching members —
and a commentary on specific youthfulness: the lean erect torso
and limbs of an adolescent, straight as a plumb line, irreducible in
space. The Idea of a boy.

But we must not carry the idea of Idea too far. Brancusi's knowledge of the history of sculpture was ample, and, as a youth in the
academy, he had copied the head of the famous *Laocoön.* The gesture of torment, head cringing into the shoulder, appeared in
Brancusi's own early characterizations called *Torment,* which metamorphosed into ovals slightly canting toward a base. The idea of
torment took many forms subsequently, and appeared in a sculpture he pointedly titled *Prometheus.* We have an amusing account by
James Johnson Sweeney, a friend and connoisseur of Brancusi, who
was struck with his first vision of *Prometheus:*

I saw no evident link between it [the sculpture], and the Fire Bringer or his eagle. On looking into the classical dictionary, I found that his mother was Clymene the Oceanid. Immediately I felt on track: here, a marble head, almost featureless, that of a child born in the sea, washed up in the shingle. But when I asked Brancusi, he explained simply that it was the head of suffering Prometheus. "If it is properly set you see how it falls on his shoulder as the eagle devoured his liver."

There is an important phrase here: *if properly set*. We always talk about sculpture in the round, and how we must perceive it from many angles while walking around the object, and how sculpture creates and is created by space, and so on. But Brancusi talked about how his work must be properly set: in other words, there is an ideal viewing point from which the Idea of the form becomes self-evident.

For instance, while the *'Young Bird* was set on a weighty base — its relative condition as a fledgling not yet able to fly emphasized by the full roundness and weight meeting the limestone plinth — the many versions of *Bird in Space* (perhaps his best-known work) were always set on smallish bases to emphasize the vertical soaring motion of the sculpture. As Brancusi said in the catalogue of the 1933 Brummer exhibition in New York, it was "a project of a bird, that once it is enlarged, will fill the sky." In other statements, he didn't say "sky," but "vault of heaven," lending an almost architectural quality to his ambition. As is repeatedly pointed out, Brancusi perceived these many attempts to arrive at the optimal shape of a flying creature as attempts to embody the sensation of flying in matter. Matter is respected, but by the act of carving and polishing, will be transcended. When Brancusi was still hopeful about realizing his project for the Maharajah of Indore in the early 1930s — the first of his total projects that envisioned both sculptural and architectural elements — he wrote to the Maharajah: "My *Birds* are a series of different objects on a central unchanging theme. The ideal realization of this theme would be an enlarged work filling the vault of the sky . . . The more I've succeeded in ridding myself of myself, the closer I've gotten to it." Many art historians have mentioned Brancusi's attraction to Buddhism, and particularly the Tibetan monk Milarepa, whom he read attentively. Unquestionably the "central theme" Brancusi referred to can be considered from a spiritual point of view — that is, the desire to transcend earthly

concerns. But the phrase "ridding myself of myself" expresses a desire familiar to many artists. There are numerous testimonies to
an experience of self-transcendence among artists who have tried
to explain the creative process. There comes a moment in the
struggle to give form to feeling when the intense absorption in
the task works to set the artist free, to bring him beyond his self.
Brancusi always craved that experience, and I think his perseverance — that is, his returning again and again to a central unchanging theme — was a quest for the ideal moment of freedom, freedom from the necessity imposed by gravity, from velleities of daily
life, from the indeterminate. Soaring, after all, is the essence of
freedom. Brancusi's recourse to metaphor is always related to this
quest. In one of his written notes he said of himself: "Like a light
object that one puts into the deep ocean, I have had to make my
way up like a blind man, not knowing why and struggling against all
currents and obstacles to reach the surface." In relation to the
birds in space, we have evidence offered by Noguchi, who, when he
entered Brancusi's studio as a dedicated apprentice, was witness to
the masters making plaster replicas from stone birds, then sending
them to be cast after having worked the plaster, and then beginning once again to polish the castings to make entirely new objects.
This may be an example of what Brancusi meant when he said he
struggled against all currents and obstacles.

There is yet another bird that Brancusi sought to characterize,
only this bird, the Gallic cock, is known to us through synthesis: it is
not the bird itself that rises but his cry, a sound become thing. Each
time Brancusi fashioned this vivid symbol, often in carved plaster
in his studio, the sound was offered in variations, much as Satie's
single sounds are multiplied into musical composition, or melody
in which slight modulations are the sole indication of its finally melodic and composed character. The forest of plaster cocks seen in
so many of Brancusi's own photographs of his studio is a haunting
reminder of Brancusi's ability to orchestrate his own environment.
In them the senses are alerted to the musical properties or the
rhythms implicit in his life's work. Those triangular cuts, marching
up triumphantly, sound into the sky. In the studio photography of
around 1945 or 1946, they arise above, and their rhythms are repeated, probably not accidentally, in the triangular cuts and ridges
of the magnificent wood sculpture *King of Kings*. I could always

hear the clatter of primitive washboard music on the king's torso. And as for the cocks, Brancusi's fellow artist, Jean Arp, wrote a little verse about them that quite perfectly covers the subject, beginning with the lines

> The cock crowed co-co-rico and each
> Sound made a zig or a zag in his neck.

We know from the numerous biographies that Brancusi loved music, had once built a violin for himself, had a huge collection of records of folk music from all over the world, including spirituals recorded in the United States, and, according to anecdote, played duets with his friend Satie. Noguchi described a phonograph that Brancusi had built for himself with the novel feature of two arms. More important, perhaps, is the historical fact that the word *musicality*, from the days of Delacroix, had entered the lexicon of visual art to designate a tendency toward abstraction. I have no doubt that Brancusi hearkened to an inner rhythm as he worked, as fundamental as the fact that each person walks in an idiosyncratic rhythm, and that folk dances, which Brancusi was said to have relished performing, spring from organic responses as simple as the beat of the heart. This difficult issue of rhythm has to do with Brancusi's work techniques and with his idealism. When he was working on his wood version of *Endless Column,* the box frame saw was thrust back and forth in a definite rhythm; otherwise, it would not have functioned well for him. And his act of polishing a bronze casting of one of his birds also had its rhythms, as Noguchi's suggestive words tell us: "The long file had to go its full length, curving over its roundness."

The most apparent use of rhythm is of course in the motif that has accumulated the most commentary — *Endless Column.* In this absolute, or perhaps Brancusi would have said, comparatively absolute, conception, the erect chain of polyhedrons, meant to pierce the vault of the heavens, has incited many musical comparisons. Brancusi himself referred to his column as a "song." Perhaps "hymn" is the right word, for in the ensemble at Tirgu Jiu there are symbolic relationships that call upon a philosophic schema of the universe and its center, in which the column climbing upward becomes an *axis mundi.* "The endless column" Brancusi wrote, "is like a timeless song that lifts us into infinity."

This timeless song inspired many sculptors in the twentieth century. The earliest significant tribute was written by the British sculptor Barbara Hepworth who, after a visit to Brancusi's studio in 1932, wrote:

> The quiet, earthbound shapes of human heads or elliptical fish, soaring forms of birds, or the great eternal column of wood, emphasized the complete unity of form and material . . . I think Brancusi's understanding of these timeless elements in sculpture is very close to Stravinsky's understanding of rhythm.

I'm sure Hepworth had in mind the thumping rhythms of *The Rite of Spring*, at whose 1913 premiere Brancusi might very well have been present. Satie's rhythms, although a hundred times lighter than Stravinsky's, were also organized on a similar plane. I can well understand why curator Carmen Gimenez organized her thoughts around the principle of musicality. In her introductory essay in the catalogue for a Brancusi exhibition at the Guggenheim Museum, Gimenez says "his sculpture extends like an unending melodic line," and, in an inspired simile, speaks of how "each piece occupies both its own place and projects itself by means of its aura as an animated 'ghost sonata.'" She was talking about a visual phenomenon that patinaed sculptural surfaces isolate, and that, to use Paul Klee's phrase, makes the invisible visible.

I turn now to a different kind of specialist — sculptors who have reported on their tremendous experience of Brancusi's masterwork, the ensemble at Tirgu Jiu. The late Christopher Wilmarth, a major twentieth-century American sculptor who even as a student revered Brancusi, made a special pilgrimage to Romania in 1974 to see the masterpiece with his own eyes. He went, he told me, in order to see "a true place." He said that *Endless Column* was the greatest public sculpture in existence, pointing out that "it is never the same in any light; it changes constantly; it seems to penetrate the sky." It is, Wilmarth said, an "ascension piece" and "quivers like the image of a spirit." In his own early work, it is clear that the geometric elements in Brancusi's work, such as the half-sphere and the circle, were carefully assessed, and their simplicity captured in the first of his wood-and-glass wall pieces. Later, some five years after the voyage to Romania, Wilmarth was still pondering Brancusi's principles and methods and effects, when he embarked on a remarkable project: the illumination of the sonnets of Mallarmé. There, the predominant image is an ovoid shape, often an emblem of the human visage. In the glass-and-bronze relief, *When Winter on Forgotten Woods Moves Somber,* the oval is pierced with an inner oval, much as *Socrate*'s head was an opening through which the universe flowed. In another in this series, *Insert Myself Within Your Story,* the luminescent oval is both suspended and perforated by a dark steel rectangular element, invoking dualities that are omnipresent in Brancusi's work as well: hard and soft, dark and light, material and ethereal. Wilmarth's intense preoccupation with making a "place," a true place, as in the case of Brancusi, led him to make many experiments with series of works. These he always exhibited with great care so that the viewer, the vertical person, felt englobed by an ideal space. For him, the way his works were "set," to use Brancusi's term, was always of signal importance.

The other specialist is the still living and remarkable sculptor William Tucker, who also made a pilgrimage to Tirgu Jiu around 1972, and reported on the experience at length in his book *Early Modern Sculpture.* Although Tucker's writings on Brancusi are, so to speak, objective — that is, he is evaluating Brancusi as a major twentieth-century sculptor in a historical context — he cannot conceal his awe, his immense emotional response to *Endless Column,* and declares finally that "If there is one piece in the history of modern sculpture which in every respect deserves the title 'masterpiece,' it is surely the Tirgu Jiu *Endless Column.* " His observations about the column are consonant with those of many others who have marveled at the perceptual transformations Brancusi anticipates — how in a certain light, the elements appear to be a fully modeled spiral, or in another light, a pure vertical plumb line, or, in still another, a series of ellipses.

But I imagine Tucker's response was tempered by his earliest investigations of Brancusi, while still a student. He would have paged through the books and seen the dramatic photographs of the earliest *Endless Column* in the garden of the photographer Steichen — a great hewn tree-trunk that Brancusi transformed — and later photographs of the many trial columns, with differing numbers of elements, and also hewn in wood by the master's own hand. Photographs of Impasse Ronsin, often reproduced, show Brancusi hoarding house timbers to be worked eventually — great, trued lengths of wood, sometimes retrieved from demolitions, sometimes from lumberyards.

When I first visited Tucker, before he settled in the United States and while he was working in London, I saw his narrow garden timbers, tarred and weathered, clearly retrieved from long-ago demolitions. After his return from Romania, Tucker did a remarkable series of sculptures derived from heavy oaken timbers, *Portraits of K* and *House* in 1975, and, six years later, the powerful *House of the Hanged Man*. Aside from an oblique allusion to Cézanne (and some commentators have likened Brancusi's work to Cézanne's), there is an oblique allusion to Brancusi in the notched interior members and the illusion induced by an irregular geometric conformation. The long side of the triangle sweeps up from a certain angle and continues beyond the crest. Then, there is a mysteriousness that does not lend itself to easy explanation, just as there is in Brancusi's oeuvre. These continuities in art history exist, and are mysteries, phantoms.

Even the repetitions in Brancusi, which some critics have thought to have inspired so-called minimalists such as Donald Judd, have served in markedly different ways the two specialists, Tucker and Wilmarth, who to my mind are Brancusi's true heirs. Cocteau had written, with Stravinsky in mind, that the same chord, often repeated, is less fatiguing to the ear than the frequent repetitions of a single gesture are to the eye. To which the composer Ned Rorem replied: "Yes, but is the same chord really the same, since each repetition occurs within a constantly shifting, asymmetrical rhythm, and the chord's 'meaning' shifts accordingly?" This, I think, sums up *Endless Column*'s meaning — the repeated elements, having been modeled before casting, would have been bound to have slight shifts in meaning — and sums up its enduring, miraculous presence in our own time.

FRED BAHNSON

Climbing the Sphinx

FROM *Fugue*

DRIVING WEST FROM Bozeman an hour before dawn, Hans and I leave the Gallatin Valley's fifty-mile-long inland sea of grain. We contour along the Madison River where I took float trips as a child, make the long climb up Ennis Pass, and drop into the remote Ennis Valley. I've spent most of my life in southwestern Montana. The mountains here are my old friends. As we drive, a group of them, Lone Mountain and the Spanish Peaks, rises to our east in greeting. South of these pyramids lies their silent watchman — and our climbing goal — the Sphinx. To reach the Sphinx we drive down the Ennis Valley, which, come summer, will swarm with hordes of East Coasters, Californians, and Texans, most arriving in RVs, descending like a plague upon the cheap diners and rubber-toma-hawk shops. But it's winter now. The shops are closed, the motor-ing public gone. All that remains is a comforting emptiness that broods over the bent world of mountain and valley like the Holy Ghost.

We turn east off Highway 287 onto a snow-drifted dirt road that leads to the trailhead at Bear Creek Ranger Station. A five-mile hike from here will bring us to our route: the Sphinx's North Face. When I get out of the car the single-digit cold jabs my nos-trils. We stuff our packs with eiderdown parkas — hedges against hypothermia if we're forced to bivouac — and swill the last of our coffee.

Winter has come early this year. It's only mid-November, and al-ready Hans and I have a month of ice climbs under our harnesses. Our tri-weekly forays into Hyalite Canyon, our training ground, have made us lean and strong. We're ready for the Sphinx. Alex

Lowe, Bozeman's local ice-climbing hero and world-renowned alpinist, claimed the first ascent back in 1987, and it was he who recommended the route to us. Known for his "sandbagging" — the old alpinist penchant for understatement — Alex described the Sphinx as "a nice day outing."

The Sphinx is aptly named: rising over eleven thousand feet above sea level, nearly two thousand of those above the valley floor, this mountain is a geologic version of that mythical creature, and one in full dominion of its landscape. Rock-buttress arms reach outward on either side. A torso of snowfields and rock cliffs supports a head forever hidden in shadow. The face itself — some five hundred feet tall and twice as wide — is concave, like an imploded wall. In winter the face is plastered with skinny drips and seeps of ice, some spilling off the summit snowfield, others emerging from cracks in the rock. Our route will follow a narrow couloir, an ice-choked gully that vertically bisects the face into roughly equal halves.

We're traveling light. *Less Is More* is our credo. Last night at my house we played our minimalist game, took all our gear — ropes, carabiners, ice screws, pitons — and laid it out on the floor. We divided that pile in half, divided the remainder in half again, and behold — our gear selection.

I close the trunk, zip the keys into my pack lid, and look up to see if Hans is ready. He's holding up the rope, eyebrows forming a question.

"We'd better bring it," I say. "For backup." Hans's perennial Scandinavian composure sags a hair, his "disappointed" look. "We can still solo it," I tell him. "I'll carry the rope." This route has never been soloed — climbed without a rope — and Hans is drawn to the untried methods, the purity of *less is more.*

Hans sets off at a fast clip. When I shoulder my pack a wave of nausea sends the coffee-bagel-cream-cheese concoction to the base of my throat. I always get queasy before a big climb. I'm eager to get going yet reluctant to leave the security of the valley. When we drove through Ennis an hour earlier, the town was still asleep. Those people will soon be waking up, stoking wood stoves, frying eggs, cradling coffee mugs. Part of me wants to be among them, among warm, sleepy-eyed souls instead of nursing my pre-climb nausea, instead of slogging up to the Sphinx.

*

I was several pints of Full Sail into a keg party in Bozeman one December night when Hans introduced himself. A wiry five feet eight inches, Hans sported the ubiquitous trio of Bozeman Outdoor Guy apparel: ponytail, bead necklace, and Carhartts. Though we both went to Bozeman Senior High School, we didn't know each other. I was eking by Year Five at Montana State and hoping not to make it Year Six. Hans, three years my senior, had just returned from Yale where he'd "picked up" a philosophy degree, cum laude.

"Chess?" he asked, pointing to a table in an empty corner. The party was low-key, the women few: another Friday night gathering of climbers and skiers. Good night for chess. Five moves in, Hans asked, "Are you sure you want to move there?" It was a question I would hear in other chess games in the coming years, always asked without irony. Hans was politely giving me a chance to change course before disaster struck. It never made a difference, though. Except for once, Hans always won.

The talk quickly moved to skiing then to climbing, where it stayed. Though already a superb skier, Hans admitted that he wasn't yet a climber but said he wanted to be. He let on that he was looking for a "rope gun" — somebody with enough experience to take the "sharp end" of the rope, to lead the hard routes. Somebody who could teach him a few things. I had been ice climbing for four years, plenty of experience, in his mind. Would I be up for taking him climbing?

In the Bozeman outdoor scene, you simply didn't admit to inexperience. Whether you were a climber, skier, or bull rider, you padded your resumé. You didn't want to be known as a Greenhorn, an Eager Beaver looking to tag along with the Big Boys. Whether you were or weren't, you pretended at veteran status.

Hans either didn't know these unspoken rules or just didn't care. He wanted to climb. Earnest, and with clear-eyed candor, Hans proposed that I take him up to Hyalite the next day. I said yes, and a partnership was formed. From then until April, Hans and I racked up some fifty days together climbing Hyalite Canyon's frozen waterfalls. It wasn't long until I was calling him "rope gun."

With Hans walking ahead beyond earshot, I slip into musing. Often on forays into the hills, I become an eight-year-old again, entering the world of trolls, lost children, magic portals that lead to safety. Forests become dark, semi-human forms; the mountains morph into a band of ogres, hunched together in conference as they argue my fate. One shakes his white mantle to reveal part of a shoulder, another sloughs ice shards to reveal a bristly back. There's menace in these gestures, but also a beckoning. The soft crunch of my plastic boots breaking hoarfrost allays my anxieties. When our trail crosses an open meadow, we follow our moon shadows running ahead across the snow.

Those glossy inspirational posters hanging in dentist's offices have made *climbing-as-metaphor-for-life* a cliché. People talk about *reaching their personal peak,* or *climbing their own Everest.* "Climbing" is what it takes to become a CEO. But for Hans and me, climbing meant climbing mountains. Climbing *was* life. It determined the shape of our flatland existence. Career (as if we had careers), love life, social life — all these had to pass through the refiner's fire of climbing. The sole test for any given job or relationship was: can I still climb five days a week?

Hans's "career" involved working night shifts at Dana Design, sewing backpacks for minimum wage. Though his Yale degree could have earned him more lucrative work, Hans preferred to man the sewing machines from 4 to 10 P.M. with other downwardly mobile outdoor-sport addicts. I oscillated between seasonal jobs: climbing-store clerk, UPS helper at Christmastime, traveling maid-cart repairman — anything to pay rent and fund climbing trips.

We never talked about it, but we wanted to see how far up — and in — climbing would take us. The passage upward was a passage *through,* a vertical portal into Meaning. The harder the route, the greater the transcendence. The vertical plane offered pure existence, an airy liminality where, with each swing of our ice axes, earthly constraints fell away. We believed that somewhere on one of those vertical faces — perhaps the Sphinx? — lay the answer to the Great Wanting.

I didn't stay the course. After climbing up mountains that promised me bliss, I retreated, rappelled back into the world before climbing could make its ultimate demand on my life.

For Hans, climbing was complete.

Midmorning under a gray sky we reach the Helmet-Sphinx col, a saddle between the Sphinx and Helmet Mountain. From the col we'll descend a few hundred feet then begin the climb up the

Sphinx's North Face. We stop for water and a quick bite of a Power
Bar. Even though the temperature hovers in the teens, we're both
overheated from the five-mile hike. We shed fleece layers and stow
them in our packs . . . A snow flurry kicks up then subsides.

After a five-minute rest we descend the backside of the col and
follow a contour line through knee-deep snow to the mountain's
north side. One minute we're in trees, the next we're standing at
the first rock band: the beginning of our route.

"The weather's looking iffy," I say, noticing a dark cloud bank
hanging over Ennis Valley to the west. Hans stares west for a time
then fixes his attention back on the route.

On the drive over from Bozeman that morning, the forecast
warned of a major low-pressure front moving east, sure to bring
storms. We'll need to move quickly. Now that we've left the safety of
the trees, I worry that a squall will trap us in a whiteout. I was
caught once in a storm above tree line. Everything became a blur
of snow and ice, my depth perception thrown. There were no trees
to offer shadow and contrast. I was nearly lost.

For the past week, though, we've had it good. A high-pressure
system spearing down from Canada has kept it clear and cold —
ideal weather for climbing. I love these high-pressure systems. While
they last, I get out. I climb mountains. I soak up all the sun and
warmth, camaraderie and good times I can, glorying in my freedom. High pressure is fleeting, though. Low pressure always seeps
its isothermal way back, bringing the dark, bone-aching cold days.

Hans eyes the western clouds again. "I think the squall will hold
off until we get up this thing," he says and starts breaking trail toward the first snowfield. I follow his tracks but hold on to my
doubts. Low pressure always returns.

The two months' snow accumulation slows us down. In some
places the snow is waist deep. It takes us nearly an hour to traverse a
section that should have taken ten minutes. Hans has been breaking trail the whole way, so I tell him I'll take a turn out front. When
I start off the snow pulls at my legs like a drowning swimmer, tugging me down with each forward step. A half-hour of slogging
through this thick soup and I entertain retreat. With conditions
like this we may not reach the summit before nightfall. We have
only a few Power Bars between us, not enough food for a bivouac.
We lack proper gear — sleeping bags, bivouac sacs, and the all-im-

portant stove to melt snow for drinking water. We'd be foolish to
risk a night in the open.

"Looks bleak," I say over my shoulder. I don't want to be the one
to say *this is leading nowhere.*

"I'll break trail again," Hans says. "If we can make it to that rock
band I think the snow will improve. Let's not give up this fast."

I soon discover he's right. We climb through a rock band, which
turns out to be a vertical choss-pile of rotten conglomerate — the
kind of thing Alex Lowe called "frozen kitty-litter" — and gain the
first of a succession of snowfields that lead to the upper face and
the couloir. The snow has turned from wet cement into a crunchy
Styrofoam. Small avalanches coming off the upper face have packed
these slopes into a firm layer of névé, ideal for climbing. We're in
the groove now, kicking crampons into the slope, swinging our
axes with verve.

We work steadily through midday, climbing the Sphinx's lower
slopes, and by noon we've reached the face. The crux of the route
— an eel-like sliver of ice spilling down a narrow scar midface —
lies before us. Stretching in either direction to our right and left
are hundreds of yards of rock, the Sphinx's weather-darkened
cheeks.

Five hours of daylight left. We shouldn't waste time, but we can't
help staring upward, wonder-struck beneath this frozen rampart.
In its 150-foot descent the ice-eel never gets wider than two body-
lengths; at its narrowest the ice is almost small enough to wrap my
arms around.

Up close the ice loses its serpentine features. It becomes one
form then morphs into another, refusing to take shape. In cold,
dry air, ice will sublimate, skipping the liquid phase to go directly
from solid to vapor. Forever in a state of *becoming,* ice is never
static. Whether forming or melting, this fluid newness holds me en-
thralled. Ice is like lava or fire — the longer you look, the more you
feel yourself on the cusp of revelation. To stare into this frozen
skein of light and shadow is to rub up against Mystery itself. By
spring, this ethereal architecture — a lone flying buttress supporting its cathedral in the sky — will be gone.

Before we start climbing, Hans takes a test swing. He tiptoes on
the front points of his crampons, crabs up the spray cone to the
base of the eel, and lands a blow with his ice ax. A deep bass note

tells us the ice is plastic — the climbing will be secure — and we decide to climb unroped. Hans climbs first and is soon fifteen feet up the initial ice curtain. His ax swings are smooth, unhurried. With a surprising lack of envy, I see that Hans has become the better climber. He is, as they say, a natural.

Ice climbing, unlike rock climbing, is possible only with equipment. In medieval times alpine shepherds used steel-pointed staffs and primitive foot spikes to cross icy passes. In the 1800s, tweed-bedecked Englishmen used the recently invented ice ax to chop steps on the lower-angled slopes around Mont Blanc in France. The early climbers used only one ice ax, but modern ice climbers, when climbing anything approaching vertical, require two. Crampons, the twelve-point spikes worn on the boots, provide purchase for the feet. Ascending vertical ice with modern gear is akin to climbing those pegboards in Fourth-Grade Gym except the holes aren't premade — you create them as you go. Each solid ax placement provides a portable anchor from which to make the next swing. "Never move on a bad placement," Alex Lowe once told us. "Each placement builds on the last; make sure every swing is bomber."

We plan to leapfrog each other, so when Hans reaches the midway point up the eel he stops, anchors himself to an ice screw, and waits for me to follow.

My muscles are stiff from cold when I begin climbing. First one tentative ax swing, then another, until I hear the telltale *thwok!* of a solid placement.

I kick in a crampon.

Swing an ax.

Breathe.

Repeat.

The old comfort of vertical orientation returns. I slip into flow.

Climbers build up a kinesthetic memory bank, a repertoire of patterns from among which the body will choose when it meets with difficulty. This corporeal knowledge instructs the limbs to pull the body over an impossibly steep overhang while the mind watches, as if from a distance. To give oneself over to this innate ability for a few seconds, minutes, even hours is to know, however briefly, a kind of bliss. A release from the burden of conscious thought.

Flow dissolves self-awareness. Gone are my flatland pedestrian worries about jobs and girlfriends — or the lack thereof. Gone my doubts and fears, even my joys and elations. Those feelings will return, all of them magnified, but in flow I just *am*. The problem with this, of course, is the same one that plagues the heroin addict: the longer I remain in bliss, the less I want to come back. I grieve when that feeling — or absence of feeling — leaves. So I search for it. And over time I build up a tolerance to it. To feed the rat, I up the fix. I push harder, climb steeper, less secure routes.

Climbing ropeless is flow distilled. To climb untethered, to set myself adrift on a sea of ice, is to achieve purity of form. Self-mastery. My life depends on the solidity of each ice ax placement, each crampon kick. The choices I make are entirely mine, and I become lord of my own universe.

I work my way past delicate flutings and chandeliers of ice, now fifty feet up the couloir. Whenever the angle eases off-vertical, I switch to the French-step position for my feet — instead of kicking straight in with my crampons, I stomp the ice at an angle with the flat part of my foot. The technique eases my burning calves.

In ten minutes I've reached Hans's perch at the halfway point. I move past him and continue up the final section of couloir. "Swinging leads," it's called in roped climbing. We mimic this pattern, climbing as though an imaginary lifeline linked us together.

The final section is as steep as the first — between seventy and ninety degrees — only more exposed. The whole north face drops away beneath my crampons, all fifteen hundred feet of it. I climb steadily, barely notice as twenty minutes slide by. Soon I pull over the vertical ice and stand at the base of the final gully that leads to the summit. I look back down the ice-choked couloir. The crux is over. I've come through the vertical gauntlet unscathed. A delicious shiver runs up my spine as I yell down, "Safe!"

I twist in two ice screws for an anchor, the foot-long hollow tubes disgorging their cores of ice onto my glove. Into the eye of each screw I clip a carabiner, tie off a bight of rope, and secure myself to the anchor. Hans begins to climb. The noise from his axes colliding into the ice is like the far-off sound of someone working their way down my street, methodically breaking windshields with a baseball bat.

Then amidst all the breaking ice I hear a different sound, metallic.

"Shit!" Hans yells. "It broke!"

"What?" I shout back. I heard him, but the gravity of what I think just happened fails to register.

He repeats his cry, this time louder and more insistent. "The pick broke on one of my axes. I can't move up or down."

"What do you want me to do?"

Hans is stuck on vertical ice with no rope, hanging on to his remaining ice ax. His only form of security, the only thing keeping him from a thousand-foot fall, is this one ax pick sunk three inches deep in ice. My mind flips through its Rolodex of rescue moves, but all the cards come up blank. He is sixty feet below, out of sight.

"Lower me one of your ice axes," Hans shouts.

I uncoil our nine-millimeter rope. Pulling out a two-foot bight, I tie that into a figure-eight knot, clip a carabiner to the bight, then clip the head of one of my ice axes onto the carabiner. I begin lowering. As I feed out rope the ax clangs against the ice.

Soon I hear a garbled cry, too faint to understand. "Did you get it?" I yell down. In the wind I hear nothing.

At this point, I assume that Hans has tied himself in to my rope. "On belay," I shout down. Still no response. I begin hauling in coils. He must be climbing fast, I think, because I don't feel any tension on the rope. I haul faster. Suddenly the end of the rope pops over the lip. The carabiner on my figure-eight knot chatters across the ice, empty. Hans got my ice ax, but he didn't tie himself in to the safety of the rope.

"What's going on?" I yell. No reply.

I try to lean over the couloir's lip, but I can't see him from my stance. The wind coming up from the valley brings only silence. Maybe he had trouble with the wrist leash on my ax. Maybe his good ax popped as he was putting on mine. These worries, then other worries, unspoken, coalesce in my head, then rattle into my gut like loose scree skittering down a talus slope.

I begin to shiver. I pull on my hood and zip it up until only my eyes are showing. I am alone and the reason for my aloneness is too appalling to admit. I am afraid.

Into that fear flows a succession of clear, rational thoughts devoid of emotional attachment:

Hans has fallen.

There is no need to rappel down to him.

No need to speed-hike out to the valley to call in a rescue.

The need for hurry is over.

I then observe in a distant sort of way that I can't feel my fingers. I swing my arms around and around until the hundreds of needles stabbing my fingers tell my brain that I have swung enough, that blood is returning life — and with life, a searing pain — to my digits. Warmed, I turn my face to the mountainside, my back to the wind. Hundreds of water rivulets are freezing around the eyes of my two anchor screws. For the longest time I watch, fascinated, as my anchor becomes entombed in ice.

I begin to hate the Sphinx. This cold, lifeless mountain has taken my friend. Hans is dead, and for what? Why am I risking my life for this? Why did Hans? Not just the Sphinx but the whole act of climbing now appears utterly absurd. I am strapped to a mountainside, helpless to aid my fallen friend. Hans has my second ice ax, my second arm; I can't move from my stance. It escapes me just what the hell I am doing here. I stomp my feet a few times, do more arm windmills. This climbing business, this search for flow, for spiritual meaning — isn't it just glorified selfishness? I think of our friend Rob Williams who died the year before while climbing in Peru. High-altitude pulmonary edema got him at twenty thousand feet. Rob literally drowned in his own lung fluids. Before he made his last climb Rob had traveled around Peru with his wife. It was their honeymoon. Where was Rob's wife now? How had she benefited from the risks he took?

A face appears over the lip.

Hans wears a grin like he's just dipped his hand in Fate's cookie jar and escaped unnoticed. Here is my friend returned to me, a veil of hoarfrost and frozen snot falling from his face, raised up like Lazarus.

Hans slogs up through the snow and clips into my anchor. He hasn't stopped grinning. Neither of us knows what to say. My anger at Hans's loss is replaced with stunned confusion. Still, we can't speak. Then Hans chuckles, and I can't help but join him. We let loose. Like a pack of coyotes, we yelp, whoop, and howl.

The head of Hans's ice ax broke where it met the shaft. He was stuck halfway up the final section of couloir. All he could do was hang on to his remaining ice ax while I lowered mine to him. With the replacement ax he set about finishing the climb. "I've never had such focus in my life," he said later, which is why he paid no attention to me yelling down to see if he was all right. Had he not the mental and physical stamina to dangle from his one good ice ax, had he tried to climb up or down, he would have fallen. In all the confusion I forgot to ask him why he never tied into the rope.

The last section of couloir leading to the summit snowfield is easy, and we climb side by side, chattering the whole way. Already the story is taking shape, the one we will tell over and over in the years to come: Hans's credentials as an alpinist are sealed. He now belongs to that elite cadre of climbers — Those Who've Escaped Death. I had already joined that club, dodging avalanches, lightning, hypothermia.

But now it's Hans who's returned from that distant shore, and I am the witness. I will be the one to corroborate Hans's tale, to tell the world that he was nearly lost but returned to life. On the final snowfield leading to the summit we climb with abandon. Our bodies move like twin skiffs riding the face of a wave, skimming a cobalt sea of ice into a welcoming sky.

When we finally stand atop the Sphinx's head, Hans strikes his classic Summit Pose — ice axes raised high, arms formed in a V for victory. His wide grin is not that of the conquering hero, not cocky. Just amazed to have passed through to the other side.

To the west the sun is almost buried under the Tobacco Root Mountains. This trip will end in the dark, with only the faint glimmer of our headlamps' glow to light the way. Twilight has fallen in the valleys, but our little summit is an island of light, the last tip of earth still sunlit. The squall is coming, moving toward us across the Ennis Valley. We'll get hit on the way down. But that doesn't worry us any longer. The biggest difficulties are over. At least for now. We linger on the summit, not wanting this day to end.

That night we ease down into a booth in a smoky pizza joint in Ennis and splurge on a large Hawaiian and a pitcher of Full Sail. We're too spent to finish the beer. On the drive back to Bozeman, Hans perks up, talks excitedly about the climb. He curses that broken ice ax, tells how he was scared shitless hanging off the Sphinx's face with no rope around his middle. I wonder if something happened to him as he dangled there, waiting for me to lower him a lifeline, some revelation about his purpose in this world. But if the Sphinx bestowed on him any distant visions, he doesn't say. I wish that I had asked.

We come down off Ennis Pass, drive past Bear Trap Hot Springs. The steam curling off the water reminds me of a guy I knew who drowned there one night after too many beers. We continue back along the now-moonlit Madison River, and Hans talks more about the climb. I keep silent. The highway's parallel yellow lines track my thoughts, as I return over and over to the near-accident. What could this mean for my life? I had one more notch on my climbing harness; I was a little wiser about how much trust to place in an ice ax; I had a wild story to tell; yet surely there was more. What that *more* is I can't say. I am still back on my airy perch high on the Sphinx, shuffling in my boots, doing arm windmills to keep warm, one of my best friends lying two thousand feet beneath me. In the space of ten minutes I had gone from wondering why Hans was taking so long, to believing him dead, to grieving his absence.

Now here he is, beside me in the passenger seat, alive as ever. But what if Hans really had died on the Sphinx? What would I have told his family, his girlfriend Helen? Would I pull out that old cliché: "he died doing what he loved"? That was the stock response of the Bozeman outdoor community when talking about a climber or skier who died in the mountains. That phrase always grated on me, though I never knew why. After climbing the Sphinx, I know. Not only is the phrase too facile; it is an Orwellian euphemism. It seeks to cover up an ugly truth about those of us who risk our lives in the mountains — that what we do is indefensibly selfish. What if one of these days on one of these peaks I get whacked? Would it be any comfort to my parents, to my brother, to my sister to hear those words, "Well, at least he died doing what he loved"?

We get back to Bozeman that night at 9:30 P.M. I drop Hans off at his place on Eighth and College, the little white house that shelters a rotating stream of climbers who need a room for a week, a month, several years.

"So, it's November. The road up to Hyalite won't be passable for much longer," Hans says. He's got a plan. "We'll have to start skiing in soon. Before the next big storm we should go hop on that mixed climb 'The Thrill Is Gone' — I heard it's in." He gets out of the car, reaches for his pack in the back seat.

The Thrill Is Gone. I think of the Sphinx, of that face scarred by eons of wind and storm. I see it staring north, guarding Lone Mountain and the Spanish Peaks, those lifeless pyramids of ice and stone. "'The Thrill is Gone.' Yeah."

"How about this Saturday? Give us time to rest up. Pick me up at seven?"

"I don't know, man. I just don't know."

We still climbed together the rest of that winter, Hans and I, and on into the summer. But I found that I climbed more out of momentum than desire. When high up on some peak or frozen waterfall, I felt something important was passing me by, like I was a traveler who had already missed several trains and couldn't afford to miss the next one. I came to think that God was on one of those trains and that perhaps I had better get on one and see if it would take me somewhere that climbing hadn't.

And so I left. I left Bozeman, the mountains, my climbing friends, Hans. The minimalist game — divide the pile in half, divide the remainder in half again — was no longer one I could play. Or rather, I played it too well. I shed all my gear. I left everything.

I tried to explain this to Hans. Over a Colombo's pesto pie and a pitcher of Full Sail, our now-ritualized postclimb meal that had assumed a near-sacramental significance, I tried to tell him. "Climbing's just not doing it for me," I said. My search was a spiritual one, I explained, which explained nothing. *Spiritual* — I thought. That word's too vague to mean anything. It gained no traction on what was missing, or on why climbing left me feeling hollow. I said something about how climbing was a quest, a seeking after something greater than myself. It was God I sought when I went to the mountains, and I wasn't finding him there. Perhaps the problem was climbing — the unnecessary risks it involved, the selfishness of my pursuit. I was like Ahab in reverse: my motive and object were sane; it was my means that were mad. I couldn't explain all this to Hans. But I think he knew. He had seen my enthusiasm wane.

"Why go to divinity school, though?" he asked.

"I'm not sure," I said, and that was true. It wasn't like I had received "the call." More like gentle tugs that became a magnetic pull toward Something I could neither explain nor comprehend. I tried out a line I'd read from Augustine: "*Fides quarens intellectum* — faith seeking understanding. That's the most I know," I said. It's still the most I know.

As I retreated from the mountains Hans headed further into them, giving his life over more completely to climbing. He climbed bigger, more difficult routes. In the storm of his youth, he made expeditions to the world's great ranges: the Peruvian Andes, the Tibetan Himalaya, the Ellsworth Mountains of Antarctica. Hans not only climbed these mountains — he began skiing them; on terrain where most would want a rope, Hans was pointing his boards downhill and letting them run. He sought the pristine chutes, the never-before-skied couloirs. Years after we climbed it, Hans would return with a friend and ski the North Face of the Sphinx.

It was on one of these First Descent skiing expeditions — September 1999, the beginning of my second year at divinity school — that Alex Lowe was killed. He was hit by an avalanche on the lower slopes of Shishapangma, a remote peak in Tibet. Hans was with Alex on that trip. He watched as Alex was buried beneath several tons of ice and snow, where he lies to this day.

And then on May 10, 2001, an avalanche hit me. It was an avalanche of words, left on my answering machine by Hans's girlfriend, Helen, words that quickly buried me beneath their weight, their finality: *Hans, Chamonix, accident.*

Between sobs Helen told me the story that I would come to hear many times in the coming weeks: Hans had been skiing the Gervasutti Couloir on Mont Blanc du Tacul in Chamonix, France, when he hit a patch of ice. He fell fifteen hundred feet down the sixty-degree couloir, suffering massive trauma. A helicopter swept him off the mountain, but his injuries proved too severe. He died en route to Geneva. He was thirty years old.

What did the mountains give, or fail to give?

"The mountains are life-giving," Alex used to say, and so they are. From the mountains comes a welling up of deep-down things, a profound sense of life's inherent majesty. Among mountains my thoughts bend toward eternity.

But the Sphinx and her pyramids had become idols. Their loosening grip on me was being supplanted by the unshakable grip of God. Augustine said that our hearts are restless until they find rest in God, but my Great Wanting was not so much a wanting to find as a wanting to be found.

When the apostle Paul arrived in Athens, he climbed Mars Hill. On the summit, in the Areopagus, he encountered a group of Athenians. He told these Athenians that earlier, while touring their

city, he had found an altar bearing the inscription TO AN UN-
KNOWN GOD. You may not know it, Paul told them, but it's really
God that you worship, the God who created the world and everything in it, who gives to mortals life and breath and all things. You
will search for God, and perhaps grope for him and find him —
the One in whom we live and move and have our being. You will
search, Paul said with surely a trace of irony, though indeed he is
not far from each one of us.

I don't climb much anymore. I have a lovely wife, a six-month-old
son, a church community to whom I'm accountable. I know my
presence among them all is cherished, that I'm depended upon.
My life is no longer my own.

Still, I wonder this: when I was climbing in flow, when my ego was
gone, when I found my body moving in sync with gravity, weather,
rock, and ice, were not my climbs small acts of worship, one creature's hymn of praise to his Creator, to a God unknown?

Before we leave the Sphinx, Hans and I take in our last aerial
view. The oblique rays of a dying winter's evening skip across Lone
Mountain and the Spanish Peaks to the north, little arrows of fire
touching down, igniting a snow cornice, a rocky arête. So lovely
this created earth, this world of mountains. Before the sun drops
behind the Tobacco Roots, there is still time to bask in the orange
light, time enough for its warmth to seep into our stiff joints, time
to revel in the glory of it all. Here on the Sphinx's summit we are
still innocent of what's to come. We can't yet trace the arc our un-
claimed lives will follow.

In the fading alpenglow as Hans and I linger on our airy perch, I
watch our shadows glide down the mountain. Their giants' arms
reach, spread over, and embrace the darkening valley. Like expec-
tant children our shadows tarry on the slope, waiting for our tired
bodies. For all must return together when we leave this warm, well-
lighted summit, when we begin making our way back toward home.

ROBERT BLY

The Head of Barley

FROM *The American Poetry Review*

I don't know if you've ever met a head of barley
In late August, protected by its spiky beards.
It sticks to your clothes from pure faithfulness.

When a farm girl picks up a Leghorn feather
And waves it in an empty barn, the storm it
Raises is as subtle as the wind of faithfulness.

The last maple leaf hanging in its tree against
The blue sky is like that angel who brought
His wing-tips in near Mary's faithfulness.

The sitar player keeps track of twelve notes
For each raga, five up and seven down. Even
With twelve brides, he maintains faithfulness.

You know a needle sticks up for itself; it's
Not a generous thing, but joining with the hand,
It starts out on the road to faithfulness.

It's hard to know what to say about the marvels
Inside the soul. Even those of us who have broken
Many promises can still hope for faithfulness.

JOSEPH BOTTUM

Christmas in New York

FROM *First Things*

THERE WAS A WOMAN screaming on Park Avenue, flecks of saliva spraying from her mouth as she raged into her cell phone, "It's not my fault." Over and over, like the high-pitched squeal of a power saw cutting bricks: *It's not my fault* and a run of foul names, *It's not my fault* and another run of names, *It's not my fault,* you *(blank)ing (blank). It's not my fault, you evil (blank). It's . . . not . . . my . . . fault.*

I don't know, maybe, whatever it was, it really wasn't her fault. But her cell phone and makeup, her dark purse and blue coat, her warm leather gloves — the accoutrements of sanity around that face of public madness — made her seem guilty, somehow. Guilty of *something,* down to the bone. The man at the Salvation Army kettle kept his tense back turned against her as he rang his Christmas bell. The crowds of passing strangers fixed their eyes at uncomfortable angles and hurried by. A child stared anxiously till his mother began chattering about breakfast, overbright and overloud as she tugged him around the corner.

I saw the screaming woman for a moment framed by the giant candy canes and white Christmas garlands soaped on the window of the storefront behind her. Then the traffic light changed, and I crossed the street, my shoulders hunched in self-protection. *It's not my fault, you evil (blank). It's . . . not . . . my . . . fault.*

Is twice a warning or only a coincidence? For I heard the phrase again that same day in the vestibule of the bank after work. New York is still one of the world's great Christmas towns. Too dirty for too long to clean up well just for the holidays, Manhattan still makes a brave show for the season. The shop-window mannequins sport their Christmas finery, and the railings on the apartment buildings don their strings of lights and tinsel. Maybe movies — from *Miracle on 34th Street* on down — are what have made New York's Christmases seem so iconic: the ice skating at Rockefeller Center, the skimpy elf costumes on the strutting Rockettes at Radio City, the sleigh bells on the horse cabs, the piles of toys at FAO Schwarz, the window displays at Lord & Taylor. But at least, as a result, New York still tries. There in the bank, while I waited in line for an automatic-teller machine, I watched the city's shoppers hurrying past, their arms full of Christmas packages, and listened to a man talking loudly on his cell phone, one foot up on the windowsill.

"It's not my fault," he explained in a confident boom. "I'm just the kind of person who has to keep after things." What is it about self-justification that always makes it seem so false? About that phrase "I'm the kind of person" that always makes it sound like the beginning of a lie? He was well dressed in loafers and slacks, a nice overcoat, and seemingly indifferent to the fact that the people at the ATMs could overhear him. With the effortless patter of a story told many times before — with the sort of smooth charm, in fact, that fails because it announces too openly just how charming it is trying to be — he launched into a long tale about how he didn't really want to sue, but then he was the kind of person who needed to see that he got his rights, and it wasn't his fault everything got so messed up.

It's not my fault — the cry we've made every day since Adam took the apple. Down somewhere in the belly, there's an awareness of just how wrong the world is, how fallen and broken and incomplete. This is the guilty knowledge, the failure of innocence, against which we snarl and rage: That's just the way things are; there's nothing I can do; I wasn't the one who started the fight; it's not my fault. What would genuine innocence look like if it ever came into the world? I know the answer my faith calls me to believe: like a child born in a cattle shed. But to understand why that is an answer, to see it clearly, we are also compelled to know our guilt for the world, to feel it all the way to the bottom.

I sometimes wonder to whom all the city's cell-phone talkers are speaking. People all around them, thousands and thousands: *there,* that angry balding man slamming past in his stained parka, and *there,* that coatless woman with the deliberately unfocused stare smokers wear as they stand with their arms crossed outside restaurants, and *there,* that tired-looking girl in the sweater trying to stop a taxi, and *there,* and *there,* and *there* — an endless stream of presence, and still they shout or murmur on the street, pouring secrets and imprecations into their clenched phones and throat microphones. Talking to the ones who aren't there. Communing with the absent, like fortunetellers with a crystal ball. Like mediums calling the dead.

Sometimes New York hints at something different. There is a strange impression the city gives after a snowstorm — a kind of epiphanic feeling, a sense of being taken for a moment out of time. People walk in the middle of the street. A few pull out their skis and slalom down First Avenue. The taxis all disappear, and for a moment the whitewashed city looks clean and small-townish.

But New York cannot play for long at being the New Jerusalem. The ultimate time-bound place, it cannot step outside the rush and rattle of commerce. The supreme City of Man, it cannot pose as the City of God. With their town bright and almost pretty, New Yorkers act for a few moments as though things have changed — or rather, as though these few moments don't count, as though the apocalypse of falling snow has lifted them out of time and the storm had left them for an instant clean and unhurried. Last winter, I saw an old-fashioned toboggan — ten or twelve feet long, the wooden slats curling to a two-foot swoosh in front — being drawn along 14th Street, filled with laughing children. Who has room to store a toboggan in Manhattan on the off-chance of snow? Someone, clearly. Someone who has been waiting years for the white apocalypse.

But most Christmases, there are only cold drizzles, the icy rain that never seems to wash anything clean. I emptied my pockets on the way home from the bank: another Salvation Army kettle, a drunk man on the sidewalk with a hand-lettered sign I couldn't read, a woman rattling change in a paper cup. I hate the city, all tarted up in its tawdry Christmas clothes. Mewing us together on its streets, it forces us to see the human stain. It forces us to know. *It's not my fault,* I muttered as I blew on my cold hands. May God have mercy on us all. *It's . . . not . . . my . . . fault.*

ERIC COHEN

The Ends of Science

FROM *First Things*

WHENEVER I MEET WITH SCIENTISTS, I'm always struck by
their optimism — and their discontent.

Mostly they are optimists, excited by the latest findings: the newly
isolated gene variant that may help explain schizophrenia, the new
telescopic images that reveal the violent births of distant galax-
ies, the geochemical discoveries that may change our understanding of Earth's formation. Armed with an endless array of Power-
Point slides, the optimists believe they are uncovering life's secrets
slice by slice, defining humanity's place in the universe, making
life better through their mastery of nature's mechanisms. Knowledge through experiment, progress through reason: They have no
doubt they are on the right side of history.

And yet, at the same time, many of these scientists seem frustrated and unhappy. Some are furious because policymakers are ig-
noring their advice and policing their laboratories, either directly,
by trying to ban all human cloning, or indirectly, by not taking bold
steps to stop global warming. Some believe that religious fundamentalists are on the march, replacing the study of Darwinian evolution with the pseudoscience of Intelligent Design. Some fear that
human beings are poised to wreck nature by polluting the atmosphere or poisoning the soil. Others feel defeated by nature's relentless brutality, by the tsunamis and earthquakes and childhood
cancers that so regularly mock man's illusions of control. "Don't
blame God," *Science* magazine exhorts us. "Better planning could
make natural disasters much less disastrous." But that hardly seems
to mitigate nature's relentless indifference to humanity or the misery of mothers left to mourn the dead infants of Java Island.

Perhaps one reason the debate about embryonic stem cells has become so prominent is that it combines scientific optimism and scientific despair so completely: the optimistic search for cures, the discontent that nature yields remedies for her afflictions so slowly, the resentment at Bush administration moralists for standing in the way of scientific progress for nonscientific reasons. The greatest animus among scientists is directed at religious believers, often defined as anyone who seeks limits on scientific freedom for ethical reasons the scientists themselves do not find compelling. The deans of major research centers feel like persecuted Galileos, yet they defend their turf in the most unscientific ways: treating the paralyzed as props in the campaign for research funding, promising cures based only on preliminary experiments, caricaturing every opponent as an irrational fanatic.

For it turns out that the methods of science cannot vindicate the ends of science, and the knowledge acquired by scientific methods cannot always justify the particular experiments used to acquire it. Yet scientists desperately want such vindication in the eyes of their fellow citizens: Good science (meaning *interesting, promising, exciting*) needs to be seen as good (meaning *virtuous, praiseworthy, compassionate*) by everyone. And so scientists have invented a new method to defend the unfettered freedom of the old one: They claim the mantle of science while making ethical claims ("embryo research is good") that rest on no special scientific basis at all, and they portray their opponents as antiscience for raising ethical questions that are entirely consistent with the scientific facts ("embryological development begins at conception").

Of course, the stem-cell fight is just one front in a long-standing conflict, not between science and religion, but between scientists who see all religion as an illusion and religious believers who desperately want the authority of science to bolster their faith's claims about the origins and destiny of man, including otherworldly claims for which there is no ordinary evidence. Both sides in this struggle make extravagant avowals about nature — especially about man's place within the natural world. And both sides are animated, in different ways, by visions of hope and despair, proof and mystery, man as elevated and man as small.

"The two world-views — science-based explanations and faith-based religions — cannot be reconciled," the esteemed biologist Edward O. Wilson recently wrote. "What then are we to do? Put the differences aside, I say." But such benign yet separate coexistence hardly seems like a viable option. The two realms mix whether we like it or not, and, to understand the meaning and limits of modern science, it is helpful to understand why modern science is often so hostile to religion — a task we can hardly leave to the scientists themselves.

Perhaps no idea offends the modern scientific mind more deeply than divine salvation. How weak we must be if we need a God to rescue us from the burdens of living in this world; how foolish we must be to let the fear of offending our imaginary savior get in the way of genuine progress. In *A Devil's Chaplain,* the biologist Richard Dawkins defines religious faith as a "virus of the mind" — or that childlike need to "suck at the pacifier of faith in immortality."

Otherworldly salvation comes in many different guises — salvation for all, salvation for those who believe in the one true God, salvation for those who lead good lives, salvation for those whom God chooses for his own inscrutable reasons. But the basic idea — "The Lord is my light and my salvation; whom shall I fear?" — is the common heritage of Jews and Christians, who yearn for redemption in a world whose many blessings always exist under a cloud of misery. And yet, the scientists, empirical to the core, know that faith is a fraud, a delusion, a prison cell for small minds. And it bothers them to the depths of their rational souls — although, curiously, for a series of contradictory reasons.

These contradictions go back to the beginnings of modern science. In *The Great Instauration,* one of the founding texts of the modern age, Francis Bacon described what he believed to be the aim and meaning of human knowledge:

> I would address one general admonition to all: that they consider what are the true ends of knowledge, and that they seek it not either for pleasure of mind, or for contention, or for superiority to others . . . but for the benefit and use of life, and that they perfect and govern it in charity . . . [From the marriage of the Mind and the Universe] there may spring helps to man, and a line and race of inventions that may in some degree subdue and overcome the necessities and miseries of humanity.

The intelligent, in other words, have a duty to their fellow men: to seek knowledge in a way that alleviates human misery, to seek power in the name of human charity. The trouble, as Bacon knew, is that the beneficiaries of his charity might not always be so amenable to his methods — methods that require violating not only the natural boundaries that exist between the species but also the divine boundaries that long divided the sacred from the profane. Where Leviticus ritually separates pure from impure with an eye to what is divine in man, Bacon's "New Atlantis" vivisects and recombines everything for the sake of healing man's animal body. "We have also parks and enclosures of all sorts of beasts and birds which we use not only for view or rareness, but likewise for dissections and trials; that thereby we may take light what may be wrought upon the body of man." On the isle of progress, the priest is replaced by the scientist, who conducts secret experiments to help his fellow citizens. This is the new charity.

Yet charity alone is hardly the only scientific motivation. For are we really to believe that the scientist's own pleasure is so unimportant to Bacon's project — the pleasure of knowing the world as it really is, taking it apart and putting it back together, coercing nature to reveal her true secrets? Are we really to believe that Descartes, who gave these fabulist visions a mathematical method, was not driven also (or primarily) by new aristocratic pleasures of the mind, pleasures that required the unfettered freedom to experiment?

From the beginning, science was driven by both democratic pity and aristocratic guile, by the promise to help humanity and the desire to be free from the constraints of the common man, with his many myths and superstitions and taboos. The modern scientist comes to heal the wretched bodies of those whose meager minds are always a threat to experimental knowledge. Salomon's House, where the elite of Bacon's scientific utopia would decide which inventions to publish and which to hide, existed both to protect men from science and science from men. It offers a new salvation and seeks to elude the oppressive trappings of the old one. It brings a new compassion and a new contempt. This was true in the beginning, and it is true today.

This double origin of modern science takes another form as well: seeing the unnecessary misery of false hope in God and the untold benefits of realism about nature — a realism often admitted to be tragic. The spiritual confidence of the believer offends those who know the twisted indifference of nature and that nature is everything. To the scientist, the believer is filled with more hope than he deserves to be, surprised by a joy that is not real, dreaming of a happy ending that will never come. Callous fate, not divine salvation, is the scientific news — and it is hardly good. As Alfred North Whitehead argued in his 1925 lectures "Science and the Modern World":

> The pilgrim fathers of the scientific imagination as it exists today are the great tragedians of ancient Athens, Aeschylus, Sophocles, Euripides. Their vision of fate, remorseless and indifferent, urging a tragic incident to its inevitable issue, is the vision possessed by science. Fate in Greek tragedy becomes the order of nature in modern thought . . . This inevitableness of destiny can only be illustrated in terms of human life by incidents which in fact involve unhappiness. For it is only by them that the futility of escape can be made evident in the drama. This remorseless inevitableness is what pervades scientific thought. The laws of physics are the decrees of fate.

Darwin put this truth in a new, biological light: Man emerged from this "remorseless and indifferent" nature, leaving us with a tragic mismatch between our spiritual longings and our mortal condition. In the Darwinian view, our origins and our destiny are little comfort to those seeking meaning beyond the imminent or seeking redemption from the wretched errors of nature that leave babies to suffer and villains to prosper. Yes, man can take a certain satisfaction and experience a certain "grandeur" in his own natural ascent, as Darwin writes at the end of his masterpiece. But faith that the human story will have a truly comic ending, that it will end in a way that satisfies man's redemptive longings, that Providence is still at work, is weakened if not shattered.

But, of course, this tragic vision of life was not the whole truth about the birth of modern science, with its eyes set from the beginning on lifesaving "invention." The greatest obstacle to progress, wrote Bacon, lies "in the despair of mankind and in the supposition of its impossibility." If Christian hope offends the scientist, so does the believer's passive acceptance of misery and active obsession with sin. To live in a godless world means that we are just as innocent as nature is blind — free not to suffer, free to alter nature's workings for our own purposes, free to challenge the cold decree of fate as best we can muster.

Thus Condorcet, the French prophet of man's self-improvement, believed he was living in the "ninth stage" of mankind's progress, when reason will "lift her chains, shake herself free from some of them, and, all the time regaining strength" from the effects of the Christian Dark Ages to "prepare for and advance the moment of her liberation." As he proclaimed in his *Sketch for an Historical Picture of the Progress of the Human Mind* (1795), "Nature has set no term to the perfection of human faculties; that the perfectibility of man is truly indefinite, and that the progress of this perfectibility, from now onwards independent of any power that might wish to halt it, has no other limit than the duration of the globe upon which nature has cast us."

Not all contemporary scientists are quite as bullish about progress as Condorcet, with his limitless optimism about human destiny within the world rather than beyond it. Some even fear that the "duration of the globe" is quickly coming to an end through man's ecological abuse. But Condorcet's spirit still pervades the modern laboratory, especially the biological laboratory, which is now the high kingdom of empirical science. Once we see (with Darwin) that men are beasts, ascendant in nature but not created in the image of God, we are free to re-create nature as if we were gods: perfecting the body and the mind.

But Condorcet's original error — call it the original sin of the scientific Enlightenment — still haunts modern science: Perpetual progress is not the same thing as perfection. Infinite progress also means infinite discontent, as man is left in a state of eternal becoming with no end. "Indefinite perfectibility," Condorcet's dream, is an irreconcilable contradiction.

Perfection, after all, is an end, a limit, something definite. Christ embodies the perfection of love. The philosopher grasps the perfection of knowledge. Yet the scientist destroys the possibility of perfection by seeing a world in permanent flux. Perhaps the only perfection available to the modern scientist is stoic acceptance of contingency on the way to oblivion — and indeed, there is no necessary contradiction between stoic philosophy and modern natural science. Yet stoic acceptance of nature is precisely what modern science, technological from the beginning, is incapable of embracing in spirit. Modern science portrays a world where acceptance of our fate within nature is all we can do, and yet it remakes knowledge in such a way that technological striving is seen as the only thing worth doing. Modern biology, like Sisyphus, is haunted by temporary successes and ultimate failure. It fends off death but cannot eradicate it; it explains death's role in natural selection but not the death of individual men still thirsty for salvation.

Writing just after World War I, when the slaughtered troops and the reality of technological war had shattered some of the Enlightenment's optimism, Max Weber describes this tragic aspect of modern science with great pathos:

> For civilized man death has no meaning. It has none because the individual life of civilized man, placed into an infinite "progress," according to its own imminent meaning should never come to an end; for there is always a further step ahead of one who stands in the march of progress. And no man who comes to die stands upon the peak which lies in infinity . . . He catches only the most minute part of what the life of the spirit brings forth ever anew, and what he seizes is always something provisional and not definitive, and therefore death for him is a meaningless occurrence. And because death is meaningless, civilized life as such is meaningless; by its very "progressiveness" it gives death the imprint of meaninglessness.

Weber's essay on "science as a vocation" is perhaps the best starting point for understanding the limits of scientific aspiration in our time. Weber praised scientists for living in the world of facts and criticized those who sought salvation by pretending that the old gods still exist. But he also reminded scientists that they have nothing privileged to say about the realm of value, the realm that matters most to human beings seeking knowledge of how to live. Like everyone else, the scientist must decide which ends to pursue, which gods to serve, which demon will "hold the very fibers of his life." And these are exactly the questions that the scientific method cannot answer. Divine salvation may be an illusion but so is believing that science can tell us how to live in the world it dissects and describes, and how to live well in a world where scientific power is so readily, so seductively, so dangerously at our disposal.

The impotence of science is perhaps most readily apparent in that realm where science is most powerful: nuclear weapons. Consider, for example, the current confrontation with Iran. Only the scientifically trained can provide accurate estimates about the state of Iran's weapons development, about the state of our own offensive and defensive military options, about the likely effects of a nuclear attack — the number of dead bodies, the hazards to the environment, the technical challenges of rebuilding. But when it comes to making decisions or evaluating the meaning of our nuclear predicament, the methods of science lead us into the nonscientific realm of interpretation.

The sociobiologist, who sees man in light of his long animal history and nature as a vast impersonal process, might say that the confrontation with Iran hardly matters in the cosmic scheme of things. Man killing man, culture clashing with culture, is inherent to nature's law of survival. Superior cultures, like superior individuals, triumph over inferior ones, at least in the long run. Life improves through death in a blind drama that continues unabated. The neuroscientist, who studies the brain to understand its mechanisms and improve its workings, might look instead to man himself as the agent for changing human nature. Perhaps our advancing understanding of neurobiology will eventually make tyranny a thing of the past. Perhaps our emerging science of the mind will bring a new age of man-made peace and stability, a "psychocivilized society." Perhaps Darwin's greatest species will triumph over Darwin's brutal laws.

Yet such interpretations are morally and strategically unsatisfying, to say the least. Human beings may be destined always to kill one another, but we leave ourselves morally impotent if we see this dark fact about the human condition as our only guide to moral action. Mankind may be destined to become something better, but discerning the difference between improvement and degradation requires some standard beyond the imminent processes of nature, lest we make ourselves into the subhuman denizens of Huxley's Brave New World. And while the unrestrained pursuit of knowledge is perhaps the core dogma of science, one imagines that any scientist with a conscience would reject the shelter of scientific freedom that even an evil regime like Iran might offer, a regime that might see the uninhibited investigation of the physical world as useful to its own perverse ends. While the *moral* obligation should be obvious, there is no *scientific* reason not to become an Iranian scientist.

In every area of public life where science and morality intersect, there are questions about the use of science that science itself can never answer. On stem cells, scientists can tell us the potential benefits of destroying human embryos but not whether the progress of medicine justifies the willful destruction of nascent human life. On drilling in Alaska, scientists can estimate the potential oil reserves and the potential harm to the ecosystem but not whether we have a moral responsibility to expand the domestic oil supply or to preserve an unsullied wilderness even with economic harm to ourselves. On human exploration of space, scientists can estimate the economic and human costs of putting a man on Mars and the potential benefits of such a mission to the advance of human knowledge, but they cannot say whether human greatness in space is more worthy of public funds than ongoing research into curing AIDS. Science is power without wisdom about the uses of power. As Hans Jonas put it: "The scientist himself is by his science no more qualified than others to discern, nor is he more disposed to care for, the good of mankind. Benevolence must be called in from the outside to supplement the knowledge acquired through theory: it does not flow from theory itself."

Yet the scientists still often want to tell us how to live, and they often claim the authority of science for their moral exhortations. Richard Dawkins, for example, ends his book with a letter of advice to his ten-year-old daughter on "good and bad reasons for believing." "Sometimes people have a strong inside feeling that somebody loves them when it is not based upon any evidence, and then they are likely to be completely wrong," he writes. These false feelings pass from one generation to another, from gullible parents to gullible children. "Could this be what has happened with religions" — this perpetuation of illusion? "Belief that there is a god or gods, belief in Heaven, belief that Mary never died, belief that Jesus never had a human father, belief that prayers are answered, belief that wine turns into blood — not one of these beliefs is backed up by any good evidence. Yet millions of people believe them. Perhaps this is because they were told to believe them when they were young enough to believe anything."

One can surely respect the integrity of the rationalist who doubts the existence of a heaven he cannot see and who is skeptical about theological claims that rest on dueling authorities rather than empirical evidence. But now imagine, say, a stem-cell biologist writing a similar letter to a ten-year-old girl in the cancer ward — a girl dying of the very disease the biologist cannot yet cure. The girl faces her demise with courage; she knows that God loves her, that the death of her body is not the end of her being. She prays every night, "Even though I walk through the valley of the shadow of death, I will fear no evil, for you are with me," and she still manages to smile every morning. What would the stem-cell biologist say to the girl he wants so desperately to rescue from the ravages of nature? Would he describe the miracle cures that will not come in time? Would he tell her that God's love is an illusion, that her prayers evaporate unheard and unanswered into the ether, that her brief transitory existence is all there is, that she is "sucking the pacifier of faith in immortality"?

Perhaps the rationalist can stomach a little bit of comforting illusion for a dying girl he cannot help. Or perhaps he believes her piety must be shattered for the greater good, since the lives of future children depend on destroying that fundamentalist faith ("embryos are sacred") that stands in the way of progress. Perhaps the young girl's courage will cause him to question his own rational certainty that the God she worships is simply an illusion, or to see her very desire for God as evidence of God's existence. Yet whatever letter the biologist writes, science cannot tell him what to say. Perhaps it would be better, at times, for the impotent scientist to say nothing.

But humility, alas, is not always a prominent scientific virtue, at least among the most prominent scientists, and especially among many modern biologists. And while science cannot decide for itself what to do and how to live, there does seem to be a prevailing pattern of scientific worship. Devotion to the scientific method seems to produce an ethos about the meaning of science. Of course, it is always dangerous to generalize, since science and scientists are so variable in spirit — consider biologists and physicists, academic scientists and corporate scientists, theoreticians and engineers. But it is also fair to say that certain general attitudes dominate the contemporary scientific mind or at least the elite organs of science (like the editorial page of *Science* magazine) that shape the influence of science on our culture.

First, *science invites us to believe in both charity and ruthlessness.* Modern biomedical research, most especially, often aims to help the weak by using the weak. It aims to help the sick, the suffering, and the desperate by using the embryonic, the dying, and the dispossessed. (Most recently, Ian Wilmut, the creator of Dolly the cloned sheep, proposed using dying patients to test unproven embryonic stem-cell therapies: a classic example of ruthless charity at work.) The experimental method blurs the line between those who benefit from scientific improvements and those who might serve as the experimental basis for such improvements. Science blurs the line between the human subject and the human object. This is especially true, perhaps uniquely true, in biology: By studying the parts of animals, the organismic whole is lost; the animal becomes simply a biological "model." And by studying human beings as animals, the line between man and the other animals is lost; man becomes simply another biological resource. The method of science becomes the ethos of science, or as Wordsworth put it, "We murder to dissect."

Second, *science invites us to believe in both human greatness and human smallness.* The greatness of man is the mind at work; our capacity for knowing is the singular measure of our dignity; the body is a machine on which science can work its wonders for the sake of the will. But science also cannot escape its understanding of human origins — emerging from the dust of the ground, without any notion of being created in the image of a perfect maker. In this view, man is both beast and angel, rather than image of God. This is why science can conduct the most ghastly experiments on animals (with godlike power) while also worrying as a guild about the effect of modern civilization on the animals of the earth, seeing man as more beastly than the beasts he destroys, or at least worth no more than the animals he uses. It is why science can devote so much energy to curing disease while believing that death is nature's way of improving itself.

Finally, *science invites us to believe in both progress and nihilism.* Most scientists believe that knowledge will advance, technology will improve, human life will get better, if only they are free to do their work, unhampered by irrational taboos. And yet the perfect freedom that science demands is also, in the end, a form of nihilism. Science in itself sets no limits to human action, except perhaps those actions that inhibit the activity of science. But since the domain of science is infinite within nature, there is no action that could not, in fact, be redefined as an experiment. Some scientists hold that human beings are hardwired to behave in certain ways, including ways that are compatible with our bourgeois values. But this faith in human nature in general is not the same as believing that particular human beings have any particular moral obligations. It is a description of how human beings tend to live, not a set of prescriptions for how human beings ought to live. It is a study of man always open to refinement, not an image of man by which all our refinements should be judged.

And this brings us back to Condorcet's haunting legacy: Science destroys perfection in the name of progress, but its progress ultimately fails to satisfy. In the end, the cost seems too high for those seeking a more perfect salvation from the miseries of nature. The hospital chapel may be an architectural afterthought, but the chaplain (not the "devil's chaplain") still usually gets the last word. Our faith in science eventually gives way to our need for faith. We choose the hope of perfection over endless progress and unfettered freedom but only after trying for as long as possible to have everything without contradiction.

Unquestionably, the modern scientific project has been a great success: Our lives would be inferior — indeed horrible — in countless ways without the technological fruits that were always its primary aim. We have gone some way toward correcting the amorality of nature, using nature as our instrument. For the sick, in particular, scientists and doctors are often the first saviors, restoring normal life when the ugliness of death seeks another victim. The scientist is, sometimes, the personification of love in a method. Yet ultimately, the modern scientific project will always be a failure: Its powers do not satisfy our deepest longings; its victories are always temporary and its losses always final.

Even while many scientists accuse religious believers of zealously imposing their values on everyone, some seem to have embraced a new fundamentalism of their own: the belief that Darwinism explains everything important about being human, combined with the passionate need to convert the unconverted and unsave the saved. Confronted by the aimless nature they so laboriously study, many scientists seem to need a universal, all-encompassing framework to explain their existence. Yet while orthodox Darwinists believe that the law of animal survival explains much of human behavior, they also believe that being a scientist is nobler than being simply a gene-spreading animal. The point of the scientific project is not simply to see ourselves clearly as the beasts we are but to imagine that we possess the cleverness and magnanimity of gods. It seeks not simply to understand the law of death (evolution as we find it) but to wield mastery over life (evolution as we make it).

Despite its inherent limits and frequent excesses, there is great dignity in the scientific vocation rightly understood — the dignity of confronting nature's facts in all their beauty and ugliness, and the dignity of seeking to make human life a little less miserable. Science is, or can be, a noble vocation, a realm of human endeavor that invites human excellence, including moral excellence. Against the sin of despair, the scientist stands for action. Against the post-modern revolt against reality, the scientist seeks truth. Thrown into a world that is mysterious, the scientist seeks to bring into light what is so often shrouded in darkness.

The trouble is that most scientists — at least most modern biologists, whose work dominates the public imagination about science — do not seem to reflect much or deeply about the limits of their method, or about the *moral* significance of the ends they seek and the means they use. The recent book by human genome pioneer Francis Collins — a memoir of faith that might have been titled *C. S. Lewis Goes to the Laboratory* — is notable precisely because it is such a striking exception to the norm. In the public realm, most biologists seem, all too often, like scientific geniuses and moral simpletons, applying rational rigor to their investigations of nature but relying on feeling as their only moral compass. And for all its appreciation of nature's complexity, the scientific mind seems no rival for the Bible or Aristotle or Machiavelli in understanding human complexity. Next to the philosopher, the neuroscientist still looks, all too often, like a fool.

The scientist is especially foolish when he is optimistic without a dose of tragic reservation. For, despite Condorcet's claims, science is perhaps most necessary precisely because of the permanence of human sin and human evil, not because scientific progress will be the tool of their eradication. We will continue to need vaccine makers because evil men will make and use biological weapons. We will need missile-defense makers because evil men will use ballistic missiles. We will need surveillance-system makers because evil men will

always be plotting the destruction of the innocent. Not the inevitable perfection of man in nature but the permanent imperfection
of the human soul makes modern science a moral necessity —
including, at times, the kind of ruthless experiments that are justifiable only in moments of supreme emergency, when civilization itself lies in the balance.

And no doubt, in the days ahead, there will be many emergen-
cies — anthrax attacks, avian flu, natural disasters, nuclear explo-
sions — when the power of science will serve both the best and
worst impulses of man in a world of great darkness. But perhaps
our greatest challenge is trying to recover an understanding of human life and human death that avoids treating existence itself as a
supreme emergency, an endless war against nature, a Sisyphean
struggle with no Sabbath in time.

Faced with the contingencies of nature and history, perhaps we
need to regain the kind of equanimity that faith often inspires.
Faced with a world that so often seems absurd, perhaps we should
not place all our hopes in science alone. In our hunger for still waters, nature offers no proof that man's redemptive hopes are justified, but also no proof that everything is hopeless.

Nature is filled with the good things it destroys; natural beings
yearn for life even as they are born toward death. And one of those
natural beings — man — knows that nature, even when mastered
by science, will never satisfy our more-than-natural longings. Amid
life's many horrors and wonders, those eternal longings will never
go away.

ROBERT CORDING

Luna Moths

FROM *The Southern Review*

The first time I woke up crying
From a puddle of sleep and found it

Fluttering against a wall
Like a dying leaf of spring green light.

The second I found lying lightly
On the ground, newly dead.

I brought it inside and placed it
On a blank piece of paper

For my study. Palest green wings.
A thin red border, like a child's outline,

On the edges of its forewings
And hindwings. A yellow inner border

On its long, tailed hindwings.
Four white eyespots ringed in yellow

And maroon. On that white
Sheet of paper, it appeared to be

Some beautiful, lost metaphor
Of an indecipherable language.

*

I'd read the facts — the one-week life span,
The way, because they do not eat,

The adults have no need of a mouth — by the time
I found the third, late last night,

High on the wall of my kitchen.
I'd had too much to drink. I spoke to it

As if it were my own Buddhist teacher
Here to teach me nonattachment,

The illusions of hunger, sex, rampant need.
I sat with it until the sun rose, toasting

Its quick beauty, then the restfulness I found
In its body, and then those bright-eyed,

Translucent green wings that seemed
To breathe more and more slowly before going

Motionless. When I lifted it in my hand
I knew just how little the space was

Between myself and nothingness.

MADELINE DeFREES

The Magdalen with the Nightlight
by Georges de La Tour

FROM *Image*

The candle plumbs a sadness in her gaze
that stems the flood of memories each night
when spirit mounts a watch the blood betrays.

Body resumes the phosphorescent haze,
Its diagram of burning appetite.
The candle plumbs a sadness in her gaze.

The holy books, the skull, the peace she prays
for; all enemies of passionate delight.
Her spirit mounts. A watch the blood betrays

transforms the glittering evil into grays.
She undergoes again the soul's dark night
as candles plumb a sadness in her gaze.

Light and reflected light are no surprise.
The painter knows art's power to translate
when spirit mounts a watch the blood betrays.

Her past is quick to challenge, calmly lays
a bet that seven devils will requite
the flame a candle plumbs in her sad gaze.
The spirit mounts a watch. The blood betrays.

DEBORAH DIGGES

The Birthing

FROM *The New Yorker*

Call out the names in the procession of the loved.
Call from the blood the ancestors here to bear witness
to the day he stopped the car,
we on our way to a great banquet in his honor.
In a field a cow groaned lowing, trying to give birth,
what he called *front leg presentation,*
the calf come out nose first, one front leg dangling from his
      mother.
A fatal sign he said while rolling up the sleeves
of his dress shirt, and climbed the fence.
I watched him thrust his arms entire
into the yet-to-be, where I imagined holy sparrows scattering
in the hall of souls for his big mortal hands just to make way.
With his whole weight he pushed the calf back in the mother
and grasped the other leg tucked up like a closed wing
against the new one's shoulder.
And found a way in the warm dark to bring both legs out
into the world together.
Then heaved and pulled, the cow arching her back,
until a bull calf, in a whoosh of blood and water,
came falling whole and still onto the meadow.
We rubbed his blackness, bloodying our hands.
The mother licked her newborn, of us oblivious,
until he moved a little, struggled.
I ran to get our coats, mine a green velvet cloak,
and his tuxedo jacket, and worked to rub the new one dry

while he set out to find the farmer.
When it was over, the new calf suckling his mother,
the farmer soon to lead them to the barn,
leaving our coats just where they lay
we huddled in the car.
And then made love toward eternity,
without a word drove slowly home. And loved some more.

GRETEL EHRLICH

What Is the Worth of the Wind River Mountains?

FROM *Shambhala Sun*

AN ALMOST-FULL MOON SWEEPS LIGHT across shadowed and white-spiked peaks, bringing into view an unbroken 120-mile-long mountain wall that sweeps down on either side to green plateaus, river valleys, and high, sage-glutted desert.

Once the Wind River Mountains were covered by a continual ice-cap that ran the length of the range, pierced only by the high peaks of the Continental Divide. Outlet glaciers spilled ice from between granite flanks, and meltwater fell from the edge of the faulted plateau. Massive terminal moraines wound down on either side of glacier-cut canyons, smoothing the landscape into wide meadows and undulating moraines — an alpine universe entirely carved by ice.

Now the view is not of ice sheets but of the sculpted body of land after the retreat of ice: bowl-like meadows, ice-scoured plateaus, uplifted Archean basement rock, polished granite walls amidst crowded peaks, towering cirques, string lakes, U-shaped canyons, and wild rivers that flow into three major watersheds — the Columbia, Colorado, and Missouri rivers, which spill into slow oxbows and hard rapids, straightening and crooking their necks like swans.

The Wind River Mountains push southeast like a thick thumb from the wilderness matrix that holds Yellowstone Park, the Tetons, and the Gros Ventres. It is an appendage of the Rocky Mountain cordillera that stretches from the Brooks Range in Alaska to the Sangre de Cristos in northern New Mexico. They carry a piece of the Continental Divide like a snake on their bold shoulders and create their own weather. At twelve, thirteen, and fourteen thousand feet, clouds curdle, pool up, spill down, and loft sideways; ribbons of stunted trees waver beneath granite walls stained by the leaking meltwater of blue tarns.

The Winds are pinned at an angle to Yellowstone Park and its active volcano at the northwestern part of the map. When the volcano blew 640,000 years ago it destroyed a mountain range bigger than the Winds, killed off prehistoric camels and mammoths, and poured a deep ash bed across Montana and Wyoming. Because the volcanoes occur in 600,000-year cycles, the Yellowstone volcano is now 40,000 years overdue. Earthquake "swarms" have been shaking the ground in the park, and the ancient caldera that holds Yellowstone Lake has begun to bulge again.

Running north-south at an angle to the Winds are the Gros Ventre Mountains, and these are connected by the Hoback River to the east-west Wyoming Range. In the sheltered cove made by these three mountain ranges lie the Upper Green River Lakes, the Green River, and the sage-steppe grasslands of an ancient migration corridor, in use for at least six thousand years; on it 100,000 animals — antelope, mule deer, and elk — move from the high country of the range to the Red Desert. This is their winter habitat — eight million acres of windblown native grass and sage.

To see is to stop. To open oneself to what is there. To open one's eyes, nostrils, ears, or as John Muir suggested, stand on one's head to see the world anew. The beauty of the natural world is given to us. We abuse the gift by not looking, by using it for profit, by not recognizing its intrinsic value. Real wealth is biological diversity: sun, grass, water, birds, antelope, elk, bear, moose, and the joys that we find living among them.

At this writing the Red Desert, the Boback, the Upper Green River Valley, and the entire Yellowstone ecosystem — every river, lake, valley, and mountain — are under siege from the oil and gas industry. To the south, on a mesa above the town of Pinedale and the New Fork River, the Jonah Field has been transformed into an industrial area with fifteen hundred gas wells and thousands more planned. They would like to put natural gas wells everywhere from the Upper Green River Valley to the southern tip of the Red Desert.

How these mountains, glaciers, rivers, deserts, and valleys connect and work together as critical habitat and a place of unique beauty tells the story of why we must work hard to protect this part of the world.

Mountains are a vertical altar and a wide barricade. They push and pull us; they dismantle confusion and reconstruct darkness as light. By thinning oxygen they go against life, and give it back in the form of elbow room. They represent danger; they give us beauty in jolts. We go up into them to experience hardship and find ourselves overcome with what the Chinese call "rustic joy." Mountains provoke a different kind of breathing, as human entanglements come unraveled and vision clears.

Mountains are both forbidding and enticing: they invite us in and throw us out. Their vertical intricacy acts as a narcotic on us. Thought to be the center of the earth in indigenous cultures, mountain environments have been celebrated in poems and songs since humans began walking their trails, bathing in their rivers, finding food in their high meadows, and taking refuge in their caves.

The first inhabitants of the Wind River ecosystem were the people called the Sheep Eaters. One was named Togwotee, a shaman for whom Togwotee Pass is named. The Sheep Eaters lived in the high country and made their winter homes on the northeastern side of the Winds near Sleeping Ledge in the Dinwoody drainage. Their medicine wheels, at the tops of mountains, were made of rocks positioned in the shape of a wheel with twenty-eight spokes, said to represent each of their tribes. In the middle was a stone hut for the tribal chief, with the participants standing and singing and dancing along the spokes to the god of beauty and the sun god.

They lived in skin lodges; ate buffalo, elk, deer, rabbit, wild carrots; roasted juniper berries, elk thistle, chokecherries, and wild strawberries; and used wild geranium for stomachaches and snowberry tea for healing after childbirth.

The Eastern Shoshone Indians arrived in present-day Wyoming by the early 1500s. It is unclear whether they were related to the earlier inhabitants, the Sheep Eaters, but after adopting the horse from the Comanche in the 1700s, they ranged as far north as Alberta and south to Mexico. Closer to home, they lived and hunted near the Green River, the Popo Agie, and the Wind River, traveling east to the Big Horn Mountains, north to the Yellowstone River, west to the Salmon Mountains, and south to the Yampa River and Brown's Hole.

The neighboring Blackfoot were shocked when they saw the Shoshone atop these powerful four-legged creatures, and called the horses "Big Dog" and "Elk Dog." Before encountering guns in the hands of their neighbors, what the Shoshone feared most were the dwarf Nunumbi, tiny creatures said to live in the unexplored recesses of the Wind River Mountains. For the Shoshone, the Winds marked the beginning and ending of life: the young rose out of its nesting glaciers, the very old flew to the tops of its peaks, and the dead floated away on its rivers.

In 1811 members of the American Fur Company, 61 people with 118 horses, were the first white people to make contact with the Shoshone. They camped in the Green River Valley far below Gannett Peak and feasted on the buffalo they hunted there.

Mountains pull at us, soul, psyche, and body. They are a vertical resting place for our eyes. The view from a west-slope meadow is into the interior of the mountain range. Behind a handful of bracketed peaks are more peaks: broken turrets, shadowed sidecanyons, polished square-top domes, and serrated granite blocks. From Pronghorn Peak above Middle Lake, there's a view past Gannett Peak of the Tetons. To the south there's a defile of rugged mountains, including Rampart Peak, Desolation Peak, and Mount Solitude.

Dome Peak rides Gannett Peak's shadow; the Cirque Towers make a bump in the Continental Divide, ballooning it out to hold a circle of peaks including Bollinger, Wolf's Head, Overhanging Tower, Shark's Nose, Block Tower, Pylon Peak, and Warbonnet, with Pingora Peak pushed out from the circle to stand sentinel by Lonesome Lake.

At dawn Mount Bonneville and Fremont peaks are orange walls, what the soldier and explorer John Frémont called "the red comb of the mountains." The peak named for him is a flat-walled front that holds tapestries of snow, icy glazes, and the unpolished glow of the sun. In every month of the year the "red comb" of corniced ridgelines strobes black against white.

Today winter snowbanks are broken into by steady threads of rain. Hard winds, glass-still mornings, directionless breezes hushing themselves, pink days that end in flame — that's a summer day in the Wind River Mountains.

To be here at any time of the year instructs us about how natural beauty saves us. The Chinese phrase for going on a pilgrimage — *ch'ao-shan chin-hsiang* — means "paying one's respect to the mountains." It is while walking in the mountains that the transformative effect of beauty, the outer becoming inner, can be felt.

On a July day the moon rises in daylight, making granite walls go blank. Night tries to hide the moon's light and fails: black ponds coin it in bright rounds. A wind rinses dawn with pewter, pushing the cloud-lid to one side until snowflakes scatter into the void.

A doe rises out of the green haze of new grass with two fawns. The sky blazes. Shoshone storytellers once said that Cottontail saved the earth from burning up. The sun was too strong and, after several tries, the rabbit knocked the glowing orb out of the sky with his fire drill. The sun fell. Cottontail cut the sun's chest open, took out its gall bladder, and from it made a new sun and a moon that would shine, but not too hard or too long in a world where day would alternate with night.

A tree-engine churns as wind roars up its white trunk and the sky is thrown into surging planes of gray and black. Lightning dangles — the sky's lost jewelry. A piece of a rainbow hangs down from a cloud. Rain drives at a diagonal from above a ridge. The night grows cold. How brief summer is here: July still feels like spring but by mid-August, there'll be snow.

The regional and global crisis we are feeling seems surreal. Climate change is being driven by human-caused pollution. Glaciers are melting, species extinctions are rampant, and the alarming warming trend of the weather is accelerating. The temperature increase at high elevations on Fremont Peak is 3.5 degrees Celsius.

At the same time, the oil and gas industry (the source for all greenhouse gas pollution) is forcing its way into these regions of extraordinary mountains and valleys. Air pollution is now a problem; the six-thousand-year-old migration of antelope, the longest migration corridor in the lower forty-eight, is severely threatened; and glaciers in the Winds have receded dramatically since 1986. The concept of beauty itself, and its necessary place in human society, is no longer recognized.

The ravages of climate change are most obvious in west Greenland, where the thickness of sea ice in midwinter has gone from three to four feet to just four to twelve inches. But if you look closely enough, you'll see it is happening everywhere. Two years ago, during an unseasonably hot summer in the fifth year of drought, there was an outburst flood — what glaciologists call a *jokulhlaup* — and a thirty-acre ice-dammed lake at the head of Grasshopper Glacier broke, spilling 650 to 850 million gallons of water down eight miles of three east-slope drainages, including Dinwoody Creek where, in the 1700s, the Shoshone made their winter camps.

Glaciologists say that these outburst floods are the result of global warming. As the Grasshopper Glacier shrank, the ice dam sank to the elevation of the natural spillway, and the lake water carved a new outlet.

Wind noise in the trees, silence on the moraine, heartbeat loud. Autumn comes. Mountains are the places where the dead reside, where the spirit circumambulates, where blizzards go blind. There's a chain-saw whine in the distance; high clouds are sliced open by sun.

By September new snow hangs like tapestries from Fremont Peak. A tarn silvers around my foot; the sky tarnishes. Wind pulls at the peaks: they are geological trees straining for the season's last light. How many octaves does thunder have? Snow and rain take turns swiping meadows and peaks. A sweeping rain is counterpoint to wind-wounds.

Migration begins. A bull moose chases four females through the timber. Two antelope spar. One is finally turned away and the other collects his harem. Sandhill cranes practice flying in formation. Willows rust in ponds. No water in them: they are dry depressions.

Meteorologists say this is the season of Dead Clouds — clouds that drift listlessly over the whole continent bearing no rain. Wind does not play or pressure them. They touch no mountains. A north wind blows Arctic air into place and it stays. When moisture-laden clouds do come, they hang like fish over scalloped peaks, fish that are still swimming. Reeds lie prostrate. The mergansers and mallards have gone. A mirage rises from sun-cured meadows making mountains move: they are root-cut from bunchgrass, antelope, and buffalo.

Before dawn, above tree line, in a wide basin surrounded by serrated peaks, there is no light and no color, no weather. The sky has been abandoned. October becomes November. A friend explains three Haida words: *xhaaydla*, alluding to the boundary between two worlds, and the words for "feather" and "snowflake" — *ttaghaw* and *ttaghun.*

Today it snows and a curtain falls over the mountain front, dividing the cordillera from the valleys, the realm of the gods from the one inhabited by humans. At any time of year when the view from a high peak of the entire ecosystem is occluded, I take the landscape inward and see it with my mind's eye. Yellowstone's volcano fumes and at the other end the Red Desert is a tongue curled up into a desert wall, holding hundreds of thousands of animals in its embrace until spring. *But up and down these valleys there are natural gas wells pumping.*

Wind stops at dawn. It is December. Day comes as slowly as an ice age, a white scrim that ties ground to sky. Winter does away with the tension between night and day. One slit in the clouds reveals a seam of something incandescent, then closes. We are almost out of light now, and when it does show, it does so sparingly.

A brisk wind knocks eyes into the sky but instead of blue, there is titanium. Aspen leaves are shifting heaps underfoot and gray trunks are sticks that wave like hair. A trail leads to ice-polished walls shouldering the whole range. Two ravens tilt and gyrate as they fly by, then they are lost inside the black reaches of a glacier-carved canyon.

Snow fills the hours. It is March now. A wolf walks the edge of the timber, itself a place of night at midday. As the storm abates snow flickers, making a kind of fire in the air. The Wyoming Range, the Gros Ventres, and the Winds sparkle. A moose breaks through ice in the Green River and drinks. There is the scent of thawing earth. To see is to stop and look, to love what is before us, and to stop its desecration: past midnight white shafts of auroral light beam up; a meteor sails down behind the mountain wall, bringing day.

JOSEPH EPSTEIN

Friendship Among the Intellectuals

FROM *Commentary*

"IT IS PAINFUL to consider," wrote Samuel Johnson about friendship, "that there is no human possession of which the duration is less certain."

Too true. Some friendships die on their own, of simple inanition, having been quietly allowed to lapse by the unacknowledged agreement of both parties. Others break down because time has altered old friends, given them different interests, values, points of view. In still others, only one party works at the friendship, while the other belongs to what Truman Capote called (in a letter to the critic Newton Arvin, his ex-lover) "some odd psychological type . . . that only writes when he is written to." And then of course there are the friendships that end when one friend betrays or is felt to betray the other, or fails to come through in a crisis, or finds himself violently disputing the other on matters of profoundest principle.

These days, such principled disagreements tend often to involve ideas, and to be endemic among supposedly educated people and especially among intellectuals. The ideas themselves are as likely as not to involve politics. Even more than differences over religion, political disputes seem to ignite ugly emotions and get things to the yelling stage quickly. That may well be why, in eighteenth-century clubs and coffeehouses, politics was often prohibited as a subject for discussion.

Ex-Friends is the title of Norman Podhoretz's 1999 memoir about his broken friendships with Lionel and Diana Trilling, Hannah Arendt, Norman Mailer, Lillian Hellman, and other eminences in the intellectual life of their time. In each case, politics was at the heart of the trouble. In each case, Podhoretz sets out the story of the friendship and, in a fairer fashion than I think I would have been capable of, recounts how it fell apart.

Over the four decades that I have known Norman Podhoretz, he has taken positions based on his beliefs that have cost him and his family much unjustified contumely, and at times, I have no doubt, true anguish; at a minimum they cost him a central place in what was once snobbishly considered the American intellectual establishment. He has also commanded great loyalty, which speaks to a true gift for friendship. But he knows only one way to take ideas — dead seriously. He is a polemicist, to the bone and beyond, and his has been a life lived in and through argument. Very near the pure type of the intellectual, he cannot avoid taking positions, and cannot say other than what he thinks; candor is in his nature, and he has in him much more charm than diplomacy.

In the introductory chapter of *Ex-Friends*, Podhoretz writes that friends can disagree about a lot, "but only provided the things they disagree about are not all that important to them." He is in interesting company here. In 1914, with World War I about to begin, Ludwig Wittgenstein wrote to Bertrand Russell:

> I can see perfectly well that your value judgments are just as good as mine and deep-seated in you as mine in me, and I have no right to catechize you. But . . . for that very reason there cannot be any real relation of friendship between us.

Of course, in the hothouse world of the New York intellectuals, few if any would be ready to concede that an adversary's "value judgments are just as good as mine," let alone forgo the right to catechize. So when Norman Podhoretz turned away from his radical-Left politics of the late 1950s and early '60s, arguing in print that America was on balance a good place in which one was fortunate to be living, the walls crashed down around him. He was looked upon by his former friends, he writes, "as a dangerous heretic, which I certainly was from their point of view" — just as, he adds, "I considered them a threat to everything I held dear, which they certainly were — and still are." Those friends who did not think him stupidly or evilly wrong considered him insane. "No wonder," he concludes, "that there is hardly a one of my old friends left among the living with whom I am today so much as on speaking terms, except to exchange the most minor civilities if we happen unavoidably to meet (and often not even that)."

Here is the question *Ex-Friends* raises in high relief: for what ideas would one be willing to give up one's friends? Most of us, I suspect, would answer: none. Ideas, after all, are but abstract things and as such are not worth even a single flesh-and-blood friend. And yet, abstract as they are, in the realm of politics ideas have consequences, and those consequences can be measured all too often and all too precisely in flesh and blood.

Communism, which began as an idea, ended up causing death and misery to scores of millions of people for nearly a century. If your friend were to advocate or defend the Communist system, could he truly be your friend? Cicero defined friendship "as nothing other than agreement over all things divine and human along with good will and affection." That is a lot to ask, but it seems undeniable that general agreement on such major matters is a great lubricant for a friction-free friendship.

For me, a person's general point of view is more important than his opinions on specific issues, though I admit that the line between the two is not always easily drawn. I do not see how an African American, for example, could ever overlook obvious racism in a person he calls a friend. Jean-Paul Sartre and Albert Camus broke up their friendship over Camus's *The Myth of Sisyphus*. The book argued against political utopianism, which Camus thought was the world's most dangerous delusion. Sartre, a utopian who lived comfortably enough with the horrors perpetrated by Joseph Stalin, felt this was going altogether too far, and closed things off. Sigmund Freud, unable to bear deviation from any of his own central ideas, broke with just about everyone in what was once called the Freudian circle.

An interesting sidelight on this point was offered by George Orwell in a letter to the poet Stephen Spender, written just after the two had met for the first time at a party. Until that point, writes Orwell, he had always thought of Spender as the sort of person he despised: a Communist fellow-traveler, an effete poet, an all-around weak type. He had attacked Spender in print on these very grounds. But in person he found Spender to be rather agreeable, and therefore felt disarmed from ever again criticizing him with a clear conscience. Orwell concluded that it was probably a bad idea to attend parties where one might meet enemies and find oneself liking them.

How many intellectual friendships dissolve over conflicts of opinion and ideas cannot be known, but the number is probably at least as great as those that fall apart through such normal perils as insults (intended or not) or wounds resulting from pride, ingratitude, feelings of abandonment, or misunderstanding. Nor are intellectuals immune from the riskiest of all maneuvers in a friendship: the effort to reshape the ideas and even the character of one's friend in one's own image.

A vivid instance of this in my own life was the insistence of my friend Edward Shils on remolding his then-friend Saul Bellow. I first came to know both men in the early 1970s, when they were already on the precipice of breakup. All three of us were unmarried at the time. I met Bellow first, and he introduced me to Shils, who had been responsible for bringing him to the Committee on Social Thought at the University of Chicago. The two men enjoyed a rough parity of prestige, Shils as an international scholar of society and politics and Bellow as a literary artist, though Shils was about four years older and a much more forceful character.

Shils appreciated Bellow's talent, but he wanted him to be somehow grander and graver in his person, and above all more circumspect in his private life — to be a kind of Thomas Mann, with a streak of Jewish jokiness added. Although Bellow was by then in his fifties and already world famous, Shils did not see this as any impediment to reform. A true teacher, he could not help setting people straight.

Samuel Johnson, an unreformable handful of humanity himself, instructs that we must accept our friends as they are — "not as we would make them." Sound advice, which Edward Shils could not quite bring himself to follow. Not that all his efforts went awry. Shils had much to do with converting Bellow politically, making him, a former Trotskyite, less sympathetic than he might otherwise have been to the student revolutionaries of the age and exercising a decisive influence on his 1970 novel, *Mr. Sammler's Planet*.

The friendship must at one time have been very close and precious to both men. By the time I came to know them, however, fissures, cracks, and fallen plaster were already discernible. Bellow took without evident resentment a number of sermonettes on what Shils considered the shabbiness of his personal conduct, especially toward women. In phone conversations with me, however, sometimes back-to-back, each would put down the other — brilliantly, I must say. Bellow felt that Shils did not respect him sufficiently; Shils, that Bellow failed to heed his advice and was continuing to behave badly. "I refuse to permit him to use the Committee on Social Thought as a retirement home for his old girlfriends," he once told me.

By the mid-1990s, the two men had pulled so far apart that Shils, who by then lay dying, refused Bellow's request to come bid him a final farewell. After his death, Bellow put him in *Ravelstein* (2000), where he is described by the title character as smelling musty and as probably a homosexual. Neither was remotely the case. But, as the poet Paul Valéry wrote, "No true hatred is possible except toward those one has loved."

I would have liked to remain friends with both Edward Shils and Saul Bellow, but their rising enmity was such that I had to choose between them; slowly, over a year or so, I chose Shils, the larger-hearted and better-natured man. But I myself was never an issue of contention between the two of them, and not for a moment do I think that Bellow, to whom I was never more than a secondary friend, was jealous of my friendship with Shils.

With intellectuals as with anybody else, jealousy is one of the ways that friendship can sadly resemble love. It is not uncommon for two close friends to resent a third person who may seem to be coming between them — or for that third party to resent a close friendship that appears to shut him out, and to seek means of retribution. The novelist Paul Theroux, for example, blamed the breakup of his friendship with V. S. Naipaul on the latter's marriage to a woman regarded by Theroux as aggressive and interfering. Theroux's *Sir Vidia's Shadow* (1998) was the vengeful and vitriolic result — a risible and finally unsuccessful attempt to reduce Naipaul by mocking his pretensions and highlighting his cold-bloodedness.

Theroux may possibly fall into another category — that of the person who, having no real talent for friendship himself, looks to others as ostensible friends in order to be let down by them. "He was inordinately vain and cantankerous," wrote Max Beerbohm about the painter James Whistler. "Enemies, as he had wittily implied, were a necessity to his nature; and he seems to have valued friendship . . . as just the needful foundation for future enmity. Quarreling and picking quarrels, he went his way through life blithely."

Beerbohm discovered a species of friendship made to be broken in the phenomenon that he named *sympat*. He took the word from a Brazilian he had met abroad who, after a few encounters, exclaimed, "Never, my friend, did I yet meet one to whom I had such a *sympat* as you!" Beerbohm used the neologism to refer especially to relationships made while traveling or on holiday, conjuring up, in an essay under that title, the initial pleasure one feels in unfamiliar surroundings upon finding someone with whom one has things in common and with whom one senses a more immediate closeness than might be the case upon meeting the same person at home. "*Sympat*," Beerbohm writes acutely, "is but the prelude to *antipat*." Not that he would have us avoid such friendships when abroad; the trick is to avoid them back home.

With Beerbohm's essay in mind, I recall a time when I might have played a role resembling that of the welcome *sympat* turned dreary *antipat*. This had to do with the novelist Ralph Ellison, who had written an essay for a magazine I then edited. The essay was both beautiful and wise, and when I thanked him for it, he responded by inviting me to lunch when next I was in New York.

We met one wintry day at the Century Club, for a lunch that lasted no fewer than four hours. Everything about the afternoon seemed magical. The flow of talk was unbroken: gossip, friends we had in common, the present state of the literary world. There were jokes, much laughter, and great good feeling on both sides. It was daylight when I walked into the Century Club and dark when I emerged. In Ralph Ellison I had met a man I long admired and found him not in the least disappointing. I felt I had made a new friend.

Returning to Chicago, I wrote Ellison a note of thanks for the meal and the splendid conversation, adding my hope that he would let me know if he planned to be in Chicago so that I could stand him to a similar lunch. He did not answer. A month or so later I wrote again, this time inviting him to write another essay for my magazine. No answer. A few months passed, and I wrote to pass along a bit of news that I thought might interest him. Again nothing. Ellison and I never had another communication of any kind.

Was it me? Apparently not. Soon after Ellison died in 1994, I received a letter from a reader asking if I had known him. This man and his wife had been on a cruise and met the Ellisons, with whom, he thought, they hit it off beautifully. Upon their return, he wrote to Ellison not once but several times, receiving no reply. Did I, he wondered, have any explanation for this strange behavior?

I now think the explanation may lie in Max Beerbohm's notion of the *sympat*, and, what is more, I understand and sympathize with Ellison. A naturally gregarious man, he was someone whom many people, I among them, would have been pleased to think of as a friend. He was also a man who, having published a fine novel, *Invisible Man*, in 1954, had not written another in all the decades since — a man, in other words, haunted by work undone. He did not need more friends filling up his days with correspondence, lunches, and the other time-consuming niceties that would follow from his natural sociability. No *sympats* for Ralph, evidently; he eliminated them before they had a chance to turn *antipat*.

I have broken off a few intellectual friendships myself, not all of them justly, and some of them much longer than an afternoon's duration. Once, a friend sent me the manuscript of a book he was writing on Ernest Hemingway. He was a critic very much attuned to Freudianizing his subjects — an interpretative line for which Hemingway, with his supermasculine bravado, was a choice victim. But my friend, I thought, was really pushing the limit, and in replying to one of the chapters he had sent me I wrote that he seemed to be on the path to discovering that Hemingway was a repressed lesbian. He did not find the comment amusing. His response was to write to my wife, suggesting that I was in need of therapy.

That snapped it: we didn't communicate again for fifteen years. But at some point, happily, my ex-friend began writing me brief, cordial notes, which I answered at first in a deliberately distant manner. Then I heard that he was ill, and arranged to meet him for a drink in Washington, D.C., where he lived. I was startled by how his illness had ravaged him, but we easily slipped back into our old friendship; we had both reached the grandfather stage of existence, and had a great deal to talk about. When he died not long afterward, I was left with a sense not so much of guilt as of wistfulness for the good times we might have had together, lost because of a stupid break in our friendship.

Very different was my experience with another friend with whom I had become trapped in a full-blown, decade-long relationship to which there was no way out but cruelly to end it over the telephone. I knew going in that my partner was obsessive and somewhat neurotic, but neurotics can have their own charm: Oscar Levant and George S. Kaufman come to mind. My friend, though, added to his neurosis a strong dose of solipsism, making for an exceptionally strong brew.

In some ways, the basis of our friendship was our shared contempt for those of our fellow intellectuals whom we thought naive or artistically uncultivated. He could talk for great uninterrupted stretches about the awfulness of this or that writer or teacher. (Having published my thoughts on these matters, I did not so much feel the need to talk about them.) The problem was in the word *uninterrupted*. My friend was a member in good standing of the club of nonlisteners; he could have been its president. Whenever I attempted to break in, to add a point or give the conversation a slight turn, he would mutter, "Yeah, yeah," obviously not listening, and resume his tirade.

He wanted to meet once a week over coffee. As time went on, I tried to get out of as many of these meetings as I could: I had heard all of his material, and had grown restive at having my own meager attempts at conversation completely ignored. To be fair, he could be amusing, often even interesting; generous and decent, he was not by any interpretation a bad fellow, or capable of mean acts. He just could not listen.

More and more frequently I made excuses for missing our regular sessions. Sometimes I would deliberately not pick up his calls (thank you, caller ID). But then he would leave messages saying he was worried about me. Was I ill? Was everything all right in my family? He was — is — a kindly man, and I would succumb once again.

To reveal the extent of my social cowardice: it took me nearly two years to muster the courage to tell him that I wanted out. I thought so much about how best to do this that it interfered with my thinking about other things. Finally, I called one afternoon and said that

I wished him well but, since he could not seem to bring his non-listening problem under control, I had decided to stop meeting with him. He felt, I sensed, that I was somehow ungrateful for what our friendship had given me — at least he used the word *ungrateful* in response to my awkward kiss-off. But in the end he manfully said, "Farewell, then, Joseph," and hung up. I felt terrible. I also felt hugely relieved.

Every broken friendship can be thought of as a failure or a defeat. Yet one must ask in each case, was the friendship itself therefore without meaning? Nietzsche, who himself had a famous broken friendship with Wagner — he began by idolizing the composer and ended by despising him — devotes a strangely fortifying paragraph to the subject in *The Gay Science*. Trying to make lemonade out of the rotted lemons of broken friendship, he suggests that perhaps, in "a tremendous but invisible stellar orbit, such friendships might be renewed and better made." One would like to think this may be so, but the odds in favor of it are only slightly better than those in favor of the return of vaudeville.

KATE FARRELL

Faithful to Mystery

FROM *The Journal for Anthroposophy*

This open channel to the highest life is the first and last reality, so subtle, so
quiet, yet so tenacious, that although I have never expressed the truth, and
although I've never heard the expression of it from any other, I know the
whole truth is here for me.

— Ralph Waldo Emerson

Lad of Athens, faithful be
To Thyself,
And Mystery —
All the rest is Perjury —

— Emily Dickinson

WHEN I WAS TEN OR ELEVEN, I made a plan to run away and live
in the woods, somehow talking my little sister Margaret into going
with me. Despite our fear of the dark, the departure was always set
for the middle of the night: the next full moon, say, at 2:30 in the
morning. We kept clothes for the trip in a special drawer, but there
were few other practical considerations. We knew the general direction of the route: across the road, then up a dirt road; maybe
stopping for the night in the big ditch there, then through the
woods we knew and beyond.

The idea was no doubt inspired by days spent exploring with our
brothers the woods near our house. "All trees say: *Vanish into us*,"
writes Ptolemy Tompkins in "Those Dark Trees,"[1] and kids know
how to accept the invitation; know how to take the hint from an old
line of trees and begin the march toward (in Tompkins's words)
"the secret heart of the world." The place my sister and I had in
mind was that kind of spot: less a place than an atmosphere, the

sort that becomes visible mainly in art — a watercolor forest by Paul Klee, maybe, with stairs to midair entrances among the trees. On the designated night, we would quietly rise, dress in our special clothes, take a loaf of bread from the pantry, and be ready to go. But opening the front door was like waking from a dream: nothing out there but icy darkness. Not tonight, I'd tell Margaret, but soon, I promise, one night very soon.

Our journey, or its mood, shows up often in poetry: "I will arise and go now, and go to Innisfree . . ." But the trips whose élan most reminds me of our plan are the real-life treks toward paradise recounted by Mircea Eliade. In his book *The Quest,*[2] for instance, Eliade tells the true story of the Guarini Indians' search for The Land Without Evil, the world as it was when people walked with the gods. During the sixteenth century, these South American tribes began looking for their lost homeland, the pure and perfect land of "the beginning," a project that went on for centuries. Certain tribes danced night and day, trying to become light enough to fly there or to obtain knowledge of the route to be taken — the way also taken during prayer and after death, a road at once natural and supernatural.

Had my sister and I thought of it at the time, we would have gladly danced to discover route information or become light enough for the journey. We never, however, actually did set out. Travel conditions remained inauspicious, and, like the Guarini, we kept rescheduling. I should add that it never felt like a game. On the contrary, the side of myself who dreamed up the plan seemed realer, more serious — and more myself — than the one who inhabited my usual school and church and neighborhood existence, with its measured-out possibilities and watchdog-protected darknesses; an existence I was already worried about growing up into.

Then again, misgivings about fitting in seem to have been written into the bones of great numbers of us who grew up in the 1950s and '60s, a generation famously determined to trust its own experience, go by its own rules, invent its own lives — have an "original relation to the universe," in Emerson's memorable phrase.[3] So that in a way I can picture throngs of us looking out from that childhood door through the dark, wondering how and when and in what direction.

In time, I came to feel that the creative imagination was at once the road through the dark to "the secret heart of the world" and the key to that free and original relation we all wanted so badly. Far from being the fantasyland that people often thought it, true imagination was *Mundus Imaginalis* (in Henri Corbin's term), a revelatory realm that bridged matter and spirit; it was Emerson's channel to truth, finally open to everyone — a route that could lead through potentially endless levels of understanding, changing the imaginer, and perhaps the world around her, in the direction of an existence there is less reason to run away from. But then, however universal the route, the pilgrimage is personal, and the best way to say more about both may be to go back to the time when I gave up on the dream forest and discovered poetry.

2.

> Was it a vision, or a waking dream?
> Fled is that music — Do I wake or sleep?
>
> —"Ode to a Nightingale," JOHN KEATS

Jorge Luis Borges says that he discovered poetry one evening when his father recited "Ode to a Nightingale" in the library of his boyhood home in Buenos Aires. Not a word of the lines did he understand at the time, but he swears he found poetry that night "as a music and a passion." For me, something like that happened during summer visits to Oklahoma, where my roughly educated, gruff-voiced grandfather quoted Whitman and Shakespeare while pointing out the constellations above his dusty little farm. Though I understood Whitman as little as Borges did Keats, I somehow got the idea that poetry was a magical language, one that had once communicated the secrets of existence. From the first, I associated poetry with nature. Like the woods, it had a mystery and freedom that introduced me to my own. And I remember the day it came to me, as I waited for the school bus, that if trees used words instead of limbs and leaves, they'd speak in poetry.

Not until high school did I read a modern-sounding poem and realize real poets were still writing. We students followed along as our English teacher read aloud the poem by E. E. Cummings that begins

In Just-
spring   when the world is mud-
luscious

and ends with the "goat-footed" balloon man whistling "far and
wee." After reading the poem, the teacher explained that no poem
could be understood until it was analyzed — here, for instance,
you needed to know that the word *goat-footed* symbolized the Greek
god Pan. A shy confrontation-hater, I surprised myself by speaking
up, saying that I'd understood the poem without analyzing anything. She denied the possibility. What was that *feeling* of understanding, I asked, if not understanding? She had no interest in the
question and I, no way of pressing my case. To say now what I
couldn't at the time: by "understanding," I meant that the spring
fever of the lines had come alive in my mind. Only a start perhaps,
but the poem was simple, and bypassing what was openly conveyed
to analyze words on a page was like investigating springtime without going outside. And I was furious to see poetry become for my
classmates a pointless exercise that had nothing to do with them or
their lives. Nonetheless the incident did me the favor of turning my
attention to a question that has stayed with me ever since: what
sort of understanding is the understanding of poetry? It got me
thinking too about gatehouses of knowledge that hinder instead of
enable understanding. Within a few years, I was wondering if my
Catholic school religion wasn't something like that: a vast gate-
house built at the border of what? The unknowable? Nothingness?

3.

Northrop Frye said that, walking to school one day, he just
sloughed off for good the oppressive, man-made picture of god
("that lugubrious old Stinker in the Sky") while holding on to the
part of religion that made deep sense to him.[4] A lightning flash like
that could have saved me endless trouble. The best I could do was
to nervously ask myself the usual questions. Wouldn't all-wise spiritual beings give us a way to know about them directly, instead of requiring faith in not-necessarily-trustworthy authorities? Was there
no better way to become a better person than by avoiding church-
defined sins? One Sunday in college, I borrowed a car to attend a

go-through-the-motions church service — and kept driving: out to the autumn woods which seemed so much holier. Then after quitting school to get married and "live my own life," I felt obliged to face, at least as a possibility, the terrifying pitch blackness of a world without meaning and a life without purpose. Before long, I had (unlike Frye) thrown the baby out with the holy water, so to speak, and like so many others who did the same thing, I had no idea that once religion was out of the picture, the ego, in a stupendous variety of disguises, would be ready to run the show; no thought that relying on my own thinking required making my thinking reliable; or that things like goodness, truth, freedom, and love were tricky achievements, as distant and elusive as that magic land in the forest.

Skip ahead a few years and I'm a mixed-up, grief-stricken, old-feeling twenty-seven-year-old widow, living with my two little kids in New York City where I'd come to study literature at Columbia. By then, I was writing poetry seriously, and questions about how and whether and how much we can know had a practical urgency. My husband had committed suicide the year before (his manic depression, clear in retrospect, never diagnosed) and within a few months of my arrival in Manhattan, my closest childhood friend would die in a motorcycle accident. I was counting on poetry — along with whatever secrets waited behind the doors of the big city — to help me tell my children why life was worth living.

Instead those first years in New York were rather like the years the poet Kathleen Raine describes spending in Cambridge back in the 1920s. After growing up in a family where imaginative vision was second nature, Raine capitulated to the positivism that dominated Cambridge in its so-called golden age. It took half her life, she writes, to rid herself of what she learned there and make her way back to Yeats and Blake and "those states of consciousness through which alone the lost paradise of the imagination can be regained."[5]

The materialism that Raine insists was the real religious faith of the twentieth century snagged me in my first writing class. In that class came the news that sophisticated, intellectually honest, post-Freudian thinkers did not read or write to find or express the truth about life. For beyond scientifically verifiable facts, there was no truth to find. In other classes, the attitude showed up as indifference to the validity of what writers actually said; the urge to pull works apart almost before they were read. The bedrock mindset was something like this. Now that we knew that our minds belonged to our bodily machinery, there was no going back. True, literature and the arts, along with love and beauty, were the very things that made life worth living, offering a temporary respite (no doubt evolutionary in origin) from the world's disappointments and miseries. But poetic vision, like the madness of religion, had nowhere to come from but the boxed-in subjectivity of a fantasy-prone brain. While writers of the past had the excuse of ignorance, today's writer had none. Who was I to disagree? By the time I graduated, I could almost think of myself as someone brave enough not to hope for the truth. Almost. For I led a double life, poring over volumes with the opposite message and never completely giving up on poetry's hints of who-knows-what saving reality; dim lights shining back through dark trees.

4.

There's a kind of dream in which you discover new rooms in your old house, rooms that are not only beautiful and interesting but also strangely familiar. To me, the rooms in those dreams stand for openings-up to new understandings — the moving past a wall that isn't a wall after all — that comes through imaginative experience. "The imagined world," writes Gaston Bachelard, "gives us an expanding home." When I began to teach, especially a college workshop called Imaginative Reading and Writing, I found that once students began to have this kind of experience, it was smooth sailing.

By now, I felt sure that imaginative reading was a creative activity that was as different from ordinary reading as imaginative writing was from newspaper prose, that imaginative works made this kind of reading possible as naturally as aquatic buoyancy made floating above the ground possible. All it took on the part of the reader was sympathetic receptivity — whereas a closed, critical attitude was like wearing iron shoes into the water. This way of reading would be second nature, I thought, if literature weren't used so exclusively for teaching critical (as opposed to imaginative) thinking and writing. As it was, it took my pressured Columbia students half a semes-

ter to remove their iron shoes and wade in and see that the inspired state of mind belonged, not just to writing, but to reading
and the contemplation that went with it, that these activities were
all of a piece, inspiring, sustaining, and shedding light on each
other. They saw too that imagination strengthened with use, helping them think more clearly and deeply, not only about books but
about everything else in life.

When asked around this time to write a poetry textbook, I decided to first figure out all I could about the workings of imagination which by then seemed to be at the heart of what poetry was actually *for.* Complicating matters was the fact that I was still living a
double life — "willingly suspending disbelief" while reading, yet
holding on to an obligatory disbelief as my official point of view. It
was a collision course. All this time, for example, I'd been secretly
hoping that science would eventually find (and prove true) the
hidden side of life. But what if scientific thinking could only find
the outsides of things — while the perhaps no-less-real things poetry disclosed *required* imaginative investigation and expression?
A possibility that suggested, what else? *Spiritual* realities and purposes. *Spiritual:* I despised the very word. And with supernatural beings out of the question, what or whose purposes were they? I was
becoming somewhat paranoid. Was I trying to know something
that wasn't meant to be known?

Then one day my husband, Bob, picked up a copy of Owen
Barfield's *History in English Words* from the front counter of Books
& Company, a legendary now-vanished Manhattan bookstore. Later
that day, I was taking in sentences I'd been waiting all my life
for, and over the next couple of years, I slowly worked my way
through the store's complete set of Barfield paperbacks. Having always assumed that philosophy was too abstract for me, I found that
Barfield's writing had the effect of poetry. There was the familiar
"felt change of consciousness" (Barfield's term for the shift to another state of mind). And, as with poetry, just following the words
brought a gradual understanding of things that at first had seemed
beyond me — "Suddenly I had the right eyes," says Rilke about
catching on to Cézanne's painting. The only drawback being that
Barfield's stranger ideas seemed a risk to my sanity.

Having put off Barfield's novel *Unancestral Voice*[6] till last, one September Sunday, I read it straight through, absolutely riveted, not

bothering to stop for what I didn't understand (which was plenty), completely caught up in the mystery of the Meggid. The Meggid is an invisible mental visitor who strikes up an inner conversation with Burgeon (the Barfield-like protagonist), offering cryptic hints about the secrets of existence, leaving Burgeon to work out the details for himself. A phrase like "interior is anterior" (that is, mind precedes matter) sets Burgeon to digging around in literature and history and gathering hints from everyday events and chance conversations while feeling his way through a series of incremental epiphanies.

Along the way, the reader learns about, among other things, the evolution of consciousness, Barfield's big subject. To sum up an idea that resists summation: ancient cultures felt themselves to be participants in a spirit-and-meaning-permeated universe. That sort of inspired group consciousness gradually narrowed to our current self-enclosed consciousness in which, in Matthew Arnold's words, "we mortal millions live alone," yanked by our thinking toward a dispiriting literalism, egotism, and materialism. On the positive side, this inner evolution made possible not only the successes of modern science but the potential for true freedom, creative love, and further stages of knowledge — in which, for instance, the lost paradise of imagination could be regained as a free and conscious attainment.

As *Unancestral Voice* progresses, the Meggid tells Burgeon that the Word, the Logos, has been the secret "transforming agent" in the evolutionary processes of both nature and consciousness. The incarnation of the Logos, he says, was the turning point of time, after which the responsibility for evolution began to be entrusted to human beings. Imperiling this vast and risky process was "the great taboo" against knowing spiritual realities on our own. Our usual self-understanding, the Meggid explains, is a sort of lifeless cover story, a shallow mirror behind which we're afraid to look, instinctively dreading to face our own destructiveness. But daring to face the worst in ourselves, we would find something else — the source of our own thinking, the inner word or logos, the creative spirit through which we could gradually change ourselves and the world now being entrusted to us.

On that September Sunday, I'd caught on to the barest gist of something like that in a disorderly, excited, walking-around-the-ceiling kind of way, when it dawned on me that I'd been *living* the great taboo. That my default agnosticism (to which my fear of "going crazy" from reading Barfield belonged) was my own cover story, that deep down I knew for a fact that his trustworthy voice would more likely drive a reader to sanity than to madness. My real fear was that taking his ideas to heart would make people *think* I was going mad (or else "taking the easy way out"), both the believers from my religious past and the disbelievers from my agnostic present. All my relationships seemed to be at stake, and what would become of my writing? There I stood, in my own darkness behind my own shallow mirror. "The soul," writes Yeats, "must become its own betrayer, its own deliverer, the mirror turn lamp."

In the book's final paragraphs, the Meggid at last identifies himself, describing his part in an intricate reverse hierarchy of mutual service: beings who serve the Logos who, in turn, serves everyone else with a washing-of-the-feet selflessness. The three final words, set off by themselves on the page:

> I am
> yours

were like a signature to a message passed through those ranks to the Meggid to Barfield to me — and who was I but the Prodigal in the pigsty.

One last hesitation: what if Barfield were mistaken? What if I made some grand effort only to be sucked back with everyone and everything else into lifeless nothingness. But by then I knew that reading Barfield "as if" spiritual truth were knowable would make me a better, saner, more useful person. That alone made me less afraid of death, even a death into nothingness. And finally it was just a matter of giving up my double life, my pretense that the search for truth wasn't built into every serious thought I'd ever had and every serious word I'd ever read or spoken.

5.

"Between two worlds life hovers like a star," writes Byron, in a line that sums up what countless poems, myths, teachings, and traditions, in one way or another, assume or hint or say. That we belong to two worlds: the invisible, hard-to-know eternal one we come from and the noisy, obvious, temporal one all around us. According to Plato's myth, we forget the first one when we drink from Lethe, the river of forgetfulness, before whizzing off like shooting stars to be born. But "not in entire forgetfulness" do we come, as Wordsworth put it, and people through the ages have tried in all kinds of ways to remember or know or find that other world while still in this one. Once, shamans climbed magic ropes and special trees to get there, and whole tribes, like the homesick Guarini, spent their lives looking for a road in that direction. As consciousness evolved, the distance between the worlds kept growing, so that today it's easy to feel with Matthew Arnold that we are homeless travelers . . .

> Wandering between two worlds; one dead,
> The other powerless to be born

. . . a rift that in Rilke's poem "Evening" has sunk deep inside us:

> The evening slowly changes into the clothes
> held for it by a row of ancient trees;
> and you watch as one world rises toward heaven
> and the other sinks down beneath your feet
>
> leaving you not at home in either one;
> not quite so dark as those silent houses,
> but not testifying to eternity with the passion
> of that part that turns to a star at night and rises —
>
> leaving you (speechlessly to disentangle)
> your life, vast and frightened and ever deepening,
> so that now closed-in, now all-encompassing
> your life is sometimes a stone in you, sometimes a star.

In Barfield's view, imagination can reconnect the two worlds, the stone and the star. For imagination is the bridge between matter and spirit. On first coming across this idea, I pictured the link as one of those worn footbridges between mountain peaks in old Chinese paintings. But Barfield depicts it, not as a solid bridge, but as a rainbow of imaginative activity "spanning the two precipices and linking them harmoniously together."[7] The chasm the rainbow spans is modern everyday consciousness. Caught in that gap, we believe only what our senses tell us: that matter is nothing but physical matter, while spirit either doesn't exist or defies understanding. Whereas from the rainbow bridge of imagination, we can become aware that matter, including our own bodies, is *coagulum spiritus* — that part of the spirit that physical senses perceive — while spirit is (among other things) the one who is doing the perceiving. For Barfield, as for Blake, Coleridge, Henri Corbin, Rudolf Steiner, Kathleen Raine, and others, true imagination, unlike mere fantasy, is an experience or capacity or way of thinking that "unveils," as Corbin put it, "the hidden reality." Not that the rational is superseded, but that it serves the more-than-rational.

For Barfield, Steiner's account of imagination was by far the most profound and complete, bringing to fruition what the Romantic revival had begun. "I am certain of nothing," John Keats had written, "but the holiness of the Heart's affections and the truth of Imagination" — but in *what way* was imagination true? The Romantic movement fell apart, says Barfield, because its poets and philosophers could not adequately answer that question — not even Shelley and Coleridge, for whom imagination was "a passion, a religion, a veritable key to the promised land." The answer had to wait, he says, for Steiner to take up where Coleridge left off, proving by his lifework that imagination, when taken seriously, does not just enrich our own lives, but enables us to better serve the world and one another. For Steiner saw imagination as the first part of "a long, sober process of cognition," a process which — in overcoming the divide between subject and object, matter and spirit, self and other — could also help us overcome the horrible predicaments that our divisive, materialistic mentality keeps getting us into.[8]

Sympathetic participation (Barfield's term) in works uttered and understood by imagination is a natural first step, drawing readers toward the level of thinking in which a work was created, perhaps with a noticeable shift of consciousness. One work may lead only a little way beyond everyday thinking; another, especially over time, may lead much further. Or rather it may if nothing stands in the way. Now that the iron shoes of abstraction are strapped on so firmly and early, there's a tendency to try to take in more-than-rational works with "merely rational" thinking, turning gold to straw and making writing that might otherwise be alive, illuminating, and transformative seem difficult, dull, or even nonsensical.

When all goes well, however, the reader may enter into a contemplative conversation with the writer on the "rainbow bridge" of imaginal thinking. Interspersed through such conversations — different every time for every reader — are typically lots of long pauses and mental digressions, as you connect what is said to your own experience, put things into your own words, picture them in your own way, and otherwise "dwell in Possibility," in Dickinson's phrase. One passage says something you've always wanted to say; another opens up a new part of the world — and a new part of yourself along with it. Sometimes there's just the barest premonition of understanding; other times, the meaning, obvious enough while you're reading, vanishes the minute you turn the page. Coming back to the page several books later, the meaning is as clear as day. Ideas come from nowhere, answering unrelated questions, filling in the larger picture. As understandings from one book sink into, enlarge, alter, and reverberate through those from various others, it's like a taste of that library in heaven (to adapt Donne's image) where all the books open to and illuminate each other. As for which writing allows this kind of reading, you know it by its effect. For me, it cuts across genres, from poetry to certain works of fiction, metaphysics, creative scholarship, visionary philosophy, and other kinds of prose.

In *Surprised by Joy,* C. S. Lewis recalls a day when he referred to philosophy as "a subject" in front of his friends Bede Griffiths and Owen Barfield. "It wasn't a *subject* to Plato," Barfield remarked; "it was a way." Nowadays someone could go to school for a very long time without discovering that poetry, say, or philosophy is "a way" — meaning of course a way to the truth. But it's that kind of quest that gives this kind of reading its momentum, passion, joy, and efficacy. It's a quest in which, as van Gogh says about the artistic quest, you never stop looking for something you never completely find. Every stage is interesting and important, not because more and more facts are at your disposal (which may happen as well) but because you are gradually answering your own deepest questions, finding out what you yourself think, discovering new square footage in the expanding home of consciousness, brightening the light that is, in Emerson's words, "supplied by the observer."

In a way, it's like drinking little by little from the River of Unforgetting. The Greek word *a-létheia* — literally "un-forgetting" —

was the word for truth when Plato pursued it; the truth that Christ told Pilate he had come to bear witness to. The Hungarian philosopher Georg Kühlewind emphasizes that in those days *alétheia* didn't mean truth as "correctness" but was at once a spiritual reality and the thinking that unveiled it; it was imaginative thinking, living thinking; thinking that moves through progressively deeper states and stages of consciousness; it was recognition as well as discovery.[9] The idea of truth as an expedition into mystery is there too in Dickinson's title poem:

> Lad of Athens, faithful be
> To Thyself,
> And Mystery —
> All the rest is Perjury —

The lines address, I think, the Lad of Athens in us all — the one who, in the days of the Greek mysteries, would have gladly vowed silence for the sake of enlightenment. The poem urges, however, not silence, but a double promise: to be true to ourselves (our own firsthand experience) *and* to mystery — the knowable unknown, the imaginal doorway through which the unconscious becomes conscious. In keeping both oaths at once, we become evolving witnesses to an unfolding truth, our deepening capacities deepening the mystery (and the self) toward and into and through which we move. "All the rest" — presumably every thought, word, and action — is perjury. Clinging to fixed opinions would be perjury. And convincing others to do so: well, that would be suborning perjury! No death penalty these days for the divulger of knowledge, but the process of unforgetting remains a tricky inner odyssey.

6.

Imagine that, instead of a starfish regenerating its missing appendage (a common occurrence), the appendage were to rebuild, not only its missing starfish body, but its whole lost undersea kingdom. Something like that happens in Rilke's poem "Archaic Torso of Apollo": a fragment of an ancient statue of the Greek god of truth and light begins to glow like a lantern, then shine like a star, finally disclosing a living universe that gazes back at the gazer. When this poem shows up in the last chapters of Ptolemy Tompkins's memoir

Paradise Fever,[10] it begets a similar epiphany — and a contemporary account of the transformative power of imaginative reading.

For much of the book, Tompkins the child has been swept along by the funny-in-retrospect adventures of his famous New Age father, whose symptoms of "paradise fever" include captaining a naked boat crew in search of the lost continent of Atlantis — and insisting on having two wives. But the core of the book is the author's childhood discovery of a secret "world-behind-the-world," a realm about which he constantly dreams and guesses, linking it with long-ago ages and the mysteries of nature; a near-yet-far dimension for which he feels — despite huge fears of its unknown intentions — a deep affinity and homesickness. Much less at home in the material dimension, by the final scenes he's a worn-out, miserable thirty-three-year-old writer who relies on drugs and alcohol to endure normal existence. Home for a visit, he heads into the woods one hot summer morning, veins full of chemistry, with a warm six-pack of beer, a copy of Steiner's *Cosmic Memory* (for a writing project about Atlantis), and a book of Rilke's poetry. After swigging a few beers, he opens Rilke at random to "Evening" — the poem quoted earlier about the abyss between worlds — then to the Apollo poem, focusing on the lines that have stopped so many readers in their tracks:

> . . . there isn't anyplace that isn't
> looking at you. You must change your life.

For Tompkins, the words awaken a familiar sensation — "at the exact midpoint between joy and fear," the feeling of being watched by the hidden side of life. They also awaken a way of thinking that, over the course of the day, bridges the rift between worlds, visible and invisible, and makes new sense of life. He thinks about Atlantis and its postparadise inhabitants, trying to manage by themselves when the gods are out of sight. Maybe, he thinks, if we could keep in mind, even in our very worst hours, the secret world-behind-the-world always out there watching, we could "live down here without its hurting so much." The next day he drives away from the flawed paradise of childhood and fake heavens of addiction, to change (the book predicts) in ways he hadn't thought possible.

Nostalgia for paradise, suggests Barfield, is nostalgia for nonphysical existence, of which paradise is the symbol; for the "matterless universe from which we all spring."[11] And perhaps the rift-healing dimension found by Rilke and Tompkins — call it *mundus imaginalis,* the dimension linking earth to the matterless universe — was the land the naked Atlantis-hunters were, without knowing it, seeking, as were my sister and I, and even the endlessly dancing Guarini.

One more story about reading. Once, immersed in a book by Nicholas Berdyaev, I stopped to read my husband a particularly remarkable passage — whereupon it instantly lost its magic, becoming a dull string of empty words. As I sat there perplexed, a funny thing happened: the lines of words on the page began to resemble those rickety roll-fences that keep beach dunes from blowing away. Not sand, in this case, was held in place, but expanses of meaning stretching back into the page, a place (or really, state) where a nomad like me could pitch her tent and think — the sort of delicately anchored mind-to-mind state that a reader, like a lover, half-creates, half-discovers. And for a little while, I could feel the difference it made: to be in that state or stranded outside it in everyday thinking; to take part, or not, in the miraculous interchange. Berdyaev says that there are two ways out of our modern aloneness: one is love, the other, communion in the mysteries of existence. This kind of reading seems both at once.

7.

When the second tower fell on 9/11, I saw it happen from my Brooklyn apartment window and, at the same time, on the television screen right beside it. Even that seemed symbolic. Minutes later, flaming to-do lists drifted across the river into our building's back yard. Even those of us who lost no one we knew took it personally. It was like getting word of a beloved relative's fatal illness — except that, in this case, it was our entire world whose days appeared to be numbered. In the weeks that followed, the beautiful September light around the smoldering skyline seemed to belong to a lost kingdom — or a vast chance squandered. The newspapers, with their shallow talk of war and revenge, just deepened the feeling. How much time did we have? Then came the news that New Yorkers were turning to poetry. What is the mysterious solace of poetry? the *New York Times* asked. But was it solace we were after?

I think of Jacques Lusseyran, the blind French resistance leader and concentration camp survivor who said that, in Buchenwald, poetry made the difference between who survived and who didn't. There, poetry was not literature but medicine; "it tied earth back to heaven," lending prisoners its wings, its inner freedom. The soul dies first, he said, and poetry kept their souls alive against all odds.[12] "It is difficult/ to get the news from poems," writes William Carlos Williams, "yet men die miserably every day/ for lack/ of what is found there."

For Barfield, what is found in poetry and other works of imagination is the thinking whose development is the hope of humanity, the power whereby the world "powerless to be born" might be born after all. We cannot change the world, he says, by "tinkering with the outside"; it can only be changed from within and we *are* its within.[13] Altered eyes, says Blake, alter everything. And in my view, New Yorkers turned to poetry after 9/11 less for solace than for emergency assistance — new eyes, deeper answers, a way of thinking adequate to the situation — however few saw the link between imaginative reading and the mind-by-mind cure of the world.

In closing, a word about my sister Margaret, childhood traveling companion, now a clinical psychologist working with the poor and mentally ill in northern California, many of them near the end of their rope. To be of real help, she says, she needs what she gets from metaphysics and meditation. We trade books. And for both of us, opening certain volumes has something of the mystery of opening the door into the dark on those long-ago nights — only these nights, travel conditions are propitious and, sooner or later, the road between stone and star starts to come into sight.

Notes

1. Ptolemy Tompkins, "Those Dark Trees," *The Sun*, September 2004.

2. Mircea Eliade, *The Quest: History and Meaning in Religion* (Chicago: University of Chicago Press, 1969), 101–111.

3. "The forgoing generations beheld God and nature face to face; we, through their eyes. Why should not we also enjoy an original relation to the universe? Why should not we have a poetry and philosophy of insight and not of tradition, and a religion by revelation to us, and not the history of theirs." From *Nature*.

4. David Cayley, *Northrop Frye in Conversation* (Toronto: House of Anansi, 1992), 3–4.

5. Kathleen Raine, *Yeats the Initiate* (London: George Allen & Unwin Ltd., 1986), 439.

6. Owen Barfield, *Unancestral Voice* (Middletown, CT: Wesleyan University Press, 1965).

7. Barfield, *The Rediscovery of Meaning* (Middletown, CT: Wesleyan University Press, 1977), 150.

8. Barfield, *Romanticism Comes of Age* (Middletown, CT: Wesleyan University Press, 1966), 15–16, 45–46.

9. Georg Kühlewind, *Becoming Aware of the Logos* (Great Barrington, MA: Lindisfarne Press, 1985), Chapter 10.

10. Tompkins, *Paradise Fever* (New York: Avon Books, 1997).

11. Barfield, *Worlds Apart* (Middletown, CT: Wesleyan University Press, 1963), 123–124.

12. Jacques Lusseyran, *Against the Pollution of the I* (New York: Parabola Books, 1999), 172–175.

13. Barfield, *History, Guilt, and Habit* (Middletown, CT: Wesleyan University Press, 1979), 92.

NATALIE GOLDBERG

On the Shores of Lake Biwa

FROM *Shambhala Sun*

I WANTED TO GO TO JAPAN to see the country that produced my
teacher. But Japan was far away. I'm terrible with languages. When
I tried to learn short Japanese phrases, it sounded like I was shred-
ding coleslaw with my tongue and not budging one inch from
Brooklyn. And all the words of that island country are written in
kanji. I wouldn't even be able to decipher signs.

People assured me that everyone in Japan learned English in
school. "No problem," they said. I didn't believe them. Hadn't I
studied French for eight years? And all I could do was conjugate
the verb "to be." Better to just spend my days on Coney Island — I
knew where the hot dogs were.

But I had a writing student who had lived in Japan for several
years and generously contacted a Japanese couple; they agreed to
take me around Kyoto. They spoke good English, so I could ask
questions. I talked my partner, Michele, into coming along.

We'd been there a week when Kenji and Tomoko picked us up at
the hotel. I already felt isolated, walking down crowded streets,
peering into unknown temples. I found myself several times towering over a young man or woman, asking something and receiving
giggles behind polite hands. The Japanese might have learned
English in school but they were too shy to speak it.

"They grind their own beans here," Kenji said as he drove us to a
coffee shop.

Just the smell cleared my sinuses. I never drink coffee — I have
enough trouble sleeping and fear chugging that dark brew would

send me running at a hundred miles per hour. But at this moment, I was so elated to speak to a native, not to feel so alone, that I too ordered a shot.

The four of us sat at a small square table, elbow to elbow. "So how do you know English so well?" I asked.

The white cups were placed in front of us. I took a sip. The black blend cut off the top of my head, hair and all. My eyes darted around the room. No tea, cookies, buns, rolls, rice cakes. Zen purity had been translated into a single-taste caffeine shop.

"We lived in England for four years. I was getting a Ph.D. in philosophy," Kenji explained.

"Really? Who did you study over there?" I'd done my master's in Western philosophy in my early twenties. But soon after I'd discovered Zen, I never thought of Bergson or Heidegger again.

"Immanuel Kant."

"You're kidding." My mouth fell open. "I did my thesis on him. You went all the way over to Europe for Kant?" I was incredulous. "In America we want to study Dogen."

It was Kenji's turn to be dumbstruck. "Ugh, no one understands Dogen. He's much too difficult." His nose crunched up.

Then I let the bomb drop. "I've been a Zen student for over two decades."

Now Tomoko grimaced. "That's awful. No one here likes Zen."

I had suddenly become peculiar to this Japanese couple.

Kenji injected, "Zen monks all die young."

I already knew, but asked, anyway, "Why?" I swallowed another gulp of coffee. I was never able to admit the answer through years of knee-aching, backbreaking sitting on little sleep.

"The training's too hard for a human being," he said.

My teacher had died in his early sixties. I could name several other Zen masters who had died too early. I had hoped it was the difficult shift they had made to America.

The conversation slid into pleasantries. Yes, I was a writer. Yes, my first book had been translated into Japanese.

Michele offered to meet them in New York the next time they visited. She described her family's apartment in that favorite of cities. I was watchful for my next opportunity to gather another crumb of information, a morsel of understanding, to slip in another question about my old practice.

My cup was almost empty. If I took one more sip I'd buzz out the window. I threw care to the neon lights above the entrance and put liquid to mouth. I leaned in close. "Can I ask you a question?" They both nodded simultaneously. Michele rolled her eyes. She knew where this was going. That morning in bed I had had a realization. Maybe I did know a little Japanese after all. In the zendo we chanted from cards that translated Japanese sounds into English syllables.

"Does this sound familiar?" I asked and then belted out the first line of the early morning chant that preceded putting on our rakusus. At this moment in the zendo our hands would be clasped in front of us with the lay ordination cloth on top of our heads. I saw the whole scene unfold as I chanted *Dai Sai Ge Da Pu Ku* in the coffee shop.

"Never heard of it." Both Kenji and Tomoko shook their heads. They must have learned that head shake in England. When I shook my head *No* here, everyone looked at me blankly.

"You're kidding." What had I been studying all these years?

"What does it mean?" Tomoko asked.

I was too disappointed to be embarrassed. "Great robe of liberation."

They both stared at me.

"This coffee is delicious," Michele quickly interjected and downed her cup.

They explained where they were going to take us. All I caught was "famous temples." I was templed out. Everyplace Michele and I went no one was meditating — just beautiful buildings, ornate altars, highly waxed, fine wood floors. I hadn't realized it, but what I'd come for was sixteenth-century Japan. I was looking for the descendants of Linji and Hakuin. Where were the kick-ass practitioners, like the wild Americans back in the States who were imitating the monks we thought were over here? We woke at 4 A.M., meditated all day, sewed robes, ate in formal style with three enamel bowls, even had miso soup for breakfast.

I let Michele do the socializing as I sat looking out the car window in the backseat next to Tomoko. Michele shifted the conversation from the dot-com explosion to a list of Japanese authors we'd been reading since we arrived. I perked up. "Yeah, we're reading these prize-winning novels and it's a surprise how often the plot is around a homosexual or a lesbian. I thought the Japanese were more uptight than that?"

Kenji lifted a hand off the steering wheel. "Oh, no, we're used to it — from the monasteries. The boys go in young."

I gulped. Is that what goes on in monasteries?

They drove us from one ancient shrine to another, all with indiscernible names. I was young again, dragged to one art museum after another. The afternoon was a blur and my eyes teared. I wanted to lie down and take a deep nap.

"I'm sorry," Kenji said. "We only have one more, but this one is important. You have to see it. Very famous."

Two young girls in navy-blue school uniforms explained the significance of the temple. All of the other visitors were Japanese. Michele and I politely stood with our hands shading our eyes. We didn't understand a word.

My mind was zinging out in the stratosphere, rejoicing that this was the last temple, when one word snapped through my daydream. Hold everything! Did that ingénue on the left say a familiar name?

"Excuse me, Tomoko," I whispered. "Who lived here in ancient days? What's his name?"

She shrugged. Even though she spoke the language this world was foreign to her.

"Please, help me," I took her hand. "I have to find out."

The student didn't know what I was talking about even through translation. She handed me the sheet she read from.

"Is the name Ikkyu here?" I turned the paper over to Tomoko. "What's the name of this temple?"

Tomoko slowly pronounced it: "Daitokuji."

My eyebrows jumped off my face. "Daitokuji. Did this temple burn down in the fifteenth century? Who rebuilt it? Does it say?"

Tomoko looked back at the paper and translated to the young hosts what I was asking. "Hai, hai," in unison. They nodded.

"Oh my god." I threw my hand over my mouth.

The thinner girl pointed to a square white building over the high stucco wall we were standing near. This time Kenji translated. "She says Ikkyu is in there."

"Ikkyu in there." My eyes widened. The eccentric Zen monk with a wild spirit whose poetry I loved. I imagined him preserved in zazen position in his ragged brown monk's robe, the one he wore when hanging out with drunks under the bridge.

My hands curled into fists. I wanted to leap the wall, burst into the tomb, bow at his feet, tell him how I'd spent a cold winter and dark spring reading his poems. They never failed me.

When a friend having a hard time would call, I'd say, "Hold on a minute," and grab *Crow with No Mouth.* "Listen to this," and I'd read them Ikkyu.

People were horrified by Ikkyu's unconventional life — he alternated between practicing hard, then frequenting brothels and bars with prostitutes and hoboes. But when he was eighty-two, he was asked to be head of Daitokuji. It was a great honor. He did not refuse. With his tremendous energy, he rebuilt the temple.

The intensity of having Ikkyu nearby was overwhelming. I was afraid I disappointed this great practitioner. He would have leaped over the barrier. He was waiting for me. I think he is still waiting.

I left Michele in Kyoto to travel north by train to Bukkokuji, one of the few Japanese monasteries willing to take Westerners and women. I thought, if I was going to be in this country, I had to experience their monasteries, even if for a short time. Michele and I went over my route many times in the hotel before I departed. The train moved fast and I was alert to hear the Obama stop announced, even though I knew it wouldn't be for quite a while.

To my right out the window was a great gray lake, reflecting the overcast sky. I heard, "Biwa."

"Biwa?" I poked the man next to me. This was very un-Japanese, but the train moved so quickly I had to act fast.

He nodded briskly, not glancing my way. "Hai."

At twenty-seven, Ikkyu, meditating alone at midnight out in a rowboat on this very lake, heard the *caw caw caw* of a crow overhead and was turned inside out, becoming totally realized.

He was a poet. It made sense that awakening would enter his body through sound. For a cook the ax might fall while tasting a particularly pungent lemon: she would drop to the ground, savoring bitter lemon in all things.

My stop was finally called and I jumped off, clutching my knapsack. I followed a path through weeds and empty lots into the monastery cemetery. Often at night monks sat at the gravestones and meditated. It was midafternoon. I was nervous. I kept repeating, "You'll be okay. You've sat six three-month difficult practice periods and this time it's just a few days."

The small building complex was a hundred yards away, built right up against a hill. I stepped into the courtyard. No one was there. A beefily built monk appeared and spoke to me in Japanese.

I shook my head. I understood not a word.

He continued to talk and motion with his hands. At this point Tangen — I recognized his face from a photo — the Zen master of the monastery, who was in his seventies and had rarely left in the past thirty-five years, glided into the courtyard, and he and the head monk (I figured out who the beefily built man was) grunted at each other. The head monk then grabbed my pack and I followed him.

Near twin sinks he stopped and pointed, holding out my sack. I took it and walked alone through a set of doors. Ten thin mattresses were on the floor and five Japanese nuns with shaved heads were lying on them. Near the entrance was a small, spare woman — the only other Western female at the monastery — who introduced herself and pointed to a rolled bed. I nervously set out my few things, unrolled the mattress, and laid down. I didn't know what the routine would be, but I knew it would be in silence. I tried to rest. How did the saying go? Rest when you rest, sleep when you sleep, cry when you cry. Et cetera, et cetera. I could have made the list go on: be nervous when you're nervous, feel your tight chest when you feel your tight chest, want to go home when you want to go home. I noticed how hot and humid it was. My straight hair was curling. No one else around me had any hair. I remembered my friend who'd been to Japan saying, there is nothing like the humidity. For emphasis he repeated himself: Trust me, Natalie, in all the world, your clothes will not get wetter than in Japan. Obama was on the sea. I was in for it.

Bells rang. All seven of us in the dormitory sprang up. They put on their robes; I put on my black long-sleeved T-shirt and black long pants, and we sat through two periods of zazen in the upstairs zendo across the court. I had no idea how long each sitting was. It could have been twenty-five minutes or forty. I was just happy to know how to do something and proud at the end to recognize the *Heart Sutra* as it was shot through at a speed no American could follow.

At dinner we ate cross-legged in the dining room in a ritualized style, with three oryoki bowls, chopsticks, napkin, and drying cloth. The actual meal was a mush of colors. What hadn't been eaten from breakfast and lunch was consumed at night. What hadn't been eaten from the meals of the days before was also in there. If mold was forming from a week ago, a high boil took care of it all.

At the end of the meal, we fingered thin slices of pickles to clean our bowls, ate the pickle slices, and drank the washing water. The bowls were then wrapped again in the lap cloth with a formal knot. I could do all this, and the Japanese nuns clucked in surprise.

We sat zazen again and went to bed. I hadn't spoken a word to anyone. I didn't know what time we would wake the next morning, but I could rely on the tight structure. Don't think, I told myself. Take care of your life — connected to all life — moment by moment.

I did not sleep for one moment the entire night. I was drenched in sweat. I think it was 3 A.M. when the bells rang and everyone popped out of bed. I ran the brush one time over my teeth. We were in the zendo fifteen minutes later.

The zendo was a comfort, but not for long. The bell quickly rang again and people ran down the stairs. Where were they going? I turned around and everyone was gone. I bolted after them and saw the monks running out the gate. I put on my shoes and dashed after them.

The streets of Obama were quiet. I heard only the swish of my rubber soles. Thank god I hadn't worn flip-flops. I chugged along, but way behind. Suddenly they turned a corner and I lost them. We were the Japanese Marx brothers. I headed east on one block, I saw them passing west on another; I darted north at the lamppost, I caught sight of them sprinting south at the turn. I was panting hard. I hadn't run like this in ten years. The sea was to my right as I galloped up an incline. Just as they neared the gate I caught up. My lungs were burning. My breath was heaving. I was soaked, hair dripping, pants and shirt stuck to my body.

I followed the monks into an empty room, where less than twenty-four hours ago the head monk had grunted at me. Another monk called out a command and everyone hit the ground flat-out; another shout and everyone was on their feet. Then we were slammed on the floor again, doing push-ups. I was already one command behind. They were down; I was up. They were up; I was down. Finally, the exercise stopped. I was a dishrag.

People stood around. Sunlight was creeping across the grave-stones. I sidled over to the Irishwoman and whispered so softly — the sound could have fit under a saltine cracker — "Can we take showers now?"

She replied with a single line: "There are no showers here."

Uh huh. I nodded. I'd heard a rumor years ago back in the com-fort of the Minneapolis zendo that baths in Japanese monasteries were taken once a week at public bath houses.

I sat on a stone step and waited for the next activity. Exhaustion allowed surrender.

The bell rang. We piled up to the zendo and sat for one period. Another bell rang and off everyone dashed down the stairs again. This time I walked. I didn't care if the fires of hell leaped at me. I found the monks in seiza, kneeling with their legs tucked under them, on the hard, wooden floor in a single row. A bell rang in an-other room and the first person in line jumped up and disap-peared. The row of people on their knees slid up to the next place.

I knelt at the end, the last person, the longest wait. My knees felt as though they were about to snap, but I didn't change positions. I crawled behind everyone else each time the first person left. I knew what was happening. This was our chance to talk to the Roshi, face to face, in his small *dokusan* room. I had heard he was clear, that just to watch him walk across a room was inspiring, that he took joy in the smallest things.

What was I doing here with this resounding pain? No one said I had to stay in this position, but everyone else was doing it and I was a stubborn person. Dedication no longer mattered, only animal will. What could I say to this man from another world? I had al-ready had my true teacher. He'd died eight years ago.

My turn came. I did the three prostrations and sat in front of Tangen Roshi. He tilted his head to peer at me. I was hopeless. I knew it. He said three English words: Not long enough.

I thought, thank god. I was fifty years old. Too old. Too tired. Too dirty.

The gesture was made for me to leave. The meeting was over. I had the urge to put my hand on his knee, to assure him I would be okay. After all, here was a man who was dedicated to waking us up. I didn't want to disappoint him but right then I wanted to go to sleep.

That afternoon after a work period when we beat mattresses and rolled blankets and towels, we had tea — and doughnuts, wrapped in cellophane, bought at a local store. I could tell this was a real treat and I abstained so the monks could have more.

Each day was long. I had no illusions that something big or deep would happen. I just wanted to make it through each day running, walking, sitting, eating in that single pair of black pants and shirt.

Young monks pounded big bells that hung from eaves and ran in the halls. Even the army knows to take boys early. Only me, only I don't know I'm not young. That is what these days taught me: I was no longer young. How easy it was for me at twenty-six, at thirty-one — but even then I complained. Now I had only a few days left in a Japanese monastery and I was thankful I would get to leave.

That day did come and there was no formality. No one said, "Oh, Natalie, we loved having you." I rolled up my mattress, deposited my scant towel and bedding in the laundry room, and slung my pack on my back.

I was thinking how I couldn't wait to return to Kyoto and take a shower when I passed the altar room. I noticed a big Buddha statue and a small inconspicuous donation box, but it wasn't necessary to pay anything for your stay.

I turned to head out. "C'mon, Nat, you can give a little something, even though these days were no fun."

I counted out yen. I was not good at figuring out the equivalent in dollars, a hundred and ten to one, too many zeros. I left what I thought was twenty-five dollars. I followed the path through weeds back to the railroad station. I was a bit early for the next train. I wandered over to the concession stand and eyed the bags of M & M's. A great compulsion overcame me. I bought two. I ripped one open; they were already melted. I shoved the colored chocolates into my mouth and they smeared over my right hand and around my lips. I had nothing to wipe them with but my dirty black sleeve.

Suddenly I looked up: one of the monks from the monastery had just entered the station, recognized me, and was walking over. He was dressed immaculately in formal traveling attire. I tried to hide my chocolate-covered hand, having already wiped my mouth. He stood in front of me in his platform sandals. He noticed my hand

and flashed a warm smile. I felt the color come to my face. He reached into the front of his robe. He pulled out some kind of bar and held it up. My eyes focused. Almond Joy. We both burst out laughing.

My train pulled up. I threw myself into a seat near the window and waved. The scenery zoomed by.

All at once, yens popped into my head. I hadn't left 2,750 — I left 27,500. Two hundred and fifty American dollars. I gasped, my stomach tightened. Then completely let go. It was fine, just fine. I was glad I'd contributed that much. And right there was everything I knew and I could not say what that was.

ADAM GOPNIK

Shining Tree of Life

FROM *The New Yorker*

WEARY OLD FAITHS make art while hot young sects make only trouble. Insincerity, or at least familiarity, seems to be a precondition of a great religious art — the wheezing and worldly Renaissance papacy produced the Sistine ceiling, while the young apostolic church left only a few scratched graffiti in the catacombs. In America, certainly, very little art has attached itself directly to our own dazzling variety of sects and cults, perhaps because true belief is too busy with eternity to worry about the décor. The great exception is the Shakers, who managed, throughout the hundred or so years of their flourishing, to make objects so magically austere that they continue to astonish our eyes and our sense of form long after the last Shakers stopped shaking. Everything that they touched is breathtaking in its beauty and simplicity. It is not a negative simplicity, either, a simplicity of gewgaws eliminated and ornament excised, which, like that of a distressed object found in a barn, appeals by accident to modern eyes trained already in the joys of minimalism. No, their objects show a knowing, creative, shaping simplicity, and to look at a single Shaker box is to see an attenuated asymmetry, a slender, bending eccentricity, which truly anticipates and rivals the bending organic sleekness of Brancusi's *Bird in Flight* or the algorithmic logic of Bauhaus spoons and forks. Shaker objects don't look simple; they look specifically Shaker.

Yet what the Shakers thought they were doing when they made their boxes and ladders and clocks, and why we think what they did was so lovely, remains something of a mystery, despite a booming market and the books to go with it. How did a sect so small make objects so sublime? Did they know what they were doing when they did what they did? Or were they doing something else, and doing this other, better thing on their way there?

The Shakers' early inheritance is English, and began with a strange visionary figure, Ann Lee, born on Leap Day in 1736. She was a woman who, in her lifetime, traveled, so to speak, from the world of E. P. Thompson to the world of William James — from a poverty-stricken and embattled sectarian North of England millennial religion to the new world of American self-made faith. At a time when Manchester was slowly becoming the industrial hell that, a hundred years later, Engels reported it to be, she was reared with seven siblings in a hovel, and her more luridly Freudian biographers suggest that hearing her father impregnate her mother again and again left her with the revulsion toward sex that distinguished her faith from competing millennial visions. Illiterate, visionary, charismatic, she took part in the swirl of "enthusiastick" sects that emerged at the time, dissenting from the Anglican Church and expecting the apocalypse; in fact, the name Shakers was given originally to a subset of the people we know as Friends, the Quakers. The Friends and the Believers — those following Ann Lee — seem to have been mixed up by the authorities, if not by themselves, into a porridge of dissenters.

After a career as an amateur sermonizer, Mother Ann, as she was known, was thrown into prison, in 1772, for disrupting the Anglican Sabbath. There she had a vision that she was the second coming of Christ; she also began to believe that sex was the root of all evil. The idea had a genuine edge not so much of feminist rage as of women's pain: she had lost her four children to illness and came of age in a working-class world in which constant pregnancy was a prime source of suffering. Her antisexual ethic was not so much antipleasure as antipregnancy.

In 1774, she and her husband and several followers emigrated to America and, after a brief stay in New York, formed a community just north of Albany. It was only then that the Believers began to emerge as a distinct cult with a distinct cult practice — a religious sect gathered around a single charismatic figure. People used to think that the Shakers recruited mostly from the poor and unhoused, eager for even a chaste roof to shelter under. It's now clear, though, that a cross-section of the American population, rich and poor and in between, joined them, for the usual mixture of reasons. And a regular intake of orphans and abandoned children gave the Shaker colonies the slightly misleading appearance of family. (There was a regular intake, as well, of people who wandered in for food and shelter in inclement times — "winter Shakers," they were called.)

Mother Ann's early followers shared her belief that she was a reborn Christ. She represented the fulfilled and completed Christ — her presence made the Messiah now sexually complete, both man and woman. Her latter-day followers tried to tone down her messianic pretensions, but they were clear, and outlasted her life. In an 1827 letter (published in 1985 by Stephen J. Stein, a Shaker historian), a young Kentucky Shaker, William S. Byrd, of the famous Virginia Byrds, admits that many "scof at the idea of Christs making his second appearance in Ann Lee" but then adds defiantly, "The same Christ that dwelt in Jesus of Nazareth, appeared the second time in this female, the spiritual Mother of all the new creation of God." Much as St. Augustine lent some of his sense of guilt and morbidity to early Christianity, Ann gave her neurasthenic desire for order and hyperorganization to all the later Shakers. Crowded poor people learn to hate disorder with a passion that for the wealthy is only a pastime; Groucho Marx, to take another important American spiritual leader, was so appalled by the chaos of his tenement childhood that, it was said, for the rest of his life he hated to have one kind of food on his plate touch another. (Whenever we see a fanatic appetite for order, there were probably once six kids in one room.)

Ann Lee became wildly controversial and was attacked several times — and once, it seems, sexually assaulted — by gangs of local men. One of these beatings may have been the cause of her sudden death, in 1784. It was left to her disciples, particularly Joseph Meacham and Lucy Wright, to organize the Believers into fully self-sustaining celibate but coed communities. They spread quickly, and through the end of the eighteenth century and the first half of the nineteenth the Shakers became American icons, establishing colonies in the Massachusetts towns of Pittsfield and Harvard, and then throughout New England and as far south as Kentucky. Still, even at their height, around 1840, the Shakers were never very many: perhaps five thousand true Believers altogether. During Ann's lifetime, the shaking of the Shakers was already legendary, not to say notorious: they would expunge the old Adam by evenings of violent dancing and rhapsodic writhing. After the establishment of the communities, the thing became more formalized: a regimented after-dinner trembling, like line dancing at a sock hop. But what the dancing represented — a sublimation of, rather than an invitation to, sex — was apparent, and undisguised, and attracted the attention of visitors from Thoreau to Charles Dickens.

So far, so weird. How did they begin to make beautiful things, and why did those things take the form they did? There is no straight line between belief and building. Both Quaker and Shaker styles came of age in the early nineteenth century, at the time of a general neoclassical revival throughout Europe and America, when linear, stripped-down, right-angle schematics were everywhere. If the Shakers were going to make objects at all, those were the kind of objects they would make; it's not as though they were imitating the Nymphenburg rococo in that other utopian colony down the road.

Yet the Shakers made specifically stylish things, where others didn't. As a fine recent anthology, *Quaker Aesthetics,* has shown, the Friends, apart from a general tendency toward the plain and suspicion of the fancy, had no real style separate from that of their fellow Americans. They wore more or less the same clothes and used the same furniture as everyone else. (They just disapproved of their own use of them more than other people did.) So why did the Shakers have a style of their own?

Most of the elements of Shakerism are common to orders and sects: the dervishes whirled, Dominican monks renounced the flesh. What seems distinctive is, first, their feminism and its insistence on coed monasticism, which made much of the sexual while also denying it. Theirs was a genuinely radical feminism. Shaker communities, though not specifically matriarchal in rule — there were plenty of male elders, too — were among the few American communities of nearly perfect sexual equality. There is even a sense, perceptible in the letters and other writings, that this made a Shaker colony a welcome place for "effeminate" men — a surviving letter reveals a code of homoerotic innuendo that is as easy to decrypt as pig Latin.

What also distinguished the Shakers was their odd join between violent antiworldliness and thoroughgoing commercial materialism. Monks and monkish communities have, of course, sold goods to the world for a long time, from medieval cheese to Moonie cappuccinos. But the Shakers, faced with the need to support large communities, worked particularly hard to manufacture things for money. Many of the objects that we think of as archetypal Shaker — the long oval boxes with their lovely triple folds, the clean brooms and chairs — were designed and made largely for outside sale. With most tribes and sects that we look to as artistic innovators, the line between cult object and commodity product — between the true African fetish and airport art — is, if often far from sharp, at least tenable. It wasn't with the Shakers. Shaker style was a commodity almost as soon as Shakerism was a cult. Contrary to Thomas Merton's romantic assertion that each Shaker chair was made as though no other chair had been made before, Shaker chairs and other wooden objects were made in semi-industrial conditions for a growing middle-class market.

It is here, ironically, in the need to make things to sell to other people, that the first stirrings of a distinct style begin. This is not to say that the objects were made insincerely, or that Shakerism in design was a scam. The built-in cupboards and chairs and ladders constructed only for other Shakers, in Shaker communities, are made in the same spirit as the things for sale. The point is that no line was drawn the other way around, either: what was made for sale looked like what was made for sacred. The urge to make consumer goods is, after all, one of the keenest spiritual disciplines that an ascetic can face: it forces spirit to take form. An ascetic drinking tea from a cup decides not to care what kind of cup he's drinking from; an ascetic forced to make a cup has to ask what kind of cup he *ought* to drink from. By the mid-nineteenth century, "Shaker" had become a brand name.

Skeptics said that the work was a form of self-coerced indenture: the Shakers could make more objects more cheaply because, as one defense of the Shakers puts it, artisans "were free of distractions" and "freed from financial worries," and, as a critic would say, were not free (or chose not to be free) to sell their skills at their true value on an open market. As Michael Downing documents in a richly human book about American spirituality, *Shoes Outside the*

Door: Desire, Devotion, and Excess at San Francisco Zen Center, the Zen community in San Francisco in the 1960s and '70s similarly produced excellence and exhaustion in equal measure. The Zen community could draw on underpaid cooks to run the Greens restaurant as the Shakers could draw on unpaid artisans to make their clocks; the proportion between beatitude found and skill exploited was left to the maker to figure. The enterprise gave the Shakers a curious double existence as a scary sect and a solid brand. And the Shaker brand *was* gold. "When a man buys a kag of apple sass of you," the humorist Artemus Ward wrote approvingly, around the time of the Civil War, "he don't find a grate many shavins under a few layers of sass."

But if that helps explain why they made so many boxes, it doesn't explain what made the boxes so fine. Some insight into what the Shakers were doing and thinking comes from the rare occasions when they were making art objects properly so called — visionary drawings. These were produced when, from the 1820s to the 1850s — around the time of the Second Great Awakening — the Shakers, within their already spiritualized environment, went through a kind of spiritual reawakening of their own.

A spiritual reawakening within a community already drawn taut by spiritual aspiration must have created a strenuous atmosphere. Visions and ghosts came down, and the Shakers, chiefly women and young girls, made "gift drawings": the drawings were gifts from above, not gifts to another. For the most part, they are conventional folk art — except for several by a Shaker woman named Hannah Cohoon, who lived in the Hancock community, and who was a kind of Emily Dickinson of drawing. Her four surviving signed drawings show a concentration on a single form rather than a chatty, anecdotal all-overness, quite outside the normal round of folk art. One of them, *A Little Basket Full of Beautiful Apples* (1856), is among the key drawings in American art, with a tonic sense of abundance — all the apples just alike, each with its rub-on of rouge, like blush applied by an adolescent girl — allied to obsessive order. Another, the famous *Tree of Light* or *Blazing Tree* (1845), shows us a vision seen in a dream: a tree with each leaf embroidered with fire, part of the normal Shaker iconography of the tree of life but also alarming in its overcharged richness. Cohoon's intensity was concentrated not on transcendental images of saints or God but on homely American objects, picnic tables and baskets of apples.

This way of imbuing the ordinary with a sense of the numinous is at the heart of the Shaker aesthetic, by far the best extended account of which can be found in *The Shaker World: Art, Life, Belief,* by the art historian John T. Kirk. Kirk argues that there are Shaker specificities, and that they reside in a series of simple design moves that are independent of the neoclassical run of the time, making a unique combination of slenderness, tenderness, and boxiness. Shaker ladders and chairs and tables tend, first of all, to be improbably long, attenuated. There was a practical reason for this: communal living demands long tables in large buildings. Things grow long naturally in dormitories. But practical necessity is always the lever of creation; the line between practical necessity and aesthetic impulse is not merely fine but nonexistent. (The last thing in the world Michelangelo wanted to paint was a ceiling. Once up there, he saw the celestial possibilities.) This constant attenuation — a pulling out of chair legs and table lengths — is one of the things that make Shaker design so seductive, in the most direct way. For attenuation in art inherently has two meanings: long, slender things are chic, as with every fashion model, and they are spiritual, as with the figures in Chartres or Blake's flamelike personages.

Shaker objects are also unusually repetitive: Kirk calls these Shaker formats "tight grids," and they infect everything the Shakers made, a last long lingering echo of Mother Ann's hatred of the collapsed and squalid mess of the one-room home. Everything in the Shaker world, from brooms to villages, is laid out in rows, grids, tightly packaged and formatted. (The insistence on the villages' grid planning was even formalized in the Shakers' "Millennial Laws" of 1821.) The grid plan of a Shaker village is unlike the seemingly similar neoclassical grid plan of, say, Quaker Philadelphia, where the regular spacing allows a rational calm to fall over the streets and squares. The plans for Shaker villages are, instead, tight and surprisingly asymmetrical, with long straight main streets and side streets that jog off abruptly at odd intersections; like Shaker furniture, Shaker plans can accept asymmetry if it is dictated by practicality. Shaker plans look less like something drawn up in an Enlightenment encyclopedia than like something sketched by a seer with an Etch A Sketch, lines sprouting and kicking out at odd but angular angles.

One sees the same principle — apparent rationality inflected with an underlying obsessiveness — in the prime Shaker objects. In an amazing midcentury case with cupboard and drawers made by the carpenters in the community in Enfield, Connecticut, two doors, above and below, mismatch, while two central drawers are broken up arrhythmically into smaller parts. It is like a cupboard in Morse code, stuttering out one half and two shorts. That Shaker box, similarly, bends around, and each element has a logic to it — the copper tacks to prevent rust, the beautiful embracing swallow-tail fingers to keep the box from cracking — but it has none of the "that's that" shortcut simplicity of folk objects; instead, a kind of underlying delirium infects it, an obsessive overcharge of finish, the sense of a will to perfection investing an otherwise humdrum object. "Trifles make perfection, but perfection is no trifle" was a Shaker motto. "God is in the details" — but the details have to provide evidence of God.

The Shakers were ascetics without being Puritans. They didn't object to color and comfort, even as they rejected ornament and luxury. (Many of the objects that look ascetic to us have simply lost their original paint.) A wonderful chair in the Hancock village is made to lean back: a rocking chair without rockers, at perpetual tilt. Yet all these elements — the flat grid patterning, the acceptance of asymmetry, the tolerance for the drumbeat repetition of similar elements without an evident hierarchy of form — add up to a simple idea: Shaker design, while reaching toward an ideal of beauty, unconsciously rejects the human body as a primary source of form. To a degree that we hardly credit, everything in our built environment traditionally echoes our own shape: we have pediments for heads and claw-and-ball feet, and our objects proceed from trunklike bases to fragile tops. Repetition and the grid are two alternatives to design that refers to classical perspective space and the roundly realized human body. They reappear in twentieth-century art through the cubist desire to make playthings that snubbed their nose at perspective, and the Teutonic urge to make a new language of pure form. Once you have got rid of the body as a natural referent for design, and no longer think "pictorially" about objects, grids and repeats begin to appear as alternative sys-

tems, whether you are in Japan, Montmartre, or Hancock. The love
of asymmetry, which seems to us so sophisticated, involves a viola-
tion of the same taboo, since symmetry is the essence of human
beauty. All Shaker design implies a liberation from "humanism" of
this kind. When we make objects that look like us, we unconsciously are flattering ourselves. The Shakers made objects that
look like objects, and that follow a nonhuman law of design.

One sees the pattern clearly in the evolution of the casement
clocks — what we call grandfather clocks — made by the Youngs
family of New York over three generations, in and out of the community of Believers. The clocks of the elder Youngses, Seth and his
son Benjamin, as described in Glendyne R. Wergland's *One Shaker
Life,* are in the manner of Greek columns, with strongly articulated
bases, long shafts, and "heads" with clock faces. Over time, the
clocks that Benjamin made became more narrowly "neoclassical":
the bases simplified and their moldings reduced, the clock head
narrowed in size, the clock's lines made neater and more geomet-
rical. But Isaac Newton Youngs, the grandson, was reared as a
Shaker, and the clocks he made became as reductive as a refrigera-
tor case, with the sides of the clock neither tapering nor swelling,
and, telltale sign, with a knob on the clock face as well as on the
clock body to allow the worker to adjust or repair the inside: the al-
lergy to putting a functional element on an object's "face" was over-
ruled, because the artisan was not thinking of it as a face. In each
case, the clocks got not merely simpler — though they did that, too
— but progressively less figural.

This doesn't mean that the Shaker objects are "inhuman" in the
sense of being cold. They aren't cold. The brooms and clocks and
boxes create an atmosphere of serenity, loveliness, calm certainty.
But these are monastic virtues rather than liberal ones. We miss the
radical edge of Shaker art if we don't see that it is not meant to be
"humanistic." (As much as the Moonies ever have, Shaker communities worked hard to exterminate individuality: people dined together, slept together, and even, in Hancock, were buried together,
in a single common grave marked "Shakers.") Most religious objects, from Baroque Catholic baldachins to Hindu temple orna-
ments, are worldly but immaterial, made with immense sophistication in order to make the ordinary physical world seem to vanish in
a smoke cloud of spirals and twists and flames. Shaker objects are,

like Zen Japanese ones, unworldly but material, far from sensuality but solid as a rock. They annihilate the body and leave us timeless form to tell the time with.

The Shakers waned as swiftly as they rose, and by the early twentieth century they were as much a relic cult as a living force. They existed in order to be in decline: the Fall and Paradise are about the same thing. (There is evidence that the Shakers themselves, even by the end of the nineteenth century, lived in conventional rooms with ordinary objects.) In this way, though, Shakerism — the enthusiasm of the Shaker design, and the accompanying cult of box and broom — is not merely a nostalgic invention. Rather, it has *always* been a nostalgic invention: the nostalgia was there almost before the experience happened. After their first blooming period, the Shakers existed to be remembered. But at the same time, consumer-goods Shakerism, which led to catalogues of Shaker chairs, cloaks, and baskets, continued to accelerate, until Shaker shopping was a major occupation, and this is a phenomenon of the late nineteenth century, not the twentieth.

The Shakers, then, did not simply survive as a path to purity never pursued. Instead, they permanently defined a curiously American composition, played in the blue key of E: enlightenment, entrepreneurialism, and exploitation all in counterpoint, with a half-heard chord of illicit eroticism. The attempt to make monastic communities that will be simultaneously asexual, industrial, and fully integrated into the entrepreneurial society around them — that will do good and do well — is so deeply embedded in our history that it recurs again and again. As Downing documents, its latest incarnation has been the Zen experience — which is uncannily like the Shaker experience, and which also involved the implantation of a slightly misunderstood alien dogma, and an immense outpouring of American spiritual yearning, a taste for commercial prosperity on the part of its leaders, and an inability to figure out what the hell to do about sex. As the Shakers made a revolution in American objects, American Zen made a revolution in American cooking, giving vegetarian food dignity. And, when the communities went into crisis, first the plates, and then the food, were what was left.

We should, perhaps, feel disappointed by this descent from the spirit, but some of us may wonder if the spirit has greater gifts to give. Food and boxes are not ethically neutral; they radiate their own aura into the harried lives of people who own them, even if only as aspiration. They were elevated, not debased, to become bourgeois amenities; they passed from the realm of false belief to the realm of spiritualized form. A forthcoming book, *Selling Shaker: The Promotion of Shaker Design in the Twentieth Century,* by Stephen Bowe and Peter Richmond, discusses, with a good deal of detailed analysis and some fine mordant humor, the slow process by which Shakerism continues to creep into the American marketplace, as Mother Ann's purities become the playthings of Oprah Winfrey. But a sneaking, not quite justifiable prejudice infects the study, in the authors' implicit belief that believing that Mother Ann was God and sex evil was intrinsically a higher-order activity than just liking to own Shaker boxes. This belief feels more Puritanical than Shakerian. Surely the aesthetic contemplation for other purposes of objects first made for cult use is more or less where the idea of art begins — the Shaker work counter in the hands of Oprah is, in this sense, not very different from the Renaissance altarpiece in the hands of Bernard Berenson — and, after all, Shakerism crept into the American marketplace by way of the American marketplace, where the Shakers placed it. In American art, the line between the goods and the good is a fine one, and doesn't benefit from being stared at too hard or cut too finely. In a commercial society, the membrane that separates spirit and store is always permeable.

Yet the blazing tree remains alight. Kirk ends his fine book with a slightly naive inquiry into the relation between Shakerism and the objects of American minimalism, and shows that the formal elements of the two — the grid, the repeated element, the entire antihumanism of the approach — rhyme if they do not repeat. Look-alikes aside, what most connects the minimal art of Judd and Serra and Stella with their very improbable predecessors is their fanaticism. The moderns are uncompromising, too: only this box now and now this box again. That same uncompromising fanaticism gives life to what might otherwise be mere Teutonic austerity and pedantic insistence. The violence done to natural form, and to the humanism it implies, creates a serene result with a perceptible violence just beneath.

American art benefits from the fanatic, as American writing does not: the visual arts threaten to disappear back into the big jumble of things we see and own unless they are marked by some kind of extremism. Writers may be Friends, but artists are Believers, or they are not much. The twin legacy of Shakerism is true to the twin roots of the Shakers' vision: they remain both as a model of wild-eyed and unreal renunciation and as makers of simple good things. The shining tree of life is a tree of light that illuminates the way for believers. It is also on fire, and can only be consumed.

MARY GORDON

My Mother's Body

FROM *The American Scholar*

1.

MY MOTHER WAS ONE OF THE AFFLICTED. She was stricken, at the age of three, with polio. I wonder if she had any bodily memory of running, of walking without labor, without anxiety: of movement as a joy. There is a picture of her, dressed to the nines in a white lace Edwardian outfit. She is trying to hide her crutch behind her body; if you didn't notice it, you might think at first she was normal. Until you saw the right leg, thinner than the other, and the right shoe, built higher than its mate.

Two of her eight siblings were stricken in subsequent polio epidemics. The merciful wing of history has brushed over our fearful memory of the terror, each summer, that one would be struck down. No more a commonplace: children in leg braces. Absent from the lexicon, the words so easily to hand, so dreadful: iron lung. Polio is no longer real to my children's generation, although carelessness or suspicion about vaccines has caused its continuance as a plague in parts of the developing world. My mother insisted that I be among the first to be vaccinated; she woke me at dawn so I would be at the head of the line for the first dosages of what she saw as the sacrament of Dr. Salk.

One of her legs, the right one, was six inches shorter than the other. She walked with a pronounced limp; she couldn't, for all the years I knew her, walk more than a block at a time. She wore one built-up shoe, really a boot, and she couldn't take a step unless she was wearing that shoe. Stairs were a difficulty. A fall was a disaster.

Her body was misshapen, asymmetrical. A body that was a problem, always. Never, a gift.

Affliction: something suffered, something done to someone from which they have no recourse, no defense. I like it much better than other words that can be used to describe what happened to my mother. *Crippled, handicapped, disabled.* Because the accent falls not on the body itself but upon its fate. Of course there were other aspects of my mother's body that were free of her affliction: her beautiful hands and arms, dappled with freckles like the skin of a young apple, her beautiful hair, her large gray-green eyes and high cheekbones, her clear smooth skin without wrinkles almost to the end, never once in my memory marked by a single blemish, no not one. Her enviable skin. It was called her "complexion." Yes, it was envied. People said to my mother, "I envy your complexion."

And other things, connected to the body but emanating from it, and desirable, a desirable feature like beautiful breasts or long legs. For example, in my mother's case, her voice, charming, lively, robust, jocular, persuasive, sure, her laughter, a laugh you could identify in a dark movie house, a laugh that made everyone want to laugh. Women who didn't like my mother criticized her laugh, called it unseemly, something that drew improper or undue attention to itself, as if she had worn a dress that was too tight or too low cut: revealing something that a proper woman knows well how to cover up.

How is it possible to speak of a mother's body?

Possible, that is, without betrayal.

And if it is possible, is it permissible?

To speak of it as if it were not a body, but something that could be turned into a work of art?

The body of the afflicted mother. The body of the work of art. The impossible desire for shapeliness, for an intact form. For harmony, radiance, wholeness. My mother's body was unharmonious. But isn't it possible to bypass harmony, bypass proportion, in the search for, if not wholeness, then radiance? The daughter, born of the mother's body, looks at it for information, curses, clues. How can a daughter talk about her mother's body? Especially when she is a writer.

I know there are a number of ways that I don't want to talk. A number of ways I don't want to write. I don't want to pity myself for being a child born of a body such as my mother's. And I don't want to describe my mother's body. Not anymore. Not now. I did it once. But she was living then. Now she is dead.

In the last years of her life, she was, in her wretchedness, my tormenter. Her body tortured me: the sight of it, its smell. Living, she was a torturer, and now, among the dead, she is entirely innocent.

There was nothing I could do to stop the torment while she lived. While I was in charge of her; in the eleven years I visited her in the nursing home once a week; while I had to supervise her care. Her presence was unbearable. The sight of her blackening teeth, rotting down to stumps, her hair, scraped down almost to her scalp — above all the smell of her — made me panic, made me want to cover my face with my hands and cry out, "I can't, I can't, I can't do this." It made me want to run in some cold wind, some scourging rain until I could lose the sight of her, the smell of her, until I could fall, exhausted. Too tired to think. To remember that the body I once loved was now the source of hatred. Except when I loved her for her helplessness. Then I loved her, to the point of weeping unstoppable, wrenching tears. Now that she is no longer among the living, I can miss her but the tears come lightly; they do not tear me apart. There is only missing. No desire to escape. No punishment, given or received.

Is it only because it no longer torments me that I no longer feel the need to describe my mother's body? Was my need to describe her body only a need for punishment? Now I feel a real aversion for the prospect. Now she is dead, the thought of describing her body makes me feel like Ham, the son of Noah, the betraying son.

This is my understanding of the story of Noah and his sons.

After his long labor, toward the end of the time on the Ark, Noah drank. Drank himself unto drunkenness. What was that like? What did he look like before he fell asleep? What was he wearing before his nakedness? Did he stagger, did he slur his words, did he curse the fates, the flood, his nagging wife, his disappointing children? Did he pity himself for his responsibility, for being born a just man in the time of the flood? Is this what enraged Ham: the admired father, chosen by God, all along a fraud? Not really a just man, just someone waiting to turn into a drunk. All along, a beast without the dignity of the pairs taken aboard. *I, Father, will expose your nakedness. I will look at what you have been all along, what you have always re-*

ally been. If I don't look, there will be no one to witness this truth. Isn't truth telling a kind of love?

He knows that it is not. He knows that it is hatred. Hatred and perhaps desire: the desire of the eyes — is it somehow connected to sex? It could be, but it doesn't need to be.

He sees what he sees.

He tells his brothers.

His brothers will not look. They enter the chamber backward, a cloak thrown over their shoulders, covering their heads. Not looking, they fling the cloak onto the naked body of their father.

The good sons.

They have not seen.

They have done the work of not seeing.

Someone had to do that work.

As someone had to do the work of seeing.

But supposing Ham had been an only child. Which work would he have chosen? The work of seeing, or the work of not seeing, the work of refusing to see?

He would have had to choose.

And then he would have had to make another choice: to speak or to be silent.

For the writer, this choice is also possible. Although we tell ourselves that it is impossible, a betrayal of our vocation.

But silence is a perfectly honorable choice. More honorable, because no one knows about it.

The most dishonorable choice: to speak and then to confess one's own (superior) knowledge of the dishonor of speaking.

I know that this is what I am doing now.

I seem unable to give up the impulse to say some things about my mother that seem to me true. And in order to do that, I must describe her body. Because only in describing her body — as something in space, as something that moved through space (awkwardly, uneasily), as something that was seen in space (misshapen, unpleasing) — can the nature, the effect of her affliction be understood. But for whom is such an understanding necessary? The answer, of course, is only myself.

For a little while, I convinced myself that I would speak about my mother's body for the good of others. For the good of other children of the afflicted. This new (false) conviction began when a friend of mine told me that her husband's father was the child of a polio victim and that his sense of his body, like mine, was greatly affected by this. She said it would be an important thing to write about, that no one had written about it.

I will do it, I said, donning my heroic cloak. I had forgotten that I had already done it. Written about my mother's body. That my friend hadn't read what I had written is another matter. I simply could have directed her to the book I had already written, the book in which I wrote about my mother's afflicted body, about being the child of such a mother. I wrote about my mother's body eleven years ago when I was writing about my father. So I was writing about my father's wife, my father's widow. A living woman. When I wrote about her then I said: *"My mother is eighty-six and something has broken or hardened and worn out. When she hasn't combed her hair, when she has lost a tooth she won't have attended to, when she won't cut or file her nails or change her clothes she is distressing to look at."*

When I wrote about my mother's body I used the word *rot.* Many readers found that shocking. I told myself I used it because it was the truth. Her body was rotting. She had allowed it to rot; she wanted it to. She forced me to deal with her rotting body because she hadn't taken off her high-laced boots for three months. I found this out when I took her to the doctor for a checkup and he told her to take her boots off. She told him she hadn't taken them off for three months, and he made her leave the office. He said the smell was not one he could allow in a professional office. In his office, he said, there could not be the smell of rot.

When we got home, I had to take her shoes off; she refused to do it herself. I knelt at her bedside, as if I were saying my night prayers, unlaced her shoes and took them off. The smell was overwhelming. I had to hold my breath so as not to take it in. And the look of them: the leprous flesh I had dreamed of martyring myself to as a pious girl. I told her I had to fill a basin of water and while the water was running, I vomited into the toilet. I came back, bathed and dried her feet. Then I phoned an agency to hire a nurse to tend to her feet every day. I could do it once, but I couldn't endure the possibility of having to do it again and again. The possibility of that made the idea of life unbearable. Made me literally long for death. The idea of death, for me, was preferable to the task of continually tending my mother's rotting feet.

Rot is one of the works of death. My mother had made it happen. She had made it happen by not taking off her shoes. She couldn't explain why she didn't take off her shoes. She said it was too much trouble.

I used the word *rot* because it was the truth. My mother's feet were rotting. Did I have to use it? What kind of daughter uses the word *rot* in relation to her mother? What is the line between truth telling and punishment? How could I want to punish my mother for something that was so clearly a sign of dementia? Was it simply the victim's impulse to take any turn that might occur to punish the one who had tortured? For whatever reason, at whatever time.

Now my mother is a skeleton, or ash. All those sites of attention, rage, despair gone now. Where did they go? Were they vaporized into the air? Absorbed into the earth? The details of the bodies of the dead turn abstract once they are no longer in the world. Abstract, therefore no longer a cause of rage. Sorrow, rather, or regret. The burning rash of rage turning to the dull tumor of sorrow.

In the days that I had to think about her uncut nails, in the days when her life consisted of sitting with her head in her hands in a stupor, a stupor punctuated by periods of anxiety, I prayed for her death. But I must remind myself that my wanting her death, even praying for it, did not end her life. I wasn't even with her when her life ended. I do not now wish her alive. Not the mother who had become entirely wretched.

My last duty toward her was to choose the clothes she would be buried in. Her own good clothes had long since disappeared. I chose an outfit of my own, one that she would look good in. A black crepe blouse with a Fortuny collar, a black silk pleated skirt. Around her neck a string of pearls. Dead, she looked beautiful. Dead, she had got back her elegance. I was glad for my part in giving it back to her.

I do not want the wretched mother back again in this life. But there is another one, desired, and desirable. A body I once yearned to be near. I once saw in the foreground of an Italian Renaissance painting a cup with the inscription "Alas, I yearned exceedingly." As a child, there were times when my entire body was a vessel of yearning for her. When she would leave me, sending me somewhere, for a day, a week's vacation, a summer with some member of her family who was meant to be doing us both a good turn by separating us. In the first years after my father's death, I felt separation from her body like a new wound on top of the old, mortal one of his death. But even before his death, I loved sitting on her lap; I loved putting my head on her firm springy bosom. I was proud of her in her suits and hats when she left the house for work. The mothers of my friends slopped around at home all day in housedresses. Carelessly coifed. Not a starched handkerchief among them, or a gold compact, or a purse with the clasp in the shape of a snake. This is the mother I want to meet again: the mother that I yearned for. I want to go back where I can meet that mother. Back past affliction, age, disease. This is the trick I want to pull: the trick of bringing the desirable mother back to life. The trick of Resurrection.

But I have no idea how I might go about it. Or if it is wrong to describe a miracle as a trick.

2.

As I am thinking about this, I travel to London to visit a friend whose lover of forty years has just died. In the duty-free shop on the way home, I spot a display advertising the perfume my mother always wore for "special occasions." Arpège by Lanvin. The young saleswoman is thin, in a short black skirt, black shirt, and black pumps with something called kitten heels. I ask if I can try a sample of Arpège. She sprays it on a little card and tells me to rub the card on my wrists. I do. I walk around with it. To see if I can bear wearing my mother's scent. To see if I can bear being my mother.

At first, the scent is sharper than I remember, less accommodating, less friendly, less sweet. And yet even as a child I valued it because as a scent it was mature, unapproachable. It was comprehensible, like the Hindu idea of God, only by what it was not: ungirlish, unfloral, unfruity, neither of the garden nor the woodland, an invented scent rather than a discovered one, composed deliberately rather than come upon (accidentally, fortuitously), an artifact, a product, and a sign of city life, not worn in the daylight, or worn casually, but something hoarded, brought out for an occasion, the seriousness of which was marked by the very act of its having been brought out.

When my mother wanted to use Arpège she would cover the

opening of the bottle with her index finger, tip it back once, twice, then press her moistened finger first to her wrists, then behind her ears. Then she would hold a linen handkerchief against the bottle's opening and tip it back until a drop or two wet the cloth. She would put the cloth into her special handbag for evenings out, and the more vivid scent that the cloth had absorbed would be taken into the leather.

When she was away at work, or out at a meeting, I would go into her drawer, open her purse, and put my nose close, close against the leather, breathing it in, the animal leather smell an undercurrent still against the sophisticated scent that had become one with its essence, with its texture: the absorption transforming them both. So I would smell the leather, then the handkerchief, and then, in a fit of terrible daring, open the bottle to smell the perfume itself. This led, once, to something terrible. I opened the bottle and knocked it over and the perfume ate through the varnish of my mother's dresser, destroying its smoothness, leaving a pocked, scratched, fuzzy, denuded surface instead of a varnished patina. The texture of the dresser top was the texture of the skin of an uncultivated peach. In all the years my mother had the dresser (thirty, perhaps, until she moved into a house that I bought for her and it was given away), nothing was ever done to make the dresser presentable once again. What could have been done? I always believed that nothing could be done. My horror when I saw the perfume eating away at the surface was the horror of despair. A despair at the inexorability of physical destruction. My conviction that nothing, nothing could be done to make it better, to repair it, was borne out. My mother's fury was negligible measured against my despair. Something in the world had ruined the beauty of something, as polio had ruined the beauty of my mother's body, and I was its minion, its agent, its stooge. From then on, the notion of the physical world's inexorability was mine.

But the accident of the perfume did not make me stop loving the perfume. And believing that this was a sign of the best way of being female that was open to me — and worth a tremendous amount, although I had no idea what the currency might be, what might have to be given up.

But I don't want to be thinking about this, a memory of ruin, of sorrow: this is everything I'm trying to get away from: the sorrowful mother, the ruined mother. I want to reach the desirable mother, the mother who is the site of pleasure. I want an alternative to biography. To history. My own and hers. I want something larger, something outside the circle I have been traveling the circumference of, like a horse with blinders, the horse in Joyce's "The Dead" who keeps traveling around the statue of King William because he can't break his habits from being the workhorse at the mill.

I want to be outside myself, and her. Or outside myself but with her and her perfume. So I decide to learn about the perfume as a research project. That will take it out of the cramped domain of my own life. A person familiar with computers in spite of myself, I begin by Googling Arpège. *Google,* a word my mother would never have heard of, that I hadn't heard of until after her death.

The first site I travel to is offering the perfume for sale. It tells me that Arpège was launched in 1927 as a soft floral fragrance for women. It describes its scent as "powdery floral." It elaborates: "a luxurious, gentle, floral fragrance, combining honeysuckle, jasmine, roses, and orange blossoms, accents of vanilla and sandalwood. It is recommended for romantic wear." I see that I was wrong about its being unfloral. All those different flowers, hinting of hot climes, tropical even: honeysuckle, jasmine, orange blossoms, but domesticated, familiarized by two of them: the vanilla and the rose. But what do they mean by powdery? Powdery implies a certain dryness, a certain enviable dryness. Absorptive. A civilizing element: it calms things down.

The business of the site, though, is selling the perfume. Whoever created the site must understand that Arpège has been absent from the larger imagination of fragrance for a number of years. They are too smart to try to sweep this under the rug; they make a charming tale of it; the passage of time, its erasures, become something that can be talked about. "This one your grandmother probably wore in her younger days. Naughty thing she is sometimes. Arpège is one of those classic fragrances that have made many a man go weak at the knees. Who says Grandma should have all the fun?"

What is this as a marketing strategy? To whom is it meant to appeal, and what might the appeal be? Obviously, to someone younger than I, someone more obviously in the sexual running. My mother wore Arpège. But they're trying to sell it to someone whose grandmother wore the scent. Someone my daughter's age. As is so frequently the case now, I see that I am too old to be the target audience.

And what glamour is being invoked? Naughty granny — naughty in the '20s, the madcap '30s. White art deco bedrooms, Irene Dunne or Carole Lombard in lounging pajamas? Secrets kept from the naughty granny's daughter, the potential buyer's mother. (Me?) A drama of exclusion. A suggestion that respectability can be kept, that its price is not the price of pleasure. That a daring past is something that can be got away with. That the knees of the powerful man, the man who pays for your perfume, can turn to rubber. And no one will be worse off. You will make a good marriage (maybe not to the man with the rubbery knees) but at least you will have children, grandchildren.

In invoking the glamorous grandmother of the '20s and '30s, I am opening a historical gap as large — eighty years — as if I had, in the 1950s, evoked a glamorous image of the belle époque. This seems wonderful to me, an encouragement to my plan for finding an alternative to history, to biographical fact.

A second Google site reminds me of the advertising slogan that went with the perfume: "Promise her anything, but give her Arpège." What did the admen have in mind with this one? That the purchase of this scent would allow, encourage, validate false statements? That as long as you gave this bottle to your honey, you could swear to marry her next month, leave your wife next year, give up men, or booze or horses? Clearly, the message is pitched toward the man, because who would want to be deceived? What woman longs to be a dupe? In failing to understand this, am I failing to understand something important in the history of women? The acceptance of deception. The faked orgasm. The faked pregnancy. Perfume itself covering the animal truth. Does my inability to enroll myself in this ancient brigade mean I have no right to wear the perfume? That I should count myself instead as part of the unglamorous sisterhood: bluestockings, do-gooders, unembellished, not a drop or particle of makeup on their natural skins, content with whatever God gave them, out to do God's work, to tell the truth, the whole truth, nothing but the truth. A life without glamour. I never wanted that. Even when I thought I would be a nun, I imagined myself glamorous in my habit. My mother, buying her suits, her face powder, her Arpège, insisted on being a part of the duplicitous world of female pleasure. As do I.

After a while I get it: it's not that I'm against deception. But I want the deception coming from me. I don't mind deceiving, but I don't want to be deceived. I don't want *anything* promised to me. It's not that I want *nothing*. I want *something*. *Many things*. But not *anything*. As if I had no choice. No scent, however desirable, is worth that. Especially when I could get the perfume for myself. Because of my mother, I always imagined myself a wage earner. Never dependent on a man for necessaries or for luxuries. No, never that.

Simultaneously proud and self-pitying, I buy the perfume for myself.

When I turn to the site called "Fascination Perfumery" I feel a shock; it tells me something I ought to have known but never knew, that the symbol on the bottle of Arpège is a symbol of mother and daughter.

I go to my own bottle. There it is; a mother and a daughter. The mother in an extravagant robe and turban absolutely dwarfing the child. Who kneels at her feet. Why did I never notice this? Perhaps because it isn't an obvious mother and daughter; the mother, so huge, so exotic, and the daughter, so insignificant, not on her mother's lap, not in her arms, but at her feet. Overwhelmed.

I determine to track down the history of this image. Where did it come from? Whose idea was it? What was it meant to evoke, to represent? I turn once more to Google; I look up Jeanne Lanvin and find a French site, untranslated.

I am astonished to learn that her career as a couturière was derived from her life as a mother, from her adoration of her daughter, Marguerite. I am told this even before I am told the details of her life, even before I learn that Jeanne Lanvin was born in 1867 (in America, the Civil War is only just over). She was the oldest of eleven children. Her father was an unsuccessful journalist. (So we have something in common, Jeanne Lanvin and I.) At thirteen she became a milliner, but her career took off when her clients saw the extraordinary garments she had made for her beloved daughter, coveted them first for their daughters, then for themselves. Adapting the lavish details — *broderie anglaise,* exotic fabrics — that she had used for her daughter's clothes made her one of the most successful couturiers in Paris. It's almost as if she didn't mean it; she was just trying to express her love for her daughter. Her brief marriage to Marguerite's father, an Italian, is barely mentioned. As if everyone knows it didn't really count.

As a gift for her daughter's thirtieth birthday, she created the perfume Arpège, the name created by the daughter, a singer herself, who upon smelling the perfume said, *"on dirait un arpège."* It's like an arpeggio. The site goes on to say that despite her passionate but suffocating love, *"amour passioné mais étouffant,"* mother and daughter were in the end *"éloignées".* — estranged, distant, separated.

I am desperate to learn more about the Lanvins, but the well of the Internet has run dry. Or not quite: I go to Amazon and find that I can order from Paris a biography of Jeanne Lanvin.

I wait six weeks for the book to arrive.

How did it happen that the mother and daughter ended up *éloignées?* When, on the back cover of the biography, we are told that *"Le nom de Lanvin baptise un bleu mythique et orne l'image devenue célébrissime, de la femme à l'enfant, image que les flaçons précieux d'Arpège multiplient à l'infini."* A new shade of blue, baptized, the image of the mother and the child, gilded, multiplied into infinity. The infinite multiplication of maternal love. Sold then, not bought though, by the daughter, who will flee from her mother, returning only after her death to head the corporation, the House of Lanvin.

But even before the estrangement, the daughter rejected the name her mother gave her, changing herself from Marguerite to Marie-Blanche. Marguerite makes a glamorous marriage into a noble family: she becomes the comtesse de Polignac. The count takes his place in the history of impoverished noblemen, supported by the wife's money, earned through commerce. Only this time, it is the wife's mother, rather than her father, whose business sense turned straw to gold.

Marguerite's husband was not the first Polignac to trade his title for money; his uncle married the ugly American heiress Winnaretta Singer (sewing machine heiress: the machine Mme Lanvin started her career with), who was one of the models for Proust's Mme Verdurin. Marguerite had a minor career as a singer of baroque opera; she was involved in bringing back into vogue the works of Monteverdi. But most important, she was a patron of the arts, a generous friend to artists. Most especially Poulenc. And she commissioned her other good friend Édouard Vuillard to paint both her portrait and her mother's.

I see Vuillard's name and I get a shock as unsettling as the one I got when I discovered that the symbol of Arpège was a mother and a daughter. For many years, Vuillard has been my favorite painter, the one I think of as mine. I have written about him; I have made pilgrimages to see his work. I chose one of his paintings to serve as the jacket art for my novel *Men and Angels*. My legacy to my children: a Vuillard pastel, an extravagant expenditure made before I even had children, an expenditure that some people I knew considered foolish. My Vuillard, whose blues and whites are the sign for me, the map for me, of everything I want to accomplish in my work, this painter who appears in Proust, Proust whom I begin each day's work by reading, how can it be that he is connected to Arpège, therefore to the body of my mother?

The web of accident, the web of association, a web spanning years, class, circumstance. Is it a web or a stream? Or a path that I have discovered, or have I just invented it? If there is a stream, or a path, in what direction does it lead? I think it is a stream, taking up whatever falls into it, whatever borders it. A stream with leaves, weeds, Proust's water lilies that approach the shore, stretch out, retract, return again. What is the source of this stream? Does it begin with the body of my mother, perfumed, with the artifacts (handbag, handkerchief, saturated with the scent) my mother carried into the world as she entered it on my father's arm?

Yes, it begins there, but where is the next step? Because I know what the last step is. A desire to be reading, writing, looking at (but not living in) the world suggested by the smell. The world of Vuillard, of Proust, of Poulenc. A world not quite ready to give up the nineteenth century: the complications, the embellishments, the difficult, elaborate forms. A world not quite ready to take up the modern world, the one perfumed by Chanel, Mme Lanvin's rival and nemesis.

The first step, the love of my mother's perfume; the last, the desire for the world it suggested. But what about the second step out of my mother's arms, the one that allowed me to imagine that I could approach the world of Proust and Vuillard as a fellow creator? The world not just of the apprehension of art but the creation of it. Because I am not the subject of the portrait but its creator. Both my father and I have written poems to my mother. No one has ever written a poem about me.

Vuillard and I are joined here, here in this writing that I make,

because of a connection forged by something that he made: portraits of both Jeanne Lanvin and her daughter. He paints Jeanne
Lanvin in her office at her desk, a worker, an elder (she is sixty-six).
Her ledgers, her pencil holder are given the same loving attention
as the fabric of her dress, the jewels around her neck, the bust
on her desk, the dog at her feet. He says that in this painting
he wanted to get *les vérités, les séverities* of green and gray. Ver-
ities, severities. Is a kind of harshness the only way to a kind of
truth? The working woman's styptic refusal of romance. If someone wanted to paint a portrait of my mother, he would have been
wise to paint her at her desk. Where she was happiest. Where she
was most at home.

The portrait of the comtesse is much less satisfactory, and Vuillard was much less satisfied with it. Marguerite is sitting on her day-
bed idle, pampered, a figure in a drawing-room comedy: her face
unformed, so unlike the face of her mother: the face of a tragic Roman emperor.

Vuillard was working on the painting of la comtesse de Polignac
when he got the news that his mother was dying. He put down the
brush that was creating, on canvas, the face of the daughter (whose
body is on the bottle my mother tipped to fragrance her body) and
ran to the deathbed of his mother. He described it in his journal:

> find Mama in her armchair . . . Ever more painful moments, "it's too
> much, it hurts too much, it's in my back"; soaked under her towel, let
> me lose consciousness, moans; long wait while Marie fetches Pantopon;
> drowsiness at last calms her; sit beside her hold her hand under the
> sheet; squeeze it from time to time; feel the pulse beating, then lose it,
> same state remainder of the day; cold sweats, wipe her forehead; eau de
> cologne; handkerchief on her head; asks me to put some scent on my
> beard; my good little mother; says I'm not good I'm wicked; convulsion,
> responds less and less to kisses; afraid to move . . . she's very bad; she's
> going to die; her back turned; I see her glassy gaze fixed sightlessly on
> the ceiling, the mouth twisted to one side; hand clenched once more
> over her stomach; and I hold her head still, my fingers near her eyes
> which I gently close after Parvu has raised a lid. Acceptance.

Vuillard said that his mother was his muse. He painted her over
and over. She was the mother who made the boiled beef that the
exhausted artists came to at the end of a hungry day. When he took
photographs, he left her in charge of his negatives; they would sit,

stewing in a soup bowl and she, vigilant, would turn them (as she turned her marinating beef?) at the proper time. Dying, she wants perfume. On her son's beard. The fragrant body: not the mother's but the son's. Many people believe that after she died, he considered his life over.

In my family, my mother was the photographer. There are only a few pictures of me and her; many more of me with my father, my grandmother. I remember the little red dot at the back of the Brownie; the excitement, the anxiety: don't open the camera: the film might be exposed. Exposed. To light: therefore ruin. At the end of her life, Vuillard's mother's degeneration was exposed by her son. Disturbing images. In the last photographs she is toothless, bald. She is washing her feet, paring her toenails. Did he have the right to photograph her like that? Vuillard and I, the exposing children, Noah's bad sons: saying that art is an excuse for exposure.

Was Vuillard enraged at his mother as I was enraged at mine? But for what? It would seem she never failed him. How I envy Vuillard saying "My mother is my muse." How I envy Vuillard the mother who was always cooking the boiled beef so that his house was the one friends wanted to come to. How I envy Vuillard a mother who kept an eye on his negatives, turned his negatives in a soup bowl.

But Mme Vuillard: Did she have wit that crackled, sparkled like champagne?

No, she was always an old woman.

Could she have made anyone go weak in the knees?

Not as her son painted her: the only mother we know.

But there is another mother, another life, the life of the woman not a mother, a woman who had a life before she was a mother, a life lived apart from the artist child. We have no knowledge of that life. Because the mother is known only through the artist child. And he or she sees only what he or she wants to see, tells only what he or she wants told.

The mother as victim of the artist child.

3.

I spray the perfume on my wrist. I put my nose to it: by it I mean both the scent and my own skin. It is always a shameful thing to be doing, at best a foolish thing: smelling yourself. Usually you are checking to see that you don't smell bad. It's nothing you ever want to be seen doing. Yet I want to be doing it all the time. Walking down the street, in order that I can smell the flesh of my wrist, I pretend I am looking at my watch. But I am looking for my mother. For my desired mother, my desirable mother (the one who made my father go weak in the knees?). I can be with her again: the one with the beautiful skin and hands and arms. The mother I never want to leave. The one I can't bear to be separated from for one second. The one I yearn for when I'm not with her, the one whose proximity I weep for: at school, at the houses of my relatives. My beguiling mother.

With a good smell: there is the desire never to stop, but not the conviction that smelling something good is enough to be doing with one's life, one's day. But why? We think that looking at a beautiful painting or landscape, listening to beautiful music, the sound of the wind or the waves, is a fine thing to be doing with our time.

But smelling? — no, it doesn't seem to be a good enough thing to be doing with time.

Is it because it is too animal?

The worst thing you can say to someone: you smell bad. You stink.

The animal in paradise. Peaceful. Among good smells.

Paradise is peace. Is safety.

But with the added ingredient: stimulation. But a stimulation that isn't frustrated. Not satiation: rather, a stimulation that never loses the edge of its desire, its desire for more, but there is no fear of disappointment.

With a good smell: no disappointment.

A good smell is paradise.

A bad one is Hades.

Paradise: the desired place. Never to leave.

Hades: the compulsion to escape.

Always present in paradise: the fear of leaving, of being forced to leave, banishment, the angel with the flaming sword.

And what is the way back into the garden? It is necessary to believe that the banishment is final, even if the banishment was self-imposed.

Must it be the way of language, or the flesh? Can't it be some way that is beyond time, beyond words? The way of the beautiful smell.

I can do it. Whenever I want I can open the perfume. I can put it on my own body. I can be with her in the smell. But what is a smell? Rousseau says it is the sense of the imagination. My imagination turns a smell into a place, a place where I can be with her.

But how can it be a place? There is no place to put your foot. No-where to step, nothing to step down on, nowhere to sit or to lie down. Nothing to swim through. To fly through. It could almost be a place of flight, a place of falling. But flying to where? Falling from what? To what? To the past? From the present to a future paradise, dreamt but ungratified. A smell is of the body, but if it is paradise it must go beyond the body. But to where? When you are in the place that is the smell, you don't believe that you will ever be anywhere else. Because to be in a smell is to be in an eternal present. Like the mind of God. Eternal desire, eternal horror. In the presence of my mother, or my mothers — the beguiling one, the repulsive one — I believed, fully, that time held no sway. I would be always where I was. Trapped. Eternally. Or in paradise.

At the end of her life, my mother's scent was a combination of a powder — called Shower to Shower — and the urine that she tried to cover up with the powder she sprinkled between her legs. From the elegant handkerchiefs and purse to the stained drawers. This was the trajectory of my mother's life, if you trace the trajectory of scent. The trajectory that moves from beguilement to recoil, from desire to horror.

In one of the more scientific studies of fragrance that I pursue, I am told that in perfumes, the top notes are floral, but the middle notes "are made from resinous materials which have odours not unlike those of sex steroids, while the base notes are mammalian sex attractants with a distinctly urinous or fecal odour." So is it re-ally the same thing, the smell of urine, the smell of perfume, only we are, unlike animals, overrefined: unable to trace the common source? When I try to type the word *urinous,* the computer auto-matically changes it to *ruinous.* It is true: when my mother's domi-nant scent was urinous, it was ruinous of my love for her.

I want to go back, beyond that. Through the sense of the imagi-nation. To that old place. The garden.

The paradise of *with.* Of a yearning that is satisfied and yet never used up: there will always be more, more yearning, more scent, and you will never go hungry, or be disappointed, sent away empty. Never enough, how could there be enough of this happiness? This is the paradise of the good smell. But the words — *smell, nose* — are comic. And the comic is the sign of falling short of the ideal. Paradise does not fall short, though. You fall into the good smell, you fall and fall and the fall is wonderful, there is no end to it, you fall, but you are carried, together. As a child, there was no desire for me to be apart from my mother. In her last years, I could barely bring myself to be with her for half an hour a week. The smell in the nursing home, *urinous, ruinous.*

I put my nose to my wrist. Arpège. The music: the arpeggio. I can follow the scent, like music, beyond the body, beyond words. I don't need to be in the ruinous place. I can be in the paradise with the mother I desire.

Mother, I want to be in the place where I was with you and you smelled so beautifully of the large world, of glittering cities, of furs and laces, of drinks in sparkling glasses, of candle lights, mirrors where women with piled hair are reflected from the funnel-shaped darkness of formal rooms.

Where are we, Mother?

I can ask that question, but of course I will hear only silence. My mother has no voice. No words. The words must be mine. I must do the talking. I must say where we are.

We are in a room. We enter it, leaning on each other's arms.

My mother is not limping. Or her limping doesn't matter.

Is that applause? Are we greeted by applause by the people sitting at the glittering tables? Are they saying, *At last, you are with us, you have always been one of us, we have been waiting?* You are the most glamorous, the most shimmering, the most radiant of us all.

In our ears, at our throats, jewels sparkle. We are dressed for the ball.

Beautiful mother.

Beautiful girl.

Where are we, Mother?

Or is there no need to name?

But why not name it; there is nothing to be afraid of here.

Here where we are:

Paradise.

Europe.

Paris.

Home.

Where we belong.

If I had been able to speak like this to my mother, words rooted in the body but beyond the degraded and degrading flesh, would it have changed anything? Prevented anything? Rage, humiliation, stupor, degradation, or despair? It doesn't matter; I was never able to speak to her like that. With that kind of love. As it was, the love I had for her, love mixed with hate, the words I could speak to her, words of love and hate, were attached to the body that degraded rather than evaporated, like the scent of her perfume. And so nothing was prevented by my love. My impure love. I couldn't prevent her fate, or ours, any more than I could have prevented the perfume eating the varnish of her dresser. Something was eaten, eaten away. There was nothing I could do about it. My love prevented nothing. Not one thing.

But if I speak of her, if I write about her, it is possible that I can prevent her disappearance. She will not evaporate, like a scent that is absorbed in air, into a nullity. My mother will not be nothing.

But no, it isn't words that will perform the miracle I need. There are no words that I can use to call her.

I put my nose to my wrist. And she is risen from the dead. She is risen indeed.

VICKI HEARNE

What Philosopher

FROM *The American Scholar*

What philosopher denies
The moods of the wind and stones?

What philosopher has learned
To fear the silent oak trees?

What philosopher can with
The fullest joy shiver when

The terrier goes for sticks?
As for the philosopher,

As for the heart of the world.
So long as ideas edge

Their way between what is good
And so extreme and happy

And what is blackest evil
And so extreme and happy

Some philosopher will learn
To deny the wind and stones

Or to accept them into
The golden truth of the world.

CAROL HUANG

Tomorrow Is Another Day

FROM *The American Scholar*

ADDIS ABABA IS NINE degrees north of the equator, a city of brutal sun and cold nights chilled by mountain air, ringed by hilltops,
and fed by springs that tumble into polluted creeks swarmed by
buzzards and hawks. It is a city of old palaces hidden by soaring
gates and of dirt alleys that vanish into neighborhoods of mud and
scrap metal. It is a city that smells of sweat and dung and diesel; a
city in which herdsmen chase goats alongside traffic and children
sell shoeshines and songs for pennies; a city of beauty as well as of
misery, clinging to hope against all odds.

More than thirty years ago this windblown, sunbaked African
capital, banked approximately seventy-seven hundred feet in the
Entoto Mountains, was reeling from revolution. A coup had top-
pled Haile Selassie, the eighty-two-year-old emperor, the only ruler
most Ethiopians had ever known, sparking a power struggle in
which a pug-nosed army colonel named Mengistu Haile Mariam
emerged as the most ruthless member of a secretive military junta
called the Derg. After executing his military rivals, Mengistu went
after the civil opposition with a series of search-and-destroy campaigns that he christened the "Red Terror." People were caught
hiding in the woods and at roadblocks, seized jumping over walls,
and plucked from demonstrations, buses, and homes. "It was a
time when many young people simply vanished into thin air," wrote
Nega Mezlekia in his memoir, *Notes from the Hyena's Belly*. "The ca-
lamity was beyond anyone's wildest imagination. The streets, public parks, and market stalls were littered with the open-mouthed
dead." Africa Watch called it "one of the most systematic uses of
mass murder by a state ever witnessed in Africa."

Nebiy Mekonnen (NEH-bee mah-KOH-nun) was a chemistry student at Addis Ababa University when Ethiopia's last emperor fell. As a member of an underground movement fighting Mengistu's emerging dictatorship, he'd already been arrested twice when Mengistu's men captured him a third time. It was May 1978, the year Fidel Castro sent twenty thousand troops to help Ethiopia fight Somalia, which had invaded the Ogaden Desert. There were so many Cubans in the Ethiopian capital that year that hotel bars served Cuba Libres and "Guantanamera" played over the state-run radio. Nebiy was en route to a secret meeting near the Ghion Hotel when he saw four white Peugeots, the vehicles favored by Mengistu's security forces. Before he could alter the direction of his footsteps, two men approached him. One man walked toward him, another came from behind, and when he ran into the street, others circled him. They shoved him into a waiting car and radioed their commander, "The sugar cane has been cut."

Inside the palace prison they blindfolded him and demanded names and addresses. When he refused to talk, they stuffed his mouth with a rag that was still damp from the blood and vomit of the previous victim. They forced his elbows and knees around a pole, which they lifted over the floor, so that Nebiy was suspended upside down, curled like a fetus, his feet turned to the ceiling. They tortured him in this position for several days, beating the bottoms of his feet until his soles bled. At first Nebiy thought he could toughen up the soles of his feet by walking after each beating. He would steady himself against the walls of his cell and put one foot in front of the other, leaving a staggered trail of bloody footprints. Eventually, he could no longer walk, so another prisoner offered to carry him. Nebiy had never met the boy before. He was short and stocky with dark, curly hair and thick, callused feet that looked as though they'd never worn shoes. For eight days Amha Getaneh carried Nebiy between their cell and the toilets, until Nebiy's feet healed enough for him to walk again.

Three months later Nebiy, Amha, and others were sent to Maikelawi, a police station in the northern part of the city that had been converted into a detention center. A wall of mud and stone blocked the compound from public view. A single-story building within contained a dozen cement rooms. Each room measured just four by four meters and held as many as fifty people. At times it was so crowded that the prisoners slept in shifts. An uncovered walkway divided the rooms into rows of six, allowing armed soldiers on the roof to see the inmates below. Toilets and showers were at one end, and a solid metal gate was at the other.

The prisoners were allowed out to use the toilets only twice a day, once at dawn and again at dusk, and that was the only time they saw the sky. When they shuffled to the toilets, Nebiy used to look up at the sky and wonder, among many other things, how long he would be in jail. It wouldn't have been so bad if they'd sentenced him to ten, twenty, or even thirty years. He could have told himself after, say, the fifth year, "You've only got five or fifteen or twenty-five to go." But they never sentenced him. They didn't kill him, either. They just left him there, as though, by simply putting him in prison, they'd obliterated him.

Years later, Nebiy and the other prisoners were allowed to sit in the open walkway. They'd play chess with pieces molded from dough and sweetened tea and talk as the sunlight slid from one side of the wall to the other. By then Mengistu's grip on the capital was firm, and each time Mengistu delivered a speech, the guards would haul in a television and make the prisoners listen. There were books then, too — Charles Dickens's *Little Dorrit;* a book on acupuncture; a copy of *Julius Caesar.* Things weren't so bad, and the nightly executions had slowed to a trickle. But that was all later, years later; in the beginning things were very tense, and the prisoners of Maikelawi had just one book — a tattered copy of *Gone with the Wind.*

When Margaret Mitchell's Pulitzer Prize–winning novel was published in 1936, Haile Selassie had been emperor of Ethiopia for six years. The Lion of Judah would remain on the throne for nearly forty more years and be the last of a line of feudal kings who'd ruled the lands of ancient Abyssinia since the earliest days of Christianity. According to a text written between the sixth and eleventh centuries, the kings descended from a tryst between King Solomon of Israel and the Queen of Sheba. They reigned over Africa's oldest independent country, a land of myth and majesty, whose waters from Lake Tana fed more than 50 percent of the Nile, and whose southwestern highlands were credited with producing one of the world's most widely drunk and profitable beverages, coffee.

Haile Selassie brought the first cars to Ethiopia, including Rolls-Royces for his private fleet, and introduced electricity, airplanes, and the country's first written constitution. As prince he'd pushed to abolish slavery so that Ethiopia was able to join the League of Nations in 1923, and as emperor he helped found the Organization of African Unity, headquartered in Addis Ababa, in 1963.

Like others of his generation, Nebiy was raised to believe that the emperor was something akin to a god. Though millions of Ethiopians starved while the emperor traveled the world in a private jet and fed fresh meat daily to the lions in his private zoo, Nebiy's parents raised him to accept the old adage "You can no more fault the emperor than you can sow the sky." Nebiy's father was a bureaucrat in the emperor's Ministry of Finance, his mother a deeply devout woman who used an upturned umbrella to collect money for the local Orthodox Christian Church. Her loyalty to the emperor ran so deep that each time the aging monarch appeared on television, she would rise from her kitchen chair and bow. His mother had given birth late in life, and Nebiy, her only child, dutifully ran errands for neighborhood housewives, attended church every Sunday, and earned good grades in school.

But it was the '60s and '70s, and the educated youth in Ethiopia, like their counterparts across the globe, were agitating for change. Despite Ethiopia's proud history of independence, its natural resources, and its rulers' claims to biblical royalty, the country seemed glaringly backward as its neighbors on the continent moved ahead from colonial rule. Few of Ethiopia's thirty million people had running water or electricity, and 90 percent of the population lived on tiny farms that barely grew enough food to feed them.

By the time Nebiy was in high school, he had started writing political poems and essays and laughing at his mother's salutes to the emperor's televised image. At Addis Ababa University he joined the Ethiopian People's Revolutionary Party (EPRP), an underground movement of students and intellectuals who wanted to overthrow the monarchy in favor of a socialist government. They published student newspapers denouncing the government and clashed with police on the streets of Addis Ababa during demonstrations that grew increasingly frequent and violent. Despite their planning and protests against the monarchy, the brute strength of the military ended it.

As an EPRP member, Nebiy was among those who opposed the creation of a military dictatorship. When the EPRP began attacking Derg supporters, Mengistu retaliated. Though the members of EPRP were his initial targets, the Red Terror campaigns rapidly escalated into indiscriminate killing. Armed neighborhood militias prowled the city for "counterrevolutionaries" and "anarchists," and each day the government radio announced the names of the newly executed and followed each broadcast with triumphant, patriotic tunes. By some estimates as many as 100,000 to 300,000 people were killed between 1977 and 1978, and thousands more were imprisoned. Those captured overwhelmed local jails and flooded prisons around the country, the most notorious of which included Karchele, otherwise known as the Central Prison, and Maikelawi, where prisoners were tortured until they confessed and were either sentenced or executed.

Other than a door and a barred window just large enough to frame a human face, each room in Maikelawi was completely enclosed. A gutter ran down the open walkway in the center, where a stream of wastewater flowed each morning as the prisoners scrubbed their rooms. There was never enough of anything in Maikelawi — not enough food, not enough room, not enough warmth. To survive, prisoners in each room divided themselves into imaginary huts, whose members pooled their money to buy a blanket, food, and eating trays. To ensure that everyone had something to eat, prisoners organized committees that equally divided any food a hut member received from his family. Prisoners never saw visiting loved ones, who could go only as far as the rear wall of Maikelawi. There runners met the families and carried their dishes of food inside the building. Prisoners poured the contents onto metal trays so that empty dishes could be returned to waiting families and used for their next trip.

The prisoners shared everything — a handful of tea leaves, a box of biscuits, lengths of yarn for darning sweaters. They called it living in the *sic,* an Amharic word that described being tightly packed, with each person pressed up against everyone ahead while being crushed by everyone behind. They ate in the *sic* and slept in the *sic,* and each person who wanted to read *Gone with the Wind* waited his turn in the *sic.*

Most of the five hundred to six hundred prisoners in Maikelawi spoke only Amharic, but others were students like Nebiy, with a proficient grasp of English. They were desperate for something to read, something to do, anything to occupy the hours as they awaited their fate. For those who could read English, the book's arrival was a miracle. Though everyone was searched upon capture, one man was brought in clutching his belongings. The man had been arrested at the airport and later executed, leaving behind his things, which included a copy of *Gone with the Wind*. With only a single book among them, Nebiy and his cellmates devised a way to share it. Each person could read the book for an hour a day before passing it to the next reader and awaiting his turn the following day. The hour that Nebiy had the book became the best hour of each day, and after reading it once, he stayed in the rotation to read it again, and then again.

Nebiy started translating the novel from English into Amharic when he began reading it the fourth time. He used the only source of paper available — the lining torn from empty packs of cigarettes. At first he tried to work discreetly in a corner, afraid that prison informants would accuse him of penning subversive messages. But it was impossible to go unnoticed in the crowded rooms, so one evening he announced to his cellmates that he was presenting them with some entertainment and brought out his translated passages. When he finished reading, people wanted to hear more. Each day he translated more of the book, and each night he read the translated passages aloud, drawing a circle around him in the room as those in other rooms stood by their doorways to listen. People began giving up their hour with the book so Nebiy could work more quickly, and because he didn't smoke, those who did passed their crumpled packs of Winstons and Rothmans to his room, where Nebiy sat on the floor, scribbling on rectangles of salvaged paper and puzzling over phrases such as "fiddle-dee-dee."

Beyond the capital, war raged. Besides fighting Somalia in the south, Mengistu's army battled uprisings from some of Ethiopia's eighty-two ethnic minorities who had long considered the country's Amhara rulers as black colonialists. Eritreans in the east fought to carve out a sovereign state along the Red Sea, Tigreans battled in the north, and the Oromos plotted their next attacks in scattered positions throughout the south. Nebiy wrote and wrote, poring over outdated, foreign words, laying down one sentence after another, blocking out the chaos, focusing on what made sense. *Ashley put down the axe and looked away . . . "In the end what will happen will be what has happened whenever a civilization breaks up. The people with brains and courage come through and the ones who haven't are winnowed out."*

Once a month Nebiy's mother boarded a bus and traveled two hours from her home in Nazareth to the capital, carrying an *agelgil,* a dish made of tightly woven leather strips with a leather cover. Though Nebiy's father had died many years before the coup, his mother was able to gather the money each month to fill the *agelgil* with injera bread, eggs, vegetables, and meat — enough, she hoped, to feed her son for a week, unaware that he shared it with as many as ten or twelve others in his hut. The dish was as big around as a man's encircled arms, so big that Nebiy and his cellmates took to calling it The Ship. Each time they saw the heavy *agelgil* from Nebiy's mother, they cried joyously, "The Ship has arrived!"

The supply of food was sporadic. Prisoners might receive food from one of their families one day, then a week or two or three would pass before their next full meal. Sometimes guards would refuse to accept a family's dish and shrug in response to the bearer's panicked questions. When guards returned a prisoner's clothing, family members would scream and sob as they realized that their loved one had been killed. Nebiy made sure that the runners took the empty *agelgil* back to his waiting mother each time she came. The empty dish was their only form of communication, his only way of letting her know that he was still inside, still alive.

By his third year in prison, Nebiy had translated Mitchell's entire novel onto three thousand scraps of paper. He kept the pages in a bag he had stitched together from two-inch squares of plastic he'd salvaged from empty pouches of milk. After a time, he could hardly fit all the pages in his satchel. Although he knew the pieces might be seized during one of the periodic searches, he was unwilling to destroy them. A fellow inmate convinced him that he had to get rid of the papers to avoid an inquiry by prison administrators. If Nebiy was unwilling to destroy the pages, he would have to get rid of them another way. Uncertain of when he'd be freed or if he'd survive, Nebiy agreed.

The pages didn't go all at once. They went in bits and pieces, folded and packed into empty packs of cigarettes. The prisoners resealed each pack with sweetened tea and made it appear like an unopened pack by sliding the bottom portion of the cellophane over the top. They even reattached the tax stamps. Although prison officials never announced their plans, prisoners learned the clues that indicated when someone was to be moved to the Central Prison or released. Surnames would be checked, and the man would be sent for a haircut and shower. Sometimes the man was gone in an hour, sometimes in a day. Those who agreed to take the pages out carried each pack up front in their shirt pockets, casually. One by one, over weeks and months, the pages of Nebiy's translation trickled out of Maikelawi, disguised as packs of cigarettes.

In an interview shortly after *Gone with the Wind* was published, Mitchell said, "If the novel has a theme, it is that of survival. What makes some people able to come through catastrophes and others, apparently just as able, strong, and brave, go under? It happens in every upheaval. Some people survive; others don't. What qualities are in those who fight their way through? I only know that the survivors used to call that quality 'gumption.'"

Nebiy is a compact, burly man with a round, heavily freckled face. When I first met him in Addis Ababa in November 2004, he seemed reluctant to discuss his translation or any of his prison experiences. As a friend of his and I talked over dinner, Nebiy listened, his expression at times attentive, and at other times seemingly lost in the drift of his thoughts.

The next morning, however, he arrived at my hotel in a lighter mood. He took my elbow as we walked down the side of a busy road swarming with taxis, buses, and trucks. Barefoot urchins tagged after women carrying baskets, and young men kicked up puffs of dust behind a soccer ball in a field across the street. As we hailed one of Addis Ababa's tiny, blue-topped taxis, Nebiy marveled at the insanity of the years under Mengistu. He recalled how prison officials once ordered him to prepare a bar chart showing the number of people they'd captured and killed so that they could demonstrate their revolutionary zeal to their commanders. But they were afraid to let it be known too widely how many people they'd killed, so they told him to leave the numbers off the chart. "A bar chart with no numbers — can you imagine?" Nebiy asked.

We arrived at a small café on the road to Bole International Airport. Like other major roads in the capital, many of which have no name, the road was known by its principal landmark and simply called Bole (BOH-lay). After Nebiy and I sat down, he reached into a briefcase and brought out three stacks of paper, each sheet about the size of an outstretched hand, each covered with tiny Amharic script.

In 1984, as another famine swept through Ethiopia, Nebiy entered his seventh year in prison. By then they'd sent his fellow prisoner Amha to Karchele, and Nebiy was the only member of EPRP arrested during the Red Terror who remained at Maikelawi. Prison officials put him in charge of their books and had him keep track of each prisoner transferred, released, or executed. They ordered him to put the names of those they'd executed under a column titled "Transferred to Other Places."

New prisoners were still being arrested, among them, members of the Oromo Liberation Front and the Tigray People's Liberation Front. Each new arrival walked into a cell crowded with bone-thin men wearing rags that hung from their hipbones like diapers. Nebiy pleaded to each newcomer, "We have run out of jokes. We have run out of smiles. We have run out of anything humanly warm, and run out of money. We have only two questions. One, can you help us with some money? And second, can you share any jokes, some songs if you have them, to enliven us? It has been too long a time since we heard any sounds from the outside."

One day the prisoners convinced the administration that they should be allowed to play table tennis in the yard so that their families could see them. They argued that after a decade of bloodshed and horror, it would be good for public opinion to see that the regime was not so evil and treated its prisoners humanely. Their plea was granted, and Nebiy finally saw his mother. She was in her seventies then, and her face appeared briefly in the distance through a crack in Maikelawi's rear wall. Nebiy smiled and waved and tried to make a great show of playing with his paddle, but failed. As the tears fell from her face, he began crying too. In seconds she was gone as other families, desperate for a glimpse of their own children, pushed forward. A guard told him later that his mother sat outside the wall for a long time afterward, unable to move.

In 1985, after nearly eight years in prison, Nebiy was released.

He went to Karchele to visit Amha and promised to return again soon. A few weeks later, he learned Amha had been killed. Nebiy knows few details of how or where Amha died. "He was like a brother to me," Nebiy said.

That same year Nebiy began looking for the pages of his translation. It seemed unlikely that he could recover every sheet, but since as many as two out of every three young men in Ethiopia had been arrested during the Red Terror, Nebiy was able to track down the pages by asking each of his acquaintances who had been in prison. "It wouldn't have been that difficult to retranslate the book, but the attachment I felt to each little leaflet — it was really very passionate," he said. "They are like your little babies. You have suffered with them, written on them. All that would be lost if I retranslated it."

When he had retrieved all the pages, he took a copy to the censorship committee to get it published. They did not like the word *baria*, the Amharic word for *slave*, because the word was also slang for Ethiopians from the south. Mengistu was a southerner, and they accused Nebiy of mocking the chairman. They told him he would have to remove the word if he wanted the translation published. "Time and again I went to the censorship chairperson, and I tried to explain, 'There is no such thing as *Gone with the Wind* without mentioning slavery. I'm not suggesting a person. I'm suggesting a whole society — black American slaves,'" Nebiy recalled. He won on the third try and, with a loan, printed twenty thousand copies in 1986, fifty years after Mitchell published her novel. It was one of the longest English books ever translated into Amharic, and sales went slowly. Shortly afterward, the price of paper skyrocketed, and Nebiy did not publish any more copies.

Beyond loving Mitchell's novel as a story, Nebiy said that he saw its historical backdrop as an allegory for Ethiopia, a promise of sorts, of what might yet come. "Whether you have black history or white history, history is history," he said. "You have to look for the outcome, which was the America that emerged. The present wouldn't have been had the Civil War not been. That was the basic thing. I really prayed that the country would reach that level. And really, if you were in prison and read that book and saw the end of it, where out of destruction reconstruction comes, where out of war comes peace — that is the utmost you can dream of."

It has been fifteen years since Mengistu fled into exile in Zimbabwe. Trials against those accused of genocide and other crimes during the Red Terror began in 1994, and though the trials were scheduled to conclude in 2004, only a third of some fifty-one hundred people charged have appeared in court. Meanwhile, Ethiopia's population in the past three decades has more than doubled to over seventy million. More than 80 percent of the country's people still live on small farms without running water or electricity, and a new killer has joined famine and war to claim lives, leaving a million children orphaned by AIDS.

Seven years ago Nebiy and a partner founded an Amharic newspaper. He serves as its editor-in-chief and works on the side for nongovernmental organizations to develop public education messages about HIV- and malaria-prevention measures. A collection of poems he wrote in prison was translated in France, and in 2003 he wrote the lyrics to an HIV-awareness song that became a local hit. On occasion he returns to Maikelawi and Karchele to visit colleagues who are still jailed.

On our last day together, I met Nebiy near the Ghion Hotel, not far from where he was arrested, and hired a taxi. We drove by the walled hilltop palace where Nebiy spent his first months in captivity. "All those trees were not there before," Nebiy noted, pointing to a driveway that vanished behind a clump of bushes. We followed the curved, sloping road past a neighborhood of unpaved streets and drove past Addis Ababa University until we turned onto an unpaved, rock-strewn road, bumping alongside a stone wall topped by razor wire. Parched, yellowing weeds grew from its crevices and clung to thin layers of dirt at the top. "There, the back side," said Nebiy. "That is where my mother brought me food." I turned and glimpsed three small windows in the stone. Though Maikelawi still serves as a prison, there were no families lined at the wall, just a small barefoot boy running down a dirt alley that disappeared beyond a row of shacks.

As we returned to my hotel, Nebiy pointed to a new high-rise under construction, where men balanced on wooden scaffolds made from eucalyptus trees. "It is a different world now," he said. "The military regime has fallen. That's one big thing. A new start has come, which is not really consolidated, but nonetheless better than the old regime. I am doing fine here, my life is good, and society is changing, moving toward democracy, I hope."

He'd shown me a copy of his published translation, a heavy book with a roughly illustrated cover depicting a woman in a red dress behind a man with a thick, dark mustache. Nebiy said the translation is as close as he could get to Mitchell's words, except for one conscious change. He named his translation *Negem Lela Ken New,* which are Scarlett's famous last words, "Tomorrow is another day."

"There is some hope in this title," he said. "Hope for us prisoners, hope for Ethiopia."

PICO IYER

This Is Who I Am When No One Is Looking

FROM *Portland*

ONCE EVERY THREE OR FOUR MONTHS, for much of my adult life now, I've gotten in my car in my mother's house in the dry hills of California, above the sea, and driven up the road, past the local yoga foundation, past the community of local sixties refugees, past the mock-Danish tourist town and the vineyards, past where Ronald Reagan used to keep his Western White House and where Michael Jackson sat imprisoned in his Neverland, past a lighthouse, past meadows of dormant cows, to another little room a thousand feet above the ocean, in the dry hills, where deer come out to graze at dusk and mountain lions come out, too, to stalk our urban fantasies.

There is a sign on the main highway down below — hanging from a large cross — and there is a saint's name on the door of the little room I enter, underneath the number. But the names are all forgotten here, especially my own, and when I step into the little "cell" that awaits me — narrow bed huddled up against one wall, closet and bathroom, wide blond-wood desk overlooking a garden that overlooks the sea — I really don't know or care what "Catholic" means, or hermitage, or monastery, or Big Sur.

There are crosses in this place, and hooded men singing the psalms at dawn (at noon, at dusk, at sunset), and there's a cross on the wall above the bed. But I go not because of all the trappings of the chapel I had to attend twice a day every school day of my adolescence, but in spite of it. I go to disappear into the silence.

My friends assume, I'm sure, that I go to the monastery to catch my breath, to be away from the phone, to drink in one of the most beautiful stretches of coastline in the world. What I can't tell them — what they don't want to hear — is that I go to the monastery to become another self, the self that we all are if only we choose to unpack our overstuffed lives and leave our selves at home.

In my cell I read novels in the ringing silence, and they are novels, often, of infidelity. In the best of them, the ones by Sue Miller, say, there is a palpable, quickening sense of the excitement of betraying others and your daily self in the world you know. I read these with recognition. This shadow story is as close to us as our dreams. All the great myths are about it, the stories of Shakespeare and Aeschylus and Homer are about it, as are our romance novels and our letters to Aunt Agony, but here in the monastery I'm committing a deeper infidelity, against the life I know and the values by which we are supposed to live. I am being disloyal in the deepest way to the assumptions of the daily round, and daring to lay claim to a mystery at the heart of me.

I step into my cell, and I step into the realest life I know. My secret life, as Leonard Cohen calls it, also happens to be my deepest and my best life. There is no will involved, no choice; this other world, and self, are waiting for me like the clothes I never thought to ask for.

I'm not a Benedictine monk, and I attend none of the services held day in, day out, four times a day, while I'm in my little room. If I make the mistake of attending one because of my longing to be good, my wish to pay, in some way, the kind monks for making the silence available to me, I soon run out again. The presence of the fifteen kindly souls in hoods, singing, takes me back, somehow, to the world, the self I've come here to escape; the words in the psalms are all of war, and I notice which face looks kind and which one bitter.

No, the flight is to something much larger than a single text or doctrine. It's to — this the word I otherwise shy from — eternity. I step into a place that never changes, and with it that part of me, that ground in me, that belongs to what is changeless. There is a self at the core of us — what some call "Christ," others the "Buddha nature," and poets refer to as the immortal soul — that is simply part of the nonshifting nature of the universe. Not in any exalted way: just like the soil or sky or air. It does not fit into our everyday notions any more than sky fits into a bed. But I steal into this better world as into a secret love, and there, as in the best of loves, I feel I am known in a way I know is true.

Thomas Merton put this best, not because he was a Christian, or even because he was a monk, but because he fell in love with silence. And he made the pursuit of that real life his lifelong mission. He knew, he saw, that it was akin to the earthly love we feel, and that the heightening, the risking up to a higher place, the making sense of things—above all, the dissolution of the tiny self we know — when we fall in love is our closest approximation to this state, as certain drugs can give us an indication of what lies beyond. But it is only an approximation, a momentary glimpse, like snapshots of a sunset where we long to live forever.

I wouldn't call this a pilgrimage, because, as Merton says, again, I'm not off to find myself; only to lose myself. I'm not off in search of anything; in fact, only — the words sound fanciful — the sense of being found. You could say it's not a pilgrimage because there's no movement involved after I step out of my car, three hours and fifteen minutes north of my mother's house, and I don't pay any of the religious dues when I arrive. But all the movements and journeys I have taken around the world are underwritten, at heart, by this: this is who I am when nobody is looking. This is who I'm not, because the petty, struggling, ambitious "I" is gone. I am as still, as timeless as the plate of sea below me.

I keep quiet about this journey, usually because it sounds as strange to other people, or to myself, as a piece of silence brought to a shopping mall. If they have an equivalent — and they surely do, in meditation, in sky-diving, in running, in sex — they will know what I'm talking of, and substitute their own terms; everyone knows at moments she has a deeper, purer self within, something that belongs to what stands out of time and space, and when she falls in love, she rises to that eternal candle in another, and to the self that is newly seen in her. But it belongs to a different order from the words we throw around at home. When we fall in love, when we enter a room with our beloved, we know that we can't really speak of it to anyone else. The point, the very beauty of it, is that it admits us into the realm of what cannot be said.

So when I come down to the monastery, I tell my friends that monks watch the film *A Fish Called Wanda* in the cloister. That most of the visitors are female, and very down to earth. The monks sell fruitcake and greeting cards and cassettes in the hermitage bookstore; they have Alcoholics Anonymous meetings once a week, and a sweet woman now lives on the property, helping care for the rooms. The monastery has a website and a fax number. There's a workout room in the "enclosure" for the monks; visiting it once, I came upon books by the Hollywood producer Robert Evans and by Woody Allen.

Everyone feels better when I assure them it's a mortal place, with regular human beings, balding, divorced, confused, with a mailing address I can send packages to. The infidelity sounds less glaring if I phrase it thus. But I can say all this only because I know I'm not talking about what I love and find; because this is the place where all seeking ends.

MICHAEL D. JACKSON

In the Footsteps of Walter Benjamin

FROM *Harvard Divinity Bulletin*

The perfidious reproach of being "too intelligent" haunted him throughout his life.
— Theodor W. Adorno

IT WAS LATE IN THE EVENING WHEN I ARRIVED, and the town was being buffeted by a stiff wind off the sea and squalls of rain. After checking into my hotel, I had dinner in the hotel restaurant and then turned in early, halyards slapping against aluminum masts in the harbor, and a lighthouse flashing in the darkness. My last thoughts before falling asleep were of a photograph I had seen that morning in a Danish newspaper of a listing wooden boat with splintered upper strakes being towed behind an Italian coast-guard cutter on whose cramped foredeck huddled thirty or forty bewildered African asylum-seekers, and of a report in another paper of a proposal by several European governments to create "holding centers" in North Africa for these clandestine immigrants who every night risked their lives[1] crossing the Mediterranean in unseaworthy boats, hoping to find work and a livelihood in Europe.

If migrants are sustained by their hope in the future, refugees are afflicted by their loss of the past. Of no one was this truer than Walter Benjamin.

I had come to Banyuls-sur-mer on the French Catalonian coast with the intention of crossing the Pyrenees on the anniversary of Benjamin's fateful journey on September 26, 1940. But though I had contemplated making this journey for at least a year, I had never fully fathomed my motives. I only knew that one must sometimes abandon any conception of what one is doing in order to do it, accepting that reasons and meanings cannot be imposed upon events but have to be allowed to surface in their own good time. Still, I was mindful of Benjamin's notion of translation "as a mode" that requires one to "go back to the original, for that contains the law governing the translation, its translatability" (1969:70). Could shadowing a writer through a landscape, or repeating a journey precisely sixty-four years after the original had taken place, enable one to know that writer's frame of mind or translate his thought? And what kind of translation is it, anyway, that seeks parallels and echoes, not between languages, but between experiences, and, as Benjamin himself suggested, between the lines?

Walter Benjamin was born in Berlin in 1892, and reborn twenty-one years later in Paris. But while Paris was where he came to feel most at home, it would be truer to say that it was the Paris of the nineteenth century that captivated him, and later became not only a refuge but also the subject of his monumental though unfinished *Passagenarbeit (Arcades Project)*. Hannah Arendt suggests that the allure of this fabulous city, for Benjamin, had something to do with the "unparalleled naturalness" with which it had, from the middle of the nineteenth century, "offered itself to all homeless people as a second home" (Arendt 1973:170); for Benjamin, however, it was more immediately the "physical shelter" afforded by its arcades, the ghostly presence of a perimeter connected by medieval gates, the village-like intimacy of its old neighborhoods, and the homeliness of the boulevard cafés that invited one to live in Paris as one lives within an apartment or house. Besides, Paris could easily be covered on foot, making it an ideal city for strollers, idlers, and browsers — that is to say, *flâneurs*. And Benjamin, who had never been successful in getting an academic job, and was obliged to lead a freelance existence that involved "the precarious, errant practices of a critic, translator, reviewer, and scriptwriter for radio" (Steiner 1998:11), living under his parents' roof until he was in his late thirties and always dependent on the support of friends, was in many ways a man who had missed his time, a would-be man of letters and leisure, with old-fashioned manners, a passion for antiquarian books, and little practical sense, someone whose idea of history never completely encompassed the unfolding tragedy of his own epoch. As he wrote in his essay on Proust, with whom he undoubtedly identified: "He is filled with the insight that none of us has time to live the true dramas of the life that we are destined for. This is what ages us — this and nothing else. The wrinkles and creases on our faces are the registrations of the great passions, vices, insights that called on us; but we, the masters, were not at home" (1969:211–212).

Did he ever feel at home in twentieth-century Germany? "One has reason to doubt it," writes Hannah Arendt. "In 1913, when he first visited France as a very young man . . . the trip from Berlin to Paris was tantamount to a trip in time . . . from the twentieth century back to the nineteenth" (1973:170).

When the Nazis seized power in January 1933, Benjamin could no longer count on an income from writing, and his attempts to write under pseudonyms such as K. A. Stampflinger and Detlef Holz proved fruitless. In March he left Germany and stayed with friends on Ibiza for six months before settling in Paris, supported by stipends from the Frankfurt Institut für Sozialforschung, where Max Horkheimer, Friedrich Pollock, and Theodor Adorno were his staunch allies. Although often isolated, and with Europe moving ineluctably toward war, Benjamin worked patiently at his projects, declining the offers and urgings of friends such as Gershom Scholem, Arendt, and Adorno to move to Palestine, England, or the United States. He was, he explained to them, no longer capable of adapting (Scholem 1982:213). Yet Benjamin was well aware of the fate of Jews in Germany after *Kristallnacht* — the mass arrests, the new edicts, the concentration camps, the panicked exodus. And even as Scholem tried to find funds to bring the reluctant Benjamin to Palestine in spring 1939, the Gestapo was ordering the German Embassy in Paris to expedite his repatriation, probably because of "Paris Letter," published in 1936, in which he made no bones about his anti-fascist views, observing, for instance, that "culture under the Swastika is nothing but the playground of unqualified minds and subaltern characters" and "fascist art is one of propaganda" (Brodersen 1996:24). Although he continued to seek naturalization in France, Benjamin's efforts in the summer of 1939 seemed to have been devoted mainly to his essay on Baudelaire, and he passed up an invitation to Sweden in order to finish it.

When war was declared on September 1, 1939, all Germans, Austrians, Czechs, Slovaks, and Hungarians of ages seventeen to fifty and living in France were subject to internment. Men rounded up in Paris were first taken to football stadiums — the Stade Colombe and the Stadion Buffalo — where they remained for ten days and nights, sleeping in the bleachers, killing time playing cards, strolling around the track, or planning how they might gain their release (women were assembled for screening in an ice-skating stadium, the Vélodrome d'Hiver). The internees were then trucked to the Gare d'Austerlitz under military escort, thence in sealed railway carriages to various hastily prepared camps throughout France. Benjamin was interned first at Nevers, where empty chateaus, vacant factories, and farms had been converted into *camps de concentration* for *ressortissants* ("enemy aliens"), including *ressortissants allemands* (those "coming from Germany"), and then at Vernuche, where three hundred prisoners were crammed into a disused furniture factory. In November 1939, thanks to the intervention of friends in Paris, notably the French poet and diplomat St.-John Perse, Benjamin was released and seemed finally reconciled to leaving France (Max Horkheimer had managed to secure for him an emergency visa to the United States). But once again, like an ostrich burying its head in the sand, Benjamin took refuge in intellectual labor, unable to break his long-standing habit of seeking security in an interiorized existence, in libraries, and in the collecting of rare books. After renewing his reader's card for the Bibliothèque Nationale, he attempted to begin researching and writing his sequel to his Baudelaire.[2]

In a letter to Gretel Adorno, dated January 17, 1940, he wrote of this tension between the exigencies of his own survival and the work that was his life:

> The fear of having to abandon the Baudelaire once I have begun writing the sequel is what makes me hesitate [to leave Paris]. This sequel will be work of monumental breadth and it would be a delicate matter to have to start and stop again and again. This is, however, the risk I would have to take. I am constantly reminded of it by the gas mask in my small room — the mask looks to me like a disconcerting replica of the skulls with which studious monks decorated their cells. This is why I have not yet really dared to begin the sequel to the Baudelaire. I definitely hold this work more dear to my heart than any other. It would consequently not suffer being neglected even to ensure the survival of its author.

In May 1940, Hitler's armies overran the French forces and in June they entered Paris. That same month, the Franco-German Armistice was signed, with its ominous Article XIX requiring the French government to "surrender on demand" anyone the Third Reich wanted extradited to Germany — an edict that effectively ended the issuing of exit visas to German refugees like Benjamin, whether in the occupied or unoccupied zones.

After entrusting his precious manuscripts to friends, Benjamin and his sister Dora joined the two million or more refugees trudging *en pagaille* toward the unoccupied zone. After spending most of that summer in Lourdes in the Basses Pyrénées, he traveled to Marseille in August to ratify his emergency visa to the United States. There, he briefly met Arthur Koestler, to whom he confided (as he had to Arendt in Paris) that he carried with him fifteen tablets of a morphine compound — "enough to kill a horse." From Marseille, Benjamin and two other refugees (Henny Gurmand and her sixteen-year-old son, José) traveled to Port Vendres where they met Lisa Fittko and her husband, Hans, who were in the process of reconnoitering, with the help of the socialist mayor of Banyuls, a new escape route across the Pyrenees. During the previous few months, refugees had fled France by taking a train to Cerbère, the last town before the Catalan frontier, and then walking to Portbou in Spain through the railway tunnel or over the steep ridge along which the border ran.

Only a week or ten days before Walter Benjamin tried to reach Spain, several other Jewish refugees — among them Lion and Marta Feuchtwanger, Alma Mahler Werfel, Franz Werfel, Heinrich Mann, and Golo Mann — had successfully used the route via Cerbère, traveling on to neutral Portugal, where they found ships to America. But with increasing Gestapo pressure on the Spanish government, and the French police obliged to collaborate under Article XIX of the Armistice, French exit visas were impossible to procure, and Cerbère was, in any event, too carefully watched by the *gardes mobiles*.

After a five-minute train journey from Port Vendres to Banyuls (although, in her memoirs, Lisa Fittko thinks they may have taken the coastal path), Lisa Fittko led Benjamin and his party on an afternoon reconnoiter of the route they would take the following day. After walking for almost three hours, they reached a clearing where Benjamin announced he intended to sleep the night and wait for the others to rejoin him in the morning. Fearing for his safety, Fittko tried to persuade him against this plan, but *der alte*

Benjamin, as she called him (although he was only forty-eight, and she thirty-one) prevailed, and she had no option but to leave him, without provisions or a blanket, clutching the heavy black leather briefcase he had brought with him and that he claimed to be "more important than I am, more important than myself" (Fittko 2000:106). Well before first light the next day, the others again left Banyuls-sur-mer. Passing through the village of Puig del Mas, and making themselves inconspicuous among the vineyard workers, they climbed to their rendezvous with Benjamin, and on across the Col de Cerbère toward Spain.[3] After a grueling twelve-hour journey, they arrived in Portbou only to find that their transit visas, which would have taken them through Spain to Lisbon, had been canceled on orders from Madrid.[4]

That night the exhausted and dispirited travelers were placed under guard in a local hotel; in the morning they were to be escorted back to France. At ten o'clock that night, unable to see any way out, Benjamin swallowed some of the morphine tablets he carried with him. He died at seven the following morning.[5] Ironically, had these refugees attempted the border crossing one day earlier or one day later, they would have made it, for the embargo on visas was lifted — possibly on compassionate grounds, possibly for some unspecified bureaucratic reason — the same day Benjamin died.

The last thing Benjamin wrote was a postcard. As Henny Gurland remembered it many months later in America, the five lines on the postcard read: "In a situation with no way out, I have no choice but to end it. My life will finish in a little village in the Pyrenees where no one knows me. Please pass on my thoughts to my friend Adorno and explain to him the situation in which I find myself. There is not enough time to write all the letters I had wanted to write" (Brodersen 1996:245).

These were the details I had gleaned from my reading. But as with so many written sources, it is often impossible to get a sense of the life that lies behind the language, or to lift the veil with which memory screens out the landscapes, faces, voices, not to mention the physical and emotional experiences, that might tell us what it was like to undergo the events that are so summarily recounted. So it was that with a faxed copy of an old map that I had been given at the tourist information office at Banyuls (I was evidently not the first foreigner to ask about the route that Walter Benjamin took across the Pyrenees), and a hastily packed lunch in my rucksack, I set out at first light along the road that led up into the hills behind the town.

Once past Puig del Mas, and climbing the narrow winding road that was marked on my map simply as Vers Mas Guillaume ("Toward Guillaume's Farmstead"), I began to feel less and less certain that I was on the right track. The steep slopes above and below the road were covered in gnarled and stunted Grenache vines that miraculously found some purchase in the dark brown schist, and whose tendrils and leaves were splayed, unsupported, over the seemingly barren ground. All this was undoubtedly the same as it had been in 1940. The workers, for example, bent over the vines, snipping bunches of grapes and placing them in panniers on their backs, which they up-ended from time to time in rectangular plastic bins along the roadside. But whereas, in 1940, the *vigneroles* walked up to the vineyards, today they came in cars or small trucks. And back then the men carried spades over their shoulders, from which hung *cabecs* — baskets for toting the stones for repairing terrace walls and storm-water ditches. Moreover, the narrow, tortuous road was probably not tar-sealed. So when I stopped to scan the slopes above me for signs of a "clearing" or for "the seven pines on the plateau" that, according to Lisa Fittko, always indicated the right direction (Fittko 2000:124), I was lost.

Well past Puig del Mas now, I asked an old man, working alone among his vines, if I could get to Spain if I continued walking up this road. He thought I was crazy. You get to Spain along the coast road, he said. This road goes nowhere. I explained that I was looking for the smugglers' track that Jewish refugees used in 1940 to avoid the frontier posts. Could he perhaps take a look at my map and set me straight? The old man appeared to have considerable trouble reading the map, or making sense of the penciled line that marked the *ruta realitzada per Walter Benjamin en el seu èxode,* and kept insisting that one could only reach Portbou via the coast road. From the way he turned the map this way and that, I concluded that he was trying to see the map as a picture that bore some natural resemblance to the landscape with which he was so familiar, and was baffled by the abstractions of cartography. This road goes nowhere, he repeated. It goes up the valley, then comes to a dead end.

I decided to retrace my steps to Puig del Mas. There, I asked another old man, walking his Labrador dog along a narrow street, if he could decipher my map and tell me how I could find the old route over the mountains. "In 1940 it was called *la route Lister*," I explained (General Enrique Lister, a commander in the Republican Army, had used it when escaping into France with his troops in 1939, after the fall of Barcelona). But though the dog owner had a dim memory of such a path, he had no knowledge of it, and knew of no one I might ask for information. So I returned, reluctantly, to the Syndicat des Initiatives in Banyuls, only to be assured that I had been on the right road after all. Just keep on going, I was told. You have to climb to the Col de Cerbère. Spain is beyond.

Two hours later I trudged past the old man who had told me that the road led nowhere. He was lugging a pail of grapes down through his vines to the roadside. Upon seeing me, he shrugged his shoulders in disbelief. *"Ô non!"*

It was windy now — the *tramontane* blustering out of a clear blue sky. Behind me, in full sunlight, were the terra cotta roofs and pale ocher walls of Puig del Mas, and ahead, in the distance, was the sea, scoured and flecked by the unrelenting wind. In the lee of a roadside wall, and shaded by cedars, I sat down, drank from the bottle of water I had brought with me, and scribbled some notes. I could hear men's voices in the vineyards below me, borne on the wind, and I caught a whiff of burning cigarettes and the stale fermented smell of grapes. Looking up at the range, I could see where the highest and steepest vineyards gave way to a wilderness of pinewoods, evergreen oaks, and scrub. I wondered where Benjamin had passed the night, and whether he might have found sanctuary in one of the many small, conical huts made of schist — called *boris* — where vineyard workers took shelter from the wind, prepared coffee or food, and sometimes slept overnight. I also found myself reflecting on his unbroken resolve to press on. Not to retrace a single step. Certainly, as he told Lisa Fittko, his weak heart and lack of fitness made it impossible for him to even contemplate the effort of making this journey more than once, and he must have been haunted not only by the degradation of internment and the disorienting weeks of flight, but also by the realization that he had long passed the point of no return, and that his whole life — apart from those remnants contained in the briefcase he would not be parted from — was irretrievably lost. As Hannah Arendt observed, this was a man who could not imagine living without his library or his vast collection of quotations, and for whom America offered no other prospect, as he confided to her in Paris, than of being carted up and down the country and exhibited as the "last European" (Arendt 1973:168).

By midmorning I had reached a fork in the road — perhaps the "junction" that Lisa Fittko refers to in her memoir. The road to my left appeared to lead toward the head of a deep valley, directly under the steep and overgrown slopes of the mountain. The other road led straight on, going east and inland; a sign indicated that it was one of the *circuits du vignoble de Banyuls.* I asked a man and a woman, hard at work among the vines, if they could tell me which route would take me up to the col. They pointed to a stony track that began where the road divided and quickly disappeared into the broom, grass, and scrub.

It was hard going. Within minutes my heart was pounding and I was out of breath, but I was confident now that this track would lead along the spur and thence to the col. But the track soon petered out, and I found myself standing on the terrace of a vineyard, trying to figure out where I had gone wrong. Rather than turn back, I decided to take a shortcut down through the vineyard to the road below in the hope that it would take me toward the head of the valley from where I might find a path up onto the range. But all my efforts to find a path or force my way through the dense scrub were unavailing, and realizing that the sealed road I had taken simply looped back toward Banyuls, I asked a man who was dumping grapes into his truck by the roadside whether he could point out to me the path that led up to the col. Without hesitation he directed my attention back to the spur I had first followed, and the highest vineyard on the western side, where a white truck was parked beneath some pines. That was the way.

Confident now of my direction, I walked quickly back along the valley road, then took a dirt track up through a stand of parasol pines, resinous in the wind, until I was once more on the path along the spur. Now, rather than forge straight ahead as I had done before, I took a turning to my right that I had ignored earlier because it seemed to be bearing west rather than south toward Spain.

This path, I now discovered, turned sharply left and led along the spur toward the summit road that was now visible, cut into the side of the mountain, and heading toward the col.

With my goal in sight, I decided to stop for lunch, enjoy the view, and write some notes. From Lisa Fittko's descriptions, I could well have been sitting where Benjamin and the others rested from their exertions, four or five hours into their ascent. She describes how they had to clamber up through a vineyard to the ridge, and how this climb defeated Benjamin, who had to be half-carried up the steep rubble slope, one arm around José's shoulder, the other around Fittko's, the black briefcase presumably in Frau Gurmand's hands. When they stopped, Fittko ate a piece of bread she had bought with bogus food stamps, and offered some tomatoes to the famished Benjamin, who, with his inimitable courtesy, said, "By your leave, *gnädige Frau,* may I serve myself?" I sat under a gnarled cork oak, out of the wind, and laid out my own lunch — some sachets of honey, bread rolls, and an apple that I had taken from the breakfast buffet at my hotel, plus a couple of bananas, a bottle of Evian water, and a cellophane bag of walnuts I had bought at a *tabac* on my second trip from Banyuls. In the distance, the Pyrenees were lost in a blue haze. Below me, the wind riffled and battered the *maquis.* Grasshoppers flickered among the stones.

Half an hour later, as I was hoisting myself up over the limestone boulders that interrupted the upward path, I marveled at the determination and patience that had enabled Benjamin to accomplish what would have been ordinarily inconceivable and impossible. Lisa Fittko was struck by what she called his "crystal-clear thinking and unfaltering inner strength," and she recalls how, during his night alone on the mountainside, he had worked out a plan of action in which he would harbor his resources by walking for ten minutes and resting for one. Hans Fittko, who had met Benjamin during their internment at Vernuche, remembered how the older man had quit smoking the better to survive his ordeal. Yet it wasn't because this might improve his physical fitness, nor even because tobacco was hard to come by; it was, Benjamin explained, because concentrating his mind on not smoking helped him distract himself from the hardships of the camp — evidence, perhaps, of his Taoist commitment to that eternal patience whereby running water finally "gets the better of granite and porphyry," wearing away stone.[6]

The track passed under a pylon, and a few minutes later I was on the old unpaved road that zigzagged up toward the crest. I stopped only to eat some wild blackberries, and to get my bearings for the return trip. Then I was on the col, and looking down over wind-swept rocky slopes to the marshaling yards at Cerbère. Portbou, I guessed, lay just over the ridge from there.

The road toward Spain, cut into the side of a hill, descended gradually above a valley in which I could make out farmhouses among plantations of pines and cedars. I sat in the long grass, and watched the wind raking the heather and brushwood on the ex-posed upper slopes of the range. The only sounds were the dis-tant barking of a dog and the wind howling in the girders of a nearby watchtower. How could one not remark the grim irony of this place, named for the three-headed dog who guards the oppo-site shore of the Styx, "ready to devour living intruders or ghostly fugitives" (Graves 1955:120)? Far beyond Cerbère lay the wind-whipped sea, with cape after cape vanishing into the haze of Span-ish Catalonia. I felt exhilarated to have made it, because I had slept badly the night before, filled with trepidation about setting off into an unknown region without a guide. And all that morning, as I stumbled along paths that led nowhere, missed critical turnoffs, and failed to reconcile my map with the terrain around me, I had felt tense with anxiety and doubt. There was, of course, no more certainty that I had taken exactly the same route Benjamin took than that my experiences bore any relationship with his, let alone afforded me any insights into his work. But perhaps such certain-ties are beside the point, since our relationships with even those closest to us are not necessarily founded on knowledge in the intel-lectual sense of the word, but rather on a sense of a natural affinity or fellow-feeling that cannot be explained.

Perhaps this is why I had mistakenly made my trip a day earlier than the actual anniversary of his own, as if I had unconsciously, magically, and belatedly sought to prevent his fate, much as some people — including Heinrich Mann's wife, Nelly, when the day came for her to cross the frontier from Cerbère to Portbou — did everything in their power to avoid traveling on Friday the Thir-teenth. In any event, I came back to Banyuls, where I had left my things at the hotel, and the following morning packed my ruck-sack, paid my bill, and set out for Portbou. My plan was to take the morning train and spend the day exploring the town where Benjamin had died, but at Banyuls railway station I checked the timetable only to discover that the 9:10 train to Portbou had stopped running a week ago, and since it was Sunday I would have to wait until 2:20 for the only train that day. It did not take me more than a few seconds to decide that I would sooner be on the move than standing still, stuck in Banyuls and waiting for a train that might never come. So I retraced my steps through the old town and back along the seafront road, heading south.

There was no footpath and scarcely any grassy verge along the narrow highway, and after hitching for an hour without success, I yielded to the road, resolved to walk the whole distance. Apart from the belligerence of the wind and the cars that often passed uncomfortably close, I was elated to be on the open road with the sea beside me, wearing its fingers to the bone on the jagged foreshore, and further out its surface annealed by the harsh light and smeared by the same incessant wind that shoved at my back. It is sometimes uncanny, the way unforeseen events turn out to be a blessing in disguise, though this seems never to have been true of Walter Benjamin. His remarks on Marcel Proust could well have been reflections on his own character — "a man in whom 'weakness and genius coincide'; a man who 'died of the same inexperience which permitted him to write his works.' He died of ignorance of the world and because he did not know how to change the conditions of his life which had begun to crush him. He died because he did not know how to make a fire or open a window" (Benjamin 1969:213). Even his dear friend Hannah Arendt confessed that he seemed destined, "with a precision suggesting a sleepwalker, to stumble into catastrophe after catastrophe" (1973:157), and she recalls a succession of Kafkaesque episodes in which, for example, the young literary critic, counting on a promised stipend for reading a manuscript, received nothing because the publisher went bankrupt; and much later, in the winter of 1939–40 when the danger of bombing made him leave Paris for a safer place, Benjamin sought refuge in Meaux, a troop center and probably one of the few places that *was* in serious danger during this period of the *drôle de guerre*. Undoubtedly, Arendt also had in mind the tragic irony of September 26, 1940, when Benjamin and his party arrived in Portbou only to be told that Spain had closed its borders that day, and that visas issued in Marseille would not, in any case, be accepted. Had he attempted the crossing a day earlier, all would have been well; a few weeks later, his visa would have been accepted. "Only on that particular day was the catastrophe possible," Arendt wrote (1973:169).

In the three days Lisa Fittko spent with Walter Benjamin she formed an impression of a man whose intellectuality gave him a certain inner strength but made him "hopelessly awkward and clumsy" (2000:109). From her teenage years, Fittko had been a political activist. A gutsy, no-nonsense young woman who had quit her university studies to fight fascism, Benjamin's mystical Marxism would have left her cold. *Faut se débrouiller!* she exclaimed. "One must know how to help oneself, to clear a way out of the debacle," which in France in 1940 meant knowing how to "buy counterfeit food stamps, scrounge milk for the children, obtain some, any, kind of permit — in short, manage to do or obtain what didn't officially exist" (2000:113).

Between May and June 1940, Lisa Fittko was in the concentration camp at Gurs, in the foothills of the Pyrenees. The camp had been built in April 1939, to accommodate Republican refugees and members of the International Brigades who were fleeing Spain after the civil war — rows of barracks in a sea of mud, each barracks containing sixty sleeping pads with straw *palliasses*, twenty-five barracks to each *îlot*, or section, each *îlot* separated from the others by barbed wire. At the end of the camp was the *îlot des indésirables* — the unwanted ones — known for their opposition to the Nazis and kept under strict surveillance. Among the *indésirables* at Gurs was Hannah Arendt, and it was through an audacious ruse, in which Lisa Fittko was actively involved (the distraught *commissaire spécial de police du Camp de Gurs*, panicked by the German advance, agreed in a drunken moment to allow Fittko and others to sort the *indésirables* into dangerous and less dangerous categories),[7] that Arendt was released from the *îlot des indésirables* and able to make good her escape from the camp.[8]

The light on the sea was like fish scales. The wind-combed grass on the hillside and a grove of cork oaks brought back memories of the East Coast of New Zealand. How strange it is, the way one's thoughts are set free by walking. I felt that I was writing a poem with my body, not my mind, by moving rather than using words. The poem was myself on the road. The *terroir* of a piece of writing, I said to myself — the way words soak up the earth and the light.

*

At Cerbère, footsore and weary, I bought an espresso and sat in a seafront café, watching the traffic wend its way slowly up the steep road that presumably led to the border. Again, I found it difficult to imagine how some of the émigrés who passed this way in 1940 managed to climb the hill. In his memoir of this time, Varian Fry speaks of his concern for the physical resources of many of the political and intellectual refugees he helped. In Marseille, Alma Mahler Werfel and Franz Werfel "never went around the block without taking a taxi, if they could help it," and when they did walk anywhere "it was always on the level, never uphill" (1945:57). It was, therefore, touch and go whether the fifty-year-old Franz Werfel, who was "large, dumpy, and pallid, like a half-filled sack of flour" (Fry 1945:5–6) and had a heart ailment, or the seventy-year-old Heinrich Mann, who escaped with his nephew Golo and the Werfels, would be able to make it over the hill. Enervated by the midsummer heat, and often having to crawl up the "sheer slippery terrain . . . bounded by precipices" (Werfel 1959:244), they nevertheless crossed the mountain, and after bribing the soldiers at the Spanish frontier with packets of cigarettes, were waved through.

I could not help but compare the fate of Walter Benjamin who, a week later, would attempt a much longer and more arduous trip across the Pyrenees, clinging to his briefcase full of notes as if it were a lifeline, and the fate of Alma Mahler Werfel, who held on to the scores of Gustav Mahler's symphonies and Bruckner's Third with similar tenacity, and whose twelve suitcases were brought by Varian Fry and Dick Ball on the train from Cerbère to Portbou, or her husband, whose period of limbo in Lourdes had inspired him to write what would become one the most celebrated pieces of émigré writing in wartime America, *The Song of Bernadette*.

And so I began the hardest part of my journey. The wind was now so strong that at times I was almost knocked off my feet or could make little headway walking into it. I chose to hug the rock face rather than walk along the outer edge of the road, even though there were few places where I could safely step aside while cars passed. But as I approached the ridge, I could see that the road doubled back, presumably descending from that point on into Spain. I passed a sign warning of *Paravent Violent*, cut across the corner of the road, and was immediately in sight of the Douane — a narrow building around which the downhill road flowed like a stream. Its offices were devoid of furniture; there was no indication that it was still in use; and I felt a momentary pang of disappointment that I could simply walk past this point where the fate of so many desperate travelers had been decided by the caprice or greed of a frontier guard, a cable from Madrid, or even the hour of the day. Perhaps nothing defines the plight of the refugee more than this overwhelming sense that one's life is no longer in one's own hands, that one is totally dependent on the goodwill of others, and yet utterly ignorant of what the future holds. I therefore found it poignant to recall that one of Benjamin's last published essays had been a commentary on Bertold Brecht's great poem *Legend of the Origin of the Book Tao Te Ching on Lao Tzu's Way into Exile,*[9] in which he pointed out that an act of pure friendship between a customs officer and the seventy-year-old sage, going into exile on an ox, was the only reason that Lao Tzu's inimitable work survived, to be passed down through the centuries to us. It is thus a reminder that the one hope we have in this world is that compassion will triumph over indifference.

As I walked quickly down the winding road I could see Portbou below me, dominated by the great barn of its railway station and its church, but with a white-walled cemetery and cypresses conspicuous above the bay. I reached the town at 11:45, having covered the eighteen kilometers from Banyuls in under four hours. But before exploring the town I decided to make sure I could get a train to Perpignan that afternoon and thereby catch my flight to Paris early the next morning. After buying a ticket for the 1:56 train I stowed my rucksack in a station locker, grateful to be rid of its weight on my back, and descended a flight of stone steps into the town. I did not have to hunt about for my destination; the "Memorial W. Benjamin" was clearly marked, and within minutes I had located the cemetery where, among the tiered white tombs, some of which had hinged windows to protect the flowers and photographs that had been placed in front of the niches, I found myself standing in front of the brown schist boulder that commemorated Benjamin's death in Portbou on September 27, 1940. Where he was actually buried no one had yet discovered. Although Henny Gurland had supposedly paid the town authorities to have Benjamin buried in the cemetery, Hannah Arendt passed through Portbou in January 1941 and found no trace of his grave. "It was not to be found," she wrote Gershom Scholem. "His name was not written anywhere." And she described the cemetery above the blue waters of the bay as "one of the most fantastic and beautiful spots I have seen in my life" (Scholem 1982:226).

Someone had inserted a rock rose between the boulder and the marble plaque in front of it, and on the boulder various visitors had placed small stones or white polished pebbles from the nearby path. I sat against a concrete wall, out of the wind, and copied into my notebook the words on the plaque:

> Walter Benjamin
> Berlin, 1892–Portbou, 1940
>
> "Es ist niemals ein Dokument der Kultur,
> ohne zugleich ein solches der Barberi zu sein"
> *Geschichtsphilosophische Thesen, VII*

The German phrase had also been translated into Spanish.

But if I had been able to choose, from Benjamin's work, an epitaph, it would have been the lines that preface the eighth thesis: "The tradition of the oppressed teaches us that the 'state of emergency' in which we live is not the exception but the rule." For as I sat there, my journey at an end, I was thinking how, as Benjamin observed so often, the presence of the now (*jetzheit*) makes it inevitable that thoughts of any one tragic death give rise to thoughts of all wrongful death. And so I thought of the nameless individuals who at that very moment were held in limbo and incommunicado, stripped of their rights, subject to torture or the degradation of interminable waiting, in places as far afield as Guantánamo Bay in Cuba, the Abu Ghraib prison near Baghdad, and the numerous "immigration camps" and "detention centers" around the world where asylum-seekers, driven from their homelands by persecution or want, were excluded not only from the protection of our laws, but ostracized from our definition of humanity.

For a moment, as I gazed at the boulder and the plaque bearing Walter Benjamin's name, I was fighting back tears. Then, bending down, I took a white stone from the path and placed it on the boulder, taking superstitious care not to dislodge any of the others that had been put there — possibly fifty, possibly a hundred — one for each of the pilgrims who had found his or her way to this place, half-hoping, perhaps, for a moment of truth, or even a sign of re-

demption. I then broke off a leaf from the small variegated cop-
rosma bush growing by the boulder, and put it in my wallet.

Why was I so moved by this place? Cemeteries are for families.
The living come to cemeteries to reconnect with kith and kin, to
keep alive — with flowers, prayers, thoughts, and the small rituals
of cleaning or tending a grave — the presence of those who have
passed away. But what kinship brought me here? What affinity drew
me to Benjamin?

And then it occurred to me that this affinity had less to do with
the inspiration I had drawn from Benjamin's ideas of allegory and
narratively coherent experience (*erfahrung*), or from the notion
that the form of our writing may imitate the "natural" or spontaneous forms in which the world appears to us; it came mostly from the
way I have taken heart, for many years, from his example, and
come to see that the maverick life of a thinker, arcane and obsolete
though it is nowadays seen to be, is as legitimate as any other vocation. Although our backgrounds and upbringings were utterly unlike, and he died the year I was born, had I not, from the beginning, been attracted to the life of the mind, only to find that such
an existence had little value in the country where I was raised? But
in contrast to Benjamin, I did not aspire to intellectual greatness.
This was not because I embraced the anti-intellectualism of my native culture, or, like Pierre Bourdieu, felt ashamed of thought; it
was because I had always been convinced that thought and language were profoundly inadequate to the world, and could neither
save nor redeem us. It may not have been Benjamin's intellectuality
that made him so maladroit. But it did offer him a kind of magical
bolthole where he could avoid taking action, and console himself
that the world was safe and secure as long as he could make it appear so in what he thought and wrote.

Perhaps we should learn to judge the intellectual life not in
terms of its practical capacity to improve the material conditions of
our lives, but in terms of whether it enlarges our capacity of seeing
the world in new ways. In his *Prison Notebooks*, Antonio Gramsci
asked: "Are intellectuals an autonomous and independent group,
or does every social group have its own particular specialised category of intellectuals?" Experience has taught me not to think of intellectuals as groups, but to celebrate originality of thought, wherever and whenever it occurs, for it is as likely to make its appearance

in an African village as in a European university. And this faculty of seeing the world in a new way, of seeing through customary jargons and received opinions, has a lot to do with living in what Karl Jaspers called "border situations," or "training one's imagination to go visiting" (Arendt 1982:43), which is to say making a conscious virtue out of the pariah status that, for example, Jews had thrust upon them in Nazi Germany and Vichy France (Arendt 1978, original 1944).

Yet for all the insights they might yield, such indeterminate situations, in which one's very identity is in doubt, are at once nightmarish and farcical. Writing in 1943, Arendt observed of "we refugees" that "the less we are free to decide who we are or to live as we like, the more we try to put up a front, to hide the facts, and to play roles" (1978:61), and went on:

> We were expelled from Germany because we were Jews. But having hardly crossed the French borderline, we were changed into "boches." We were even told that we had to accept this designation if we were really against Hitler's racial theories. During seven years we played the ridiculous role of trying to be Frenchmen — at least, prospective citizens; but at the beginning of the war we were interned as "boches" all the same. In the meantime, however, most of us had indeed become such loyal Frenchmen that we could not even criticize a French governmental order; thus we declared it was all right to be interned. We were the first "*prisonniers volontaires*" history has ever seen. After the Germans invaded the country, the French government had only to change the name of the firm; having been jailed because we were Germans, we were not freed because we were Jews (61).

Hannah Arendt was an optimist, albeit a cynical one, aware that the intellectual advantages of not being at home in the world were offset by the subterfuge and pretense to which the pariah must have recourse. Every attempt to reinvent oneself, learn a new language, respect the advice of one's saviors, and pretend to forget that one ever had another life, or that one dreams nightly of those that perished, poems known by heart, places one called home, was in part a carefully managed performance, calculated to appease those in whose homeland one had no option but to make a new beginning and to fool oneself into thinking that new beginnings were possible. That Benjamin was not alone, among these refugees, in refusing the illusion of another life, and in deciding to end his life rather than endure further humiliation and loss, is something for which Arendt felt the greatest sympathy, for behind the compliant and optimistic façade of the grateful migrant is a constant struggle with despair of themselves — since deep down they do not believe that their misfortune is a result of political events outside their control, but the result of some mysterious shortcoming in themselves, a defect in their personalities, an inability to maintain the social appearances to which they have for so long been accustomed. And so they kill themselves, not, as Camus might have said, as a declaration that life is absurd and that the game is not worth the candle, but because, as Arendt puts it, "of a kind of selfishness" (1978:60).

With Benjamin there was, I think, an inability to embrace the illusion of a future. Yet without an investment in what might be, one is doomed to dwell solely on what was, and, in the case of those in extremis, to see the hardships one is presently forced to endure as the only reality. I have always shared Adorno's and Horkheimer's view that Benjamin's social criticism was compromised by his religious idealism, and I have, in particular, never accepted the idea that the present is simply a site of eternal return for all that has gone before, and that the possibility of renewal lies in meditating on a dismembered past.[10] In this view, entropy is inescapable (the debris piling up at our feet as the storm of progress hurls us away from paradise), and redemption dependent on the appearance of a savior. But perhaps it was Benjamin's unworldliness I found so unsettling — the accusation that the intellectual is by definition maladapted to real life, to practical tasks, to marriage, to human relationships, his head in the clouds, his life in an ivory tower, his ideas of no earthly use. Yet I shared the view of Hannah Arendt and Theodor Adorno that the thinker does not owe it to society to demonstrate how it might be changed for the better. Although Marx had taken exception to the notion that the task of the philosopher was simply to understand the world, not change it, I had a deep aversion to prescriptions and exhortations as to how one should lead one's life, and was drawn to Anna Akhmatova's desire to describe, before all else, and to "stand as witness to the common lot."

And I was mindful, as I left the Portbou cemetery and descended the hill toward the bay, that at the same time Walter Benjamin was being hounded from pillar to post through Vichy France, Anna Akhmatova was waiting in line, as she had done for seventeen months, outside the Leningrad prison where her son Lev Gumilev was held without trial, and where, one freezing day a woman recognized her and asked in a hoarse whisper whether she could describe it. Akhmatova later wrote: "I said, 'I can.' And something like a smile passed fleetingly over what had been her face."

After lunch in a seafront café, I returned to the station and retrieved my rucksack. The train took me to Cerbère within minutes, and with an hour and a half to kill before my connection to Perpignan, I wrote up my notes in the station waiting room, before going for a stroll through the streets from where I could see, high on the col, the tower where I rested yesterday after my walk from Banyuls.

On the train to Perpignan, I found myself in a carriage with only two or three other passengers. A young deaf-mute woman was sitting across the aisle and sending text messages on her cell phone. Each time she hit a key the phone beeped loudly, until a young man, perhaps a student, who had kicked his shoes off, and had been lounging sideways in his seat and reading a paperback novel, got up and asked her to turn the phone off. She pointed to her ears, miming that she could not hear him.

I turned to look out my window, peering through my own reflection at the ruined towers of thirteenth-century Cathar castles on the conical hills, relics of yet another epoch of intolerance and violence, and beyond, in the blue sky, a curiously distorted hogsback cloud that resembled a teased-out inverted comma — a portent, perhaps, of a change in the weather; I did not really know. And I fell to wondering why we expend so much effort on interpreting signs, reading the sky, the sea, the faces of those we love, for insights into some inner and normally invisible state, or set such great store by trying to divine or alter the course of the future.

Notes

1. The UN High Commissioner for Refugees estimates that between 1994 and 2004 more than five thousand asylum-seekers drowned in the Mediterranean.

2. Benjamin's famous *Theses on the Philosophy of History* was written during this winter of 1939–40 — reflections, he noted in a letter to Gretel Adorno, that were part of his "methodological preparation" for the sequel to the Baudelaire book, and not intended for publication.

3. According to Henny Gurland, they were joined at some stage by "Birmann, her

sister Frau Lipmann, and the Freund woman from Das Tagebuch" (Grete Freund) (Scholem 1982:225).

4. Hannah Arendt writes that the problem was not that the refugees' transit visas were invalid, but that (1) the Spanish border had been closed that very day, and (2) the border office did not honor visas made out in Marseille (1973:169).

5. Benjamin was not the only émigré to take his own life during those dark times. Ernst Weiss, the Czech novelist, took poison in his room in Paris when the Germans entered the city, as did Irmgard Keun, a German novelist. Walter Hasenclever, the German playwright, took an overdose of veronal in the concentration camp at Les Milles, and Karl Einstein, the art critic and specialist on Negro sculpture, hanged himself at the Spanish frontier when he found he couldn't get across (Fry 1945:31).

6. See Benjamin's commentary of Brecht's poem, *Legend of the Origin of the Book Tao Te Ching on Lao Tzu's Way into Exile* (1983:70–74), which itself references section 78 of the Tao Te Ching: "In the world there is nothing more submissive and weak than water. Yet for attacking that which is hard and strong nothing can surpass it. This is because nothing can take its place" (Lao Tzu 1963:140).

7. After interrogating the detainees, they designated the pro-Nazis "dangerous" and ensured that the others were given clearances.

8. Arendt escaped with Fittko but chose to make her own way to Montauban where she had friends with whom she could stay, and where, astonishingly, her husband, Heinrich Blücher (who had been interned in northern France), found her.

9. "On the 'Legend of the Origin of the . . . Tao Te Ching,'" first published in the *Schweizer Zeitung am Sonntag*, April 23, 1939.

10. As Martin Jay reminds us, Benjamin never overcame, or wanted to forget, his traumatic loss of his closest friend, Friedrich (Fritz) Heinle, who killed himself in protest of the war in 1914, or the terrible specter of the industrialized war itself (2003:11–24).

References

Adorno, Theodor W. 1981. *Prisms*. Trans. Samuel and Shierry Weber. MIT Press.

Akhmatova, Anna. 1974. *Poems*. Trans. Stanley Kunitz. Collins and Harvill Press.

Arendt, Hannah. 1973. *Men in Dark Times*. Penguin.

———. 1978; 1944. *The Jew as Pariah: Jewish Identity and Politics in the Modern Age*. Ed. Ronald H. Feldman. Grove Press.

———. 1982. *Lectures on Kant's Political Philosophy*. Ed. Roland Beiner, University of Chicago Press.

Benjamin, Walter. 1969. *Illuminations*. Trans. Harry Zohn. Schocken.

———. 1983. *Understanding Brecht*. Trans. Anna Bostock. Verso.

Brodersen, Momme. 1996. *Walter Benjamin: A Biography*. Trans. David Koblick. Northwestern University Press.

Fittko, Lisa. 2000. *Escape Through the Pyrenees*. Trans. David Koblick. Northwestern University Press.

Fry, Varian. 1945. *Surrender on Demand*. Random House.

Graves, Robert. 1955. *The Greek Myths*. Vol. 1. Penguin.

Jay, Martin. 2003. *Refractions of Violence*. Routledge.

Lao Tzu. 1963. *Tao Te Ching*. Trans. D. C. Lau. Penguin.

Lowry, Malcolm. 1969. *Hear Us O Lord from Heaven Thy Dwelling Place & Lunar Caustic*. Penguin.

Scholem, Gershom. 1982. *Walter Benjamin: The Story of a Friendship*. Faber and Faber.

Steiner, George. 1998. Introduction, *The Origin of German Tragic Drama*, by Walter Benjamin. Verso.

Werfel, Alma Mahler. 1959. *And the Bridge Is Love*. Hutchinson.

PHILIP JENKINS

Liberating Word

FROM *Christian Century*

GATHERINGS OF the worldwide Anglican Communion have been
contentious events in recent years. On one occasion, two bishops
were participating in a Bible study, one from Africa, the other from
the United States. As the hours went by, tempers frayed as the African expressed his confidence in the clear words of scripture, while
the American stressed the need to interpret the Bible in the light of
modern scholarship and contemporary mores. Eventually, the African bishop asked in exasperation, "If you don't *believe* the scripture,
why did you bring it to us in the first place?"

Fifty years ago, Americans might have dismissed the conservatism of Christians in the global South as arising from a lack of theological sophistication, and in any case regarded these views as strictly
marginal to the concerns of the Christian heartlands of North
America and western Europe. Put crudely, why would the "Christian world" have cared what Africans thought? Yet today, as the center of gravity of the Christian world moves ever southward, the
conservative traditions prevailing in the global South matter ever
more. To adapt a phrase from missions scholar Lamin Sanneh:
Whose reading — whose Christianity — is normal now? And whose
will be in fifty years?

Of course, Christian doctrine has never been decided by majority vote, and neither has the prevailing interpretation of the Bible.
Numbers are not everything. But overwhelming numerical majori-
ties surely carry some weight. Let us imagine a (probable) near-
future world in which Christian numbers are strongly concentrated
in the global South, where the clergy and scholars of the world's

most populous churches accept interpretations of the Bible more conservative than those normally prevailing in American mainline denominations. In such a world, surely, southern traditions of Bible reading must be seen as the Christian norm. The culture-specific interpretations of North Americans and Europeans will no longer be regarded as "real theology" while the rest of the world produces its curious provincial variants — "African theology," "Asian theology," and so on. We will know that the transition is under way when publishers start offering studies of "North American theologies."

The move of Christianity to the global South might suggest a decisive move toward literal and even fundamentalist readings of the Bible. Traditionalist themes are important for African and Asian Christians. These include a much greater respect for the authority of scripture, especially in matters of morality; a willingness to accept the Bible as an inspired text and a tendency to literalistic readings; a special interest in supernatural elements of scripture, such as miracles, visions, and healings; a belief in the continuing power of prophecy; and a veneration for the Old Testament, which is often considered as authoritative as the New. Biblical traditionalism and literalism are even more marked in the independent churches and in denominations rooted in the Pentecostal tradition, and similar currents are also found among Roman Catholics.

Several factors contribute to a more literal interpretation of scripture in the global South. For one thing, the Bible has found a congenial home among communities that identify with the social and economic realities the Bible portrays. To quote Kenyan feminist theologian Musimbi Kanyoro, "Those cultures which are far removed from biblical culture risk reading the Bible as fiction." Conversely, societies that identify with the biblical world feel at home in the text.

The average Christian in the world today is a poor person, very poor indeed by the standards of the white worlds of North America and western Europe. Also different is the social and political status of African and Asian Christians, who are often minorities in countries dominated by other religions or secular ideologies. This historic social change cannot fail to affect attitudes toward the Bible. For many Americans and Europeans, not only are the societies in the Bible — in both testaments — distant in terms of time and place, but their everyday assumptions are all but incomprehensible. Yet exactly the issues that make the Bible a distant historical record for many Americans and Europeans keep it a living text in the churches of the global South.

For many such readers, the Bible is congenial because the world it describes is marked by such familiar pressing problems as famine and plague, poverty and exile, clientelism and corruption. A largely poor readership can readily identify with the New Testament society of peasants and small craftspeople dominated by powerful landlords and imperial forces, by networks of debt and credit. In such a context, the excruciating poverty of a Lazarus eating the crumbs beneath the rich man's table is not just an archaeological curiosity.

This sense of recognition is quite clear for modern dwellers in villages or small towns, but it also extends to urban populations, who are often close to their rural roots. And this identification extends to the Old Testament no less than the New. Madipoane Masenya, a shrewd feminist thinker from South Africa, comments, "If present-day Africans still find it difficult to be at home with the Old Testament, they might need to watch out to see if they have not lost their Africanness in one way or the other." Could an equivalent remark conceivably be made of contemporary Europeans or North Americans?

While some resemblances between the biblical world and the world of African Christians might be superficial, their accumulated weight adds greatly to the credibility of the text. The Bible provides immediate and often material answers to life's problems. It teaches ways to cope and survive in a hostile environment, and at the same time holds out the hope of prosperity. For the growing churches of the South, the Bible speaks to everyday issues of poverty and debt, famine and urban crisis, racial and gender oppression, state brutality and persecution. The omnipresence of poverty promotes awareness of the transience of life, the dependence of individuals and nations on God, and distrust of the secular order.

In consequence, the "southern" Bible carries a freshness and authenticity that adds vastly to its credibility as an authoritative source and a guide. In this context, it is difficult to make the familiar Euro-American argument that the Bible was clearly written for a totally alien society with which moderns could scarcely identify, and so its detailed moral laws cannot be applied in the contemporary world. Cultures that readily identify with biblical worldviews find it easier to read the Bible (including the laws of Leviticus) not just as historical fact but as relevant instruction for daily conduct. This fact helps us understand the horror of quite moderate African Christians when Euro-American churches dismiss biblical strictures against homosexuality as rooted in the Old Testament, and therefore outmoded.

Before northern liberals despair at the future, some qualifications are in order. I have written here of religious and scriptural conservatism, but that term need not carry its customary political implications. Though most African and Asian churches have a high view of biblical origins and authority, this does not prevent a creative and even radical application of biblical texts to contemporary debates and dilemmas. Such applications cause real difficulties for any attempt to apply northern concepts of *liberal* and *conservative, progressive* and *reactionary, fundamentalist* and *literalist.*

According to popular assumptions, liberal approaches to the Bible emphasize messages of social action and downplay supernatural intervention, while conservative or traditionalist views accept the miraculous and advocate quietist or reactionary politics. The two mindsets thus place their main emphases in different realms, human or supernatural.

Even in the United States that distinction is by no means reliable. There are plenty of left-wing evangelicals, deeply committed to social and environmental justice. In churches of the global South, the division makes even less sense. For example, *deliverance* in the charismatic sense of deliverance from demons can easily be linked to political or social *liberation,* and the two words are of course close cognates in some languages. The biblical enthusiasm so often encountered in the global South is often embraced by exactly those groups ordinarily portrayed as the victims of reactionary religion, particularly women.

In his magnificent book *Transfigured Night,* a study of the Zimbabwean night-vigil movement, the *pungwe,* Titus Presler reports: "Charismatic renewal, conflict with demons, and the liberation of women are other fruits bearing directly on the churches' mission in Zimbabwe." How often do American Christians place women's social emancipation in the context of spiritual warfare and exorcism? But in African churches both are manifestations of "loosing," of liberation, of deliverance.

At one of these vigils, a woman preacher drew extraordinary lessons from an unpromising text, the story of Jesus ordering his disciples to untie a donkey for his entry into Jerusalem. She applied the passage directly to the experience of African women: "I have seen that we are that donkey spoken of by the Lord . . . Let us give thanks for this time we were given, the time in which we were blessed. We were objects . . . We were not human beings . . . Some were even sold. To be married to a man — to be sold! . . . But with the coming of Jesus, we were set free . . . We were made righteous by Jesus, mothers."

Women play a central role in southern churches, whether or not they are formally ordained. They commonly constitute the most important converts and the critical forces making for the conversion of family or of significant others. Women's organizations and fellowships, such as the Mothers' Unions, represent critical structures for lay participation within the churches and allow women's voices to be heard in the wider society. So do prayer fellowships and cells, which can be so independent as to unnerve church hierarchies. Female believers look to the churches for an affirmation of their roles and their interests, and they naturally seek justification in the scriptures, which provide a vocabulary for public debate.

Some texts — like the story of the donkey — have to be tortured in order to yield the desired meaning, though given the pervasive interest in deliverance, any passage that can be linked, however tenuously, to "loosing" is too good to be ignored. With other texts, however, liberating interpretations are readily found. Throughout this process, literalist readings that may appear conservative in terms of their approach to scriptural authority have practical consequences that are socially progressive, if not revolutionary. Reading the Bible teaches individual worth and human rights, and it encourages mutual obligation within marriage, promoting the Christian "reformation of machismo" described by scholar Elizabeth Brusco. Leaving women to pursue domestic piety through Bible reading is like forbidding a restive population to carry weapons while giving them unrestricted access to gasoline and matches.

Think of the implications of Bible reading for widows, who in many traditional communities are excluded and despised, and who are tied to their husbands' clans even after the husbands die. The New Testament notion of "till death do us part" is burningly relevant. So is this claim by Paul in Romans: "If the husband be dead, she is loosed from the law of her husband." In the West, Romans 7:2 is scarcely a well-known scriptural text, certainly not a reference that enthusiastic evangelists wave on placards at sports stadiums. Yet in a global context, this verse may be a truly revolutionary warrant for change.

Reading as such also carries great weight. In a neoliterate community, access to the Bible betokens power and status, and there is no reason why this gift should be confined to traditional elites. Women — and young people of both sexes — have most to gain by achieving literacy. The more conspicuous one's knowledge of the scriptures, the greater one's claim to spiritual status.

But beyond any single text, the Bible as a whole offers ample ammunition for the cause of outsiders, to the dismay of the established and comfortable. People read of the excluded who become central to the story, of the trampled and oppressed who become divine vehicles — and of how God spurns traditional societies, hierarchies, and ritual rules. As David Martin famously wrote in his account of global South churches, Pentecostalism gives the right and duty to speak to those always previously deemed unworthy on grounds of class, race, and gender. In the new dispensation, outsiders receive tongues of fire. The same observation can be applied across denominational frontiers.

Only when we see global South Christianity on its own terms — as opposed to asking how it can contribute to our own debates — can we see how the emerging churches are formulating their own responses to social and religious questions, and how these issues are often viewed through a biblical lens. And often these responses do not fit well into our conventional ideological packages.

The socially liberating effects of evangelical religion should come as no surprise to anyone who has traced the enormous influence of biblically based religion throughout African American history. Black American politics is still largely inspired by religion and often led by clergy, usually of charismatic and evangelical bent; black political rhetoric cannot be understood except in the context of biblical thought and imagery. African American religious leaders are generally well to the left on economic issues, as are many evangelicals in Latin America, and also independent and Protestant denominations across Africa. All find scriptural warrant for progressive views, most commonly in prophetic and apocalyptic texts.

When viewed on a global scale, African American religious styles, long regarded as marginal to mainstream American Christianity, seem absolutely standard. Conversely, the worship of mainline white American denominations looks increasingly exceptional, as do these groups' customary approaches to biblical authority. Looking at this reversal, we are reminded of a familiar text: the stone that was rejected has become the cornerstone.

For a North American Christian, it can be a surprising and humbling experience to try to understand how parts of the Bible might be read elsewhere in the world. To do so, we need to think communally rather than individually. We must also abandon familiar distinctions between secular and supernatural dimensions. And often we must adjust our attitudes to the relationship between Old and New Testaments.

Any number of texts offer surprises. Read Ruth, for instance, and imagine what it has to say in a hungry society threatened by war and social disruption. Understand the exultant release that awaits a reader in a society weighed down by ideas of ancestral curses or hereditary taint, a reader who discovers the liberating texts about individual responsibility in Ezekiel 18. Or read Psalm 23 as a political tract, a rejection of unjust secular authority. For Africans and Asians, the psalm offers a stark rebuttal to claims by unjust states that they care lovingly for their subjects — while they exalt themselves to the heavens. Christians reply simply, "The Lord is my shepherd — you aren't!" Adding to the power of the psalm, the evils that it condemns are at once political and spiritual, forces of tyranny and of the devil. Besides its political role, Psalm 23 is much used in services of healing, exorcism, and deliverance.

Imagine a society terrorized by a dictatorial regime dedicated to suppressing the church, and read Revelation — and understand the core message that whatever evils the world may produce, God will triumph. Or read Revelation with the eyes of rural believers in a rapidly modernizing society, trying to comprehend the inchoate

brutality of the megalopolis. Read Hebrews and think of its doctrines of priesthood and atonement as they might be understood
in a country with a living tradition of animal sacrifice. On these
grounds, a Ghanaian theologian has described Hebrews as *our* epistle — that is, Africa's. Apply the Bible's many passages about the
suffering of children to the real-world horrors facing the youth of
the Congo, Uganda, Brazil, or other countries that before too long
will be among the world's largest Christian countries.

Read in this way, the letter of James is particularly eye-opening.
James is one of the most popular sermon texts in Africa. Imagine
reading this letter in a world in which your life is so short and peril-
ous that it truly seems like a passing mist. What implications does
that transience hold for everyday behavior? The letter is a manual
for a society in which Christianity is new and people are seeking
practical rules for Christian living. The references to widows appear not as the history of an ancient social welfare system but as
a radical response to present-day problems affecting millions of
women.

As a particularly difficult test for northern-world Christians, try
reading two almost adjacent passages in chapter five of James —
one condemning the rich, the other prescribing anointing and
prayer for healing. Both texts, "radical" and "charismatic," are inte-
gral portions of a common liberating message.

Think of the numerous forms of captivity entrapping a poor inhab-
itant of a Third World nation — economic, social, environmental,
spiritual — and appreciate the promise of liberation and loosing
presented in Jesus' inaugural sermon in the Nazareth synagogue.
Understand the appeal of this message in a society in which — to
quote a recent journalistic study of poverty in Lagos — "the frustration of being alive . . . is excruciating."

When reading almost any part of the Gospels, think how Jesus'
actions might strike a community that cares deeply about caste and
ritual purity, and where violating such laws might cost you your life
— as in India. Read the accounts of Jesus interacting so warmly
with the multiply rejected. In many societies worldwide, the story
of the Samaritan woman at the well can still startle. He *talked* to
her? And debated?

Or use the eighth chapter of Luke as a template for Christian healing and a reaffirmation of the power of good over evil. Or take one verse, John 10:10, in which Jesus promises abundant life, and think of its bewildering implications in a desperately poor society obviously lacking in any prospect of abundance, or indeed, of any certainty of life. This one verse may be the most quoted text in African Christianity, the "life verse" of an entire continent.

Now recognize that these kinds of readings, adapted to local circumstances, are quite characteristic for millions of Christians around the world. Arguably, in terms of raw numbers, such readings represent the normal way for Christians to read the Bible in the early twenty-first century.

After I wrote *The Next Christendom* in 2002, I had a bizarre encounter with an elderly and rather aristocratic Episcopal woman, who praised me for how effectively I had delineated the growth of new kinds of Christianity in the global South, with its passion and enthusiasm, its primitive or apostolic quality, its openness to the supernatural. She then asked my opinion: as Americans, as Christians, as Episcopalians — what can we do to stop this?

I understand her fear and see why some northern-world Christians might have concerns about the emerging patterns of global South Christianity, with its charismatic and traditional quality. But the prognosis is nowhere near as bad as she imagined. As so often in the past, Christianity must be seen as a force for radical change rather than obscurantism, for unsettling hierarchies rather than preserving them. On second thought, perhaps she was exactly right to be alarmed.

GALWAY KINNELL

Everyone Was in Love

FROM *The Atlantic Monthly*

One day, when they were little, Maud and Fergus
appeared in the doorway, naked and mirthful,
with a dozen long garter snakes draped over
each of them like brand-new clothes.
Snake tails dangled down their backs,
and snake foreparts in various lengths
fell over their fronts, heads raised
and swaying, alert as cobras. They writhed their dry skins
upon each other, as snakes like doing
in lovemaking, with the added novelty
of caressing soft, smooth, moist human skin.
Maud and Fergus were deliciously pleased with themselves.
The snakes seemed to be tickled too.
We were enchanted. Everyone was in love.
Then Maud drew down off Fergus's shoulder,
as off a tie rack, a peculiarly
lumpy snake and told me to look inside.
Inside that double-hinged jaw, a frog's green
webbed hind feet were being drawn,
like a diver's, very slowly as if into deepest waters.
Perhaps thinking I might be considering rescue,
Maud said, "Don't. Frog is already elsewhere."

PATRICK MADDEN

On Laughing

<small>FROM *Portland*</small>

MY THREE-MONTH-OLD daughter is just beginning to laugh. She
is not ticklish; she is not mimicking us. As far as I can tell, she is just
delighted by the world. She sees a funny face, sees her brother in a
giant witch's hat, sees me with my glasses on upside down, sees
her mother dancing to the funky music of a commercial, and she
laughs.

I have loved her since she was born — since before she was
born, when she was only an idea — and yet I feel I haven't known
her until now. Her laughter has become a common ground for
us, a mutual realization that the world is an interesting and silly
place.

According to a third-century B.C. Egyptian papyrus, "When [God]
burst out laughing there was light . . . When he burst out laughing
the second time the waters were born; at the seventh burst of
laughter the soul was born." Man as the height of God's laughter:
that explains a lot.

Max Beerbohm, in his essay on laughter, wonders that "of all the
countless folk who have lived before our time on this planet not
one is known in history or in legend as having died of laughter."
But Beerbohm is wrong. Bulwer-Lytton's *Tales of Miletus* speak of
Calchas, a soothsayer who was told by a beggar that he would never
drink of the fruit of his vineyard. Moreover, the beggar promised
that if the prophecy did not come true, he would be Calchas's
slave. Later, when the grapes were harvested and the wine made,

Calchas celebrated by laughing so hard at the beggar's folly that he died before he took a sip.

The word *laughter* is like any other word: if you say it enough, it begins to sound strange and wondrous. Listen to the sound as it separates from meaning; feel your tongue jump away from your front teeth, the way you bite your bottom lip slightly, the quick strike of the tongue against the teeth again — *ter!* If you say *laughter* fast enough and long enough it will make you laugh.

Animals that laugh: hyenas, monkeys, the kookaburra or laughing jackass, an Australian bird whose call is so similar to raucous laughter that early European explorers of that continent were tormented by it. There is the laughing frog (which is edible), the laughing bird (or green woodpecker), the laughing crow, the laughing thrush, the laughing dove (or African dove), the laughing goose (or white-fronted goose), the laughing gull, the laughing falcon, the laughing owl. Democritus (460–357 B.C.), called the Laughing Philosopher, proposed that matter was not infinitely divisible, that there existed a basic unit of matter, the atom, which was indivisible. It turns out that atoms can be further broken down into protons, neutrons, and electrons, which in turn consist of quarks, which name comes from the James Joyce novel *Finnegans Wake*, because Murray Gell-Mann, originator of quark theory, loved the line *Three quarks for Muster Mark!* This makes me laugh.

In English, laughter as dialogue is often portrayed as *ha ha ha*. Santa Claus's laugh is *ho ho ho*. The Green Giant's laugh is also *ho ho ho*. Children are said to laugh *he he he*. The laughter of connivers and old men is *heh heh heh*. In Spanish, laughter is *ja ja ja, jo jo jo, ji ji ji*, and *je je je*. The same holds true for laughs in Romanian, French, Japanese, and Chinese, and I'd be willing to bet it's the same in most other languages too. Always a vowel sound introduced by an *h*, the sound closest to breathing, as if laughter were as basic as respiration.

Some synonyms for *laughter: cackle, chuckle, chortle, giggle, guffaw, snicker, snigger, titter, twitter*. These words make my children laugh.

*

Many things are laughable only later, after everything has turned out fine and we can reflect on our good fortune or our dumb luck. Such as my son's many trips to the emergency room for foreign objects in his nose: raisins, rubber, paper, a toy snake's tail. "See," I once overheard a nurse telling her coworker when she saw him in the waiting room, "I *told* you it would be him."

Laughter heals; it can change the flavor of tears. When our cat died after nineteen years with us, my family was stricken with grief. My brothers dutifully prepared to bury him, digging a grave near the woods where he once romped. The former cat waited in a plastic bag inside a cooler from the vet's office. Everyone was crying silently, speaking in whispers. When the diggers rested for a moment, my father prepared to deposit the body in the hole. But we weren't done, the hole was too shallow, and my brother shouted, *Wait! Don't let the cat out of the bag!*

On a train one afternoon, Fourth of July, hot, tired, my son can't sit still. He can never sit still, but he is extra-can't-sit-still today. He jumps, hangs, clambers, throws his grandfather's hat, drops his crackers, chatters. I plead with him to be still as he wriggles and twists. He laughs, thinking I am trying to tickle him. The woman behind ducks to where he can't see her. He steps on my leg to peer over the edge of the seat. She jumps up and whispers, "Boo!" He falls limp to the seat below, convulsing with laughter. She does it again. He does it again. She does it again. He does it again. His baby sister stares intently at her brother. Her eyes radiate something I want to call admiration. Each time he falls to the seat beside her, she laughs heartily, uncontrollably. Pretty soon the whole train car is laughing. My children's laughter is so bright and clear and pure and unselfconscious that I suddenly understand why a cool mountain brook might be said to laugh.

"And God said unto Abraham," according to the book of Genesis, "as for [Sarah] thy wife . . . I will bless her, and give thee a son also of her: yea, I will bless her, and she shall be a mother of nations; kings of people shall be of her. Then Abraham fell upon his face, and laughed."

*

The next passage, you will remember, is Sarah also laughing at the prospect of bearing a child at her age (supposedly ninety). Lesson: God has a sense of humor, a special kind of love. God also chooses the name of their son: Isaac, which means "he laugheth."

We laugh at, with, about: clowns, jokes, funny faces, children, ourselves, contortions, misfortunes, wordplay, irony, other laughs, others' joy, good fortune, madness, sickness, health, debilitation, recovery, things we can't change, things we can change, sports, games, circuses, animals, drunkenness, sobriety, sex, celibacy, errors, equivocations, mistakes, blunders, bloopers, boners, double meanings.

The late Norman Cousins, editor of *The Saturday Review,* when stricken with ankylosing spondylitis, treated himself with Marx brothers movies. He recovered almost completely. Doctors were not sure why. Cancer and heart patients at Loma Linda University's medical center today are treated with episodes of *I Love Lucy* and *The Honeymooners.* Laughter apparently increases levels of disease-fighting T cells, the very cells killed off by AIDS. Doctors are not sure why.

"Among those whom I like," said the great poet W. H. Auden, "I can find no common denominator, but among those whom I love, I can; all of them make me laugh." That laughter is sweetest which is unexpected, which takes one unawares. "To that laughter," says Max Beerbohm, "nothing is more propitious than an occasion that demands gravity. To have good reason for not laughing is one of the surest aids." In church, then, in a foreign land, in a foreign language, one might reach such heights of laughter as to lose entirely any semblance of reverence.

A hot Sunday morning in Carrasco, the rich neighborhood of Montevideo, Uruguay. I am one of two gringos among nearly a hundred Uruguayans. The chapel is filled with families in summer dresses and breezy shirts. After a solemn hymn a member of the congregation approaches the podium to say an opening prayer. "Our kind and gracious Heavenly Father," he begins, and I bow my head, close my eyes, try to keep my mind from wandering as I listen to his invocation. Slowly I become aware of a muffled, tinny music in the air. Appalled, I open my eyes and slyly look around me to find the blasphemer with a Walkman. All other heads are bowed, none with headphones. I close my eyes and try to focus again, but by now the music is clearer; it's the egregiously awful "She's an Easy Lover," by Phil Collins and Phillip Bailey. Then I realize that the speakers in the chapel ceiling are channeling the music along with the prayer.

I slide down the bench away from my friend, so as not to laugh, and I fold over in airplane-emergency-landing position, biting my tongue, casting my mind, feebly, to serious thoughts, solemn thoughts, when I feel the pew start to rumble and shake with my friend's silent convulsions. With that the dam bursts, and no amount of biting our tongues and holding our noses shut can stop the laughter. The tears roll down our faces, we snort profusely. Finally the prayer ends, and as the members of the congregation lift their heads and open their eyes, everyone turns toward us, on every face an expression of dismay.

As I write, I can hear my daughter's laughter behind me. She is lying in bed, sucking on her whole hand, eyes bright with the morning sun through the window, and she is laughing. It is not clear to me what she is laughing about, but her laughter is beautiful. I listen closely, I watch her, and I start to laugh too. Amen.

FREDERICA MATHEWES-GREEN

Loving the Storm-Drenched

FROM *Christianity Today*

IF YOU HANG AROUND with Christians, you find that the same topic keeps coming up in conversation: their worries about "the culture." Christians talk about sex and violence in popular entertainment. They talk about bias in news reporting. They talk about how their views are ignored or misrepresented. "The culture" appears to be an aggressive challenger to "the church," and Christians keep worrying what to do about it. You soon get the impression that Church Inc. and Culture Amalgamated are like two corporations confronting each other at a negotiating table. Over there sits Culture — huge, complex, and self-absorbed. It's powerful, dangerous, unpredictable, and turbulent. Church is smaller, anxious; it studies Culture, trying to figure out a way to weasel in.

But there are flaws in this picture. For one thing, neither party is as monolithic as it seems. There are many devout believers among the ranks of journalists and entertainers, and there are even more culture-consumers among the ranks of devout believers. Indeed, it's almost impossible to avoid absorbing this culture; if you sealed the windows, it would leak in under the door. I once heard a retreat leader say she'd attempted a "media fast," but found the gaudy world met her on every side. "I may be free in many ways," she said, "but I am not free to not know what Madonna is doing."

Furthermore, the church is not a corporation; rather, it is incorporate, or better, incarnate, carried in the vulnerable bodies of fallible individuals who love and follow Jesus Christ. The culture is even less of an organization. It is more like a photomosaic composed of tiny faces, faces of the millions of people — or billions, rather, thanks to the worldwide toxic leak of American entertainment — who are caught up in its path.

The influence of the culture on all those individuals, including Christians, is less like that of a formal institution and more like the weather. We can observe that, under current conditions, it's cloudy with a chance of cynicism. Crudity is up, nudity is holding steady, and there is a 60 percent chance that any recent movie will include a shot of a man urinating. Large fluffy clouds of sentimental spirituality are increasing on the horizon, but we have yet to see whether they will blow toward or away from Christian truth. Stay tuned for further developments.

As Mark Twain famously remarked, everyone talks about the weather, but no one does anything about it. I think much of our frustration is due to trying to steer the weather, rather than trying to reach individuals caught up in the storm.

It's possible to influence weather within limits, to seed clouds for rain, for example. And it is right for us to consider what we can do to provide quality fiction, films, and music, and to prepare young Christians to work in those fields. We can do some things to help improve ongoing conditions. But it is futile to think that we will one day take over the culture and steer it. It's too ungainly. It is composed of hundreds of competing sources. No one controls it.

What's more, it is already changing — constantly, ceaselessly, seamlessly — changing whether we want it to or not, in ways we can't predict, much less control. If you take the cultural temperature at any given moment, you will find that some of the bad things are starting to fade, and improvement is beginning to appear; simultaneously, some good things are starting to fall out of place, and a new bad thing is emerging.

Not only can we not control this process, we can't even perceive it until changes are so far developed as to be entrenched. Chasing the culture is a way to guarantee that you will always be a step behind the times.

One of my favorite classic films is *It Happened One Night* (1934), starring Clark Gable and Claudette Colbert. This comedy won five Academy Awards and deserved them; it has some of the most original characters and clever writing you'll find in any American film. The underlying premise is that a couple will not have sex before marriage, and this romantic tension drives the plot.

Yet that does not guarantee uniform "positive values." Everyone in the movie smokes, including the heroine (while wearing her wedding gown). It's not even safe smoking: we see the hero light up in a haystack. What's more, the hero regularly directs physical threats at the heroine; he says, for example, "She needs someone to take a sock at her once a day, whether she's got it coming to her or not." While the cultural barometer in recent decades has been falling on sexual morality, indicators for smoking and violence against women have indisputably improved.

But the most striking element is the attitude toward drunkenness. The first time we see Gable's character he is roaring drunk, and this is assumed to be hilarious. His drunkenness is encouraged and subsidized by other characters. In the post-Prohibition decades, being drunk (as opposed to merely drinking) was seen as rebellious, cool, and fashionable, and people who objected were depicted as prudes and squares. That fad eventually passed, when the damage done by alcoholism could no longer be romanticized away.

Now, in the post-sexual-revolution decades, being promiscuous is seen as rebellious, cool, and fashionable, and people who object are depicted as prudes and squares. That fad will eventually pass, too, when the damage done by abortion, divorce, and sexually transmitted diseases can no longer be romanticized away.

We cannot instigate this change by appealing to morality, but simple common sense has a stubborn tendency to reemerge. By the '70s it was becoming apparent that alcoholism dealt too much disease, divorce, and family disintegration to be all that funny. This change was not achieved by the Woman's Christian Temperance Union (WCTU) finally coming up with the bulls-eye slogan that would "change hearts and minds." Instead, people just came to their senses.

But note that when the WCTU is mentioned today, it's still seen as a bastion of prudes and squares. They were not vindicated, even though they turned out to be right. And it may be the same with us. We may always be seen as prudes and squares. Despite this, sexual common sense is likely to reemerge. (It happened once before: films of the 1920s through the 1950s reflect an acceptance of male adultery that would be horrifying today. We presume that these old movies will showcase "old-fashioned values," and they do; we just don't realize what those values were.) So sometimes cultures shift

for the better. When so-called fun hurts enough, people stop doing it.

The culture, then, is like the weather. We may be able to influence it in modest ways, seeding the clouds, but it is a recipe for frustration to expect that we can direct it. Nor should we expect positive change without some simultaneous downturn in a different
corner. Nor should we expect that any change will be permanent.
The culture will always be shifting, and it will always be with us.

God has not called us to change the weather. Our primary task as
believers, and our best hope for lasting success, is to care for individuals caught up in the pounding storm. They are trying to make
sense of their lives with inadequate resources, confused and misled
by the Evil One, and unable to tell their left hand from their right
(Jonah 4:11). They are not a united force; they are not even in solidarity with each other, apart from the unhappy solidarity of being
molded by the same junk-food entertainment. They are sheep without a shepherd, harassed and helpless (Matthew. 9:36). Only from
a spot of grounded safety can anyone discern what to approve and
what to reject in the common culture.

But we must regretfully acknowledge that we, too, are shaped by
the weather in ways we do not realize. Most worryingly, it has induced us to think that the public square is real life. We are preoc-
cupied with that external world, when our Lord's warnings have
much more to do with our intimate personal lives, down to the
level of our thoughts.

So, when Christians gather, there's less talk about humility, patience, and the struggle against sin. Instead, there's near-obsessive
emphasis on the need for a silver-bullet media product that will
magically open the nation to faith in Jesus Christ. Usually, the product they crave is a movie. Now, I'm delighted that Christians are
working in Hollywood; we should be salt and light in every community that exists, and so powerful a medium clearly merits our powerful stories. But it's telling that the media extravaganza so eagerly
awaited is not a novel or a song, something an individual might un-
dertake, but a movie: something that will require enormous physical and professional resources, millions of dollars, and, basically,
work done by somebody else.

This focus on an external, public sign is contrary to the embod-
ied mission of the church. Christ planned to attract people to him-

self through the transformed lives of his people. It's understandable that we feel chafed by what media giants say about us and the things we care about, and that we crave the chance to tell our own side of the story. It's as if the world's ballpark is ringed with billboards, and we rankle because we should have a billboard too. But if someone should actually see our billboard, and be intrigued, and walk in the door of a church, he would find that he had joined a community that was just creating another billboard.

One excellent way to see how much our culture's passing weather patterns have influenced us is to read old books. If you receive all your information from contemporary writers, Christian or secular, you will never perceive whole concepts that people in other generations could see. (For example, earlier generations of Christians perceived a power in sexual purity that eludes us completely; we can only fall back on "don'ts.") Every Christian should always have at his bedside at least one book that is at least fifty years old — the older the better.

Sure, you can make yourself read the contemporary magazines and authors you disagree with, but even they share the same underlying assumptions. It's as if we see our "culture war" opponents standing on the cold peak of an iceberg. From our corresponding peak, all we can discern between us is an expanse of dark water. But underneath that water, the two peaks are joined in a single mass. The common assumptions we share are invisible to us, but they will be perceived, and questioned, by our grandchildren.

C. S. Lewis has a wonderful passage on this phenomenon in his introduction to Athanasius's *On the Incarnation:* "Every age has its own outlook. It is specially good at seeing certain truths and specially liable to make certain mistakes. We all, therefore, need the books that will correct the characteristic mistakes of our own period. And that means the old books."

The "old books" can help us discern the prevailing assumptions of our cultural moment, not only concerning the content of our discussions, but also their style. We expect that combatants will be casual, rather than formal. We expect that their arguments will be illustrated by popular culture, rather than the classics or history. Conservatives and liberals agree that it is admirable to be rebellious and challenge authority, and both sides are at pains to present the other side as authority.

More serious, however, is a tone of voice we adopt from the culture: sarcastic, smart-alecky, jabbing, and self-righteous. We feel the sting of such treatment and give it right back; we feel anger or even wounded hatred toward those on the "other side." But God does not hate them; he loves them so much he sent his Son to die for them. We are told to pray for those who persecute us and to love our enemies. The weight of antagonistic and mocking big-media machinery is the closest thing we've got for practicing that difficult spiritual discipline. If we really love these enemies, we will want the best for them, the very best thing we have, which is the knowledge and love of God.

Smart-alecky speech doesn't even work. It may win applause, but it does not win hearts. It hardens the person who feels targeted, because he feels mocked and misrepresented. It increases bad feeling and anger. No one changed his mind on an issue because he was humiliated into it. In fact, we are misguided even to think of our opponents in the "culture wars" as enemies in the first place. They are not our enemies, but hostages of the Enemy. We have a common Enemy who seeks to destroy us both, by locking them in confusion and by luring us to self-righteous pomposity.

Culture is not a monolithic power we must defeat. It is the battering weather conditions that people, harassed and helpless, endure. We are sent out into the storm like a St. Bernard with a keg around our neck, to comfort, reach, and rescue those who are thirsting, most of all, for Jesus Christ.

DARA MAYERS

Love Divine

FROM *Tricycle*

FOUR HUNDRED OF US, all wearing white, gather in a field somewhere between Ahmedebad and Bhopal in the late afternoon. We've been on buses without air-conditioning since 7 A.M., so even though the Indian midsummer heat is oppressive, the fresh air is a relief. We turned in relatively early last night and got a few hours of rest, which is good because it is impossible to sleep on the bus, so packed with devotees that women lie, for endless, bumpy hours, on the floor. They believe their discomfort burns off bad karma, but I have my doubts.

There is a buzz in the crowd as Amma emerges from her white Mercedes. She is coming to have tea with us — a sort of reward for the endless bus ride, which is only half over. This is my third day on tour with Mata Amritanandamayi, the Mother of Immortal Bliss. She is one of the most famous gurus in India today, a Hindu who preaches a doctrine of love and charity and who followers believe is the living incarnation of the Divine Mother.

So far it has been almost unbelievably unpleasant, from the terrible food, the endless work, the accommodations — horrible even by Indian standards — to the bus rides, which can only be described as torturous. Until now I have only glimpsed her through crowds of thousands, people lining up each night to receive her famous hugs in all-night love marathons. Amma stands for a moment among us, small, silent, and perfectly calm in the midst of the frenzy, as people jockey for positions close enough to absorb her divine energy. All eyes are on her, each face holding a peculiar mixture of adoration and need. Her gaze moves through the crowd slowly. When she looks at me she raises her arms in a shrug. I have joined the tour as an observer, a journalist, a skeptic. "What in the world are you doing here?" she seems to be asking me. This is the exact question I have been asking myself since I made the dubious decision to join the caravan. But when she looks at me there is simply no doubt — I have been seen.

How I ended up here is debatable. To me it seems like sheer coincidence, against a backdrop of desperation. To the devotees it is the act of Amma, calling me to come and write about her divinity. I'm willing to meet them somewhere in between. It is undeniable that when I ran into Betsy, an old friend and a devotee, in New York last month, I was heartbroken and looking for comfort. And it *was* rather amazing that my month-long assignment, which took me all over the north of India, ended in Pune, a small nowhere town, on the very same day that Amma happened to be visiting. Betsy's e-mail, telling me they were in Pune, could not have come at a better time. And what American, post-1965, has not fantasized about going to India to follow a guru? It had seemed like a good idea — I had no plans and was not looking forward to going home, where only my couch and my heartbreak awaited.

It seems clear, here, in the complete and swirling chaos, that I am not alone in my emotional state. At some level, all the devotees are heartbroken. What other reason could there be to give up everything for a woman you never actually get to be near for more than a passing moment, someone you wouldn't be able to understand even if she were to speak to you? Even most of the Indian devotees, who make up half the crowd, don't speak Amma's dialect.

For the second half of the bus ride I decide to do what everyone else is doing: I pray to Amma. I pray for general things — happiness, prosperity. But mostly I pray that the source of my heartbreak will wake up and realize what I know is true — that he loves me. I know he does because when we are together I feel it. He just hasn't realized it yet. Amma, I pray, open his eyes.

"Amma is my husband," says Kamala-Ja, originally Elizabeth Handler, a twenty-one-year-old from Wisconsin. "When I pray, I think only of her. When I look at the ocean, I imagine Amma is there swimming like a dolphin in the waves. When I see birds flying I wonder, 'Are they flying near to Amma?' I wish I could jump on their backs and fly with them to Amma." She says she loves to think of Amma's beautiful feet. "Amma is the universe," she tells me. "When I love Amma, I am loving the whole universe."

Despite my pretensions to journalistic detachment, I find myself wanting what Kamala-Ja has. I want to dedicate my life solely and wholly to one thing and give up everything else for it. I want single-minded focus on someone I believe is God. I want to exhaust myself through service, as Kamala-Ja does, in her endless days and nights of work.

However, as the days pass, it appears that my desire to cleanse myself through labor is largely theoretical. Cooking and cleaning for four hundred people and setting up for each night's program take a tremendous amount of effort. Just moving all of us from one place to another is a Herculean task, and then there are the thousands of apples that Amma gives out each evening, which need to be polished. Endless piles of vegetables need to be chopped for our communal meals. Just looking at them fills me with a sense of hopelessness. I find myself sneaking off into town during seva — the endless period of "selfless service" when the chopping occurs — to buy scarves.

This bedlam has nothing at all to do with my fantasy. There's no quiet contemplation. There's no striving toward inner peace. There's nothing peaceful about the scene at all. And the devotees are driving me mad. I can't stand all the singing and chanting, and everything is "Amma said don't do this, Amma said don't do that." The only other topic open to conversation seems to be their inability to properly digest the local fare. They are a veritable Greek chorus of gastrointestinal distress, and it is becoming unbearable.

They seem almost universally either insane or pathetic, or both. But me, I'm no nut job. It's his fault that I'm doing this. This is what I tell myself as I take a cold bucket shower in the mildewed, drafty bathroom of the Bombay middle school where we are staying, tears streaming down my face.

It is very funny to read about the places we are going. According to *Lonely Planet,* "On 26 January 2001, India's independence day, an earthquake measuring 7.9 on the Richter scale hit Gujarat, causing massive loss of life and widespread damage. Visitors should bear in mind the derisive title given the city by the Mughal emperor

Jehangir: 'City of dust.'" All of our destinations sound similarly awful.

The devotees don't have any interest in seeing the cities we go to anyway. Most of them don't have guidebooks at all. "I am just not interested in being a tourist," says Emma, an innocent-looking twenty-four-year-old from New York. "I only want to be with Amma. Everything else is just a distraction." Amma frowns on devotees venturing out on their own, so most have only the vaguest notion of where we are and where we're going, one more thing that irritates me.

But I find that mostly I am jealous of the true believers. I have spent a year and a half with a man I know is meant for me. I know it. It's what my gut tells me. It doesn't seem possible that I am wrong about this — except that apparently I am. The first time I told him I loved him he kissed me, but said nothing.

The young devotees know their love is returned. They glow with it. You can practically see the clouds beneath their feet. They can't stop talking about Amma, how they have fallen utterly and completely, head over heels, in love with her.

"It's not a sexual love," says Kamala-Ja, "But I am in love with her. I think about her all the time. All I want is to be close to her." The younger girls are derisively called "bliss bunnies" by the older women, many of whom seem strangely embittered and isolated. Whatever kind of love they have received from Amma and from the world, it has not been enough. Yet they keep going back, every night to the program, the endless, all-night program, for more, waiting for little shreds of the divine. Waiting, hanging on the smallest sign of her recognition. To this I can relate.

In Bhopal I find myself thinking about Amma more and more. The devotees are so passionate. Many of them seem to carry out deep and complex relationships with her almost entirely in their heads. "She visited me in New York," Elizabeth tells me. "I was waiting for the subway at Canal Street, and all of a sudden I could smell her beautiful scent. I knew she was there for me, even though I couldn't see her. That was when I decided to come to India."

"I am having a hard time with Amma today," Lucy tells me. "I am praying for her to come back to me, but right now she is so far away."

I'm engaging in a similar drama in my mind. The second time I told him I loved him he sat there blankly, then suggested we have Ethiopian for dinner. I said, "Okay, that sounds good." I want to go back in time and end it, right there.

I met Amma before I ever went to India, the previous summer in New York. I'd gone with my ex's sister. For almost a year already I'd been waiting for a sign from him. As each day passed, I became less hopeful. Nonetheless, when he suggested that I go with his sister to visit her guru, I jumped at the chance. I figured ingratiating myself with his family was as good a tactic as any.

I met the sister at the Manhattan Center, right next to Penn Station, at 7 P.M. There was a huge crowd, mostly the type I am not ordinarily attracted to: aggressively spiritual New Yorkers wearing long white robes, self-righteous vegetarian types. I knew it was going to be a long evening — the sister had prepared me. First there would be the speeches introducing Amma, then her spiritual talk (called a satsang), then hours of devotional call-and-response singing (bhajans), and then, finally, darshan would begin.

It was darshan that we were all there for. *Darshan*, literally "viewing," is an occasion when the guru's grace is transmitted; often a guru will simply look at the disciples. Amma's darshan is different. She actually hugs all those who come before her. Because so many people show up to be hugged, each devotee receives a number, and then waits. Our numbers were in the high thousands.

We waited until 4 A.M. at the Manhattan Center for our hugs, climbing onto the stage finally, exhausted, and kneeling before her. When the swamis placed me in her arms, she whispered "Ma, ma, ma, ma" in my ear.

It hadn't done much for me. I didn't really feel anything. I wondered if this was how my man felt about me when we were together. Purely a physical act, nothing more.

The air in Varanasi is so bad I can practically see the particulates. One devotee unabashedly wears a gas mask — a reasonable choice under the circumstances. Tonight the program begins at 6:30. As usual, it is quite a scene. It is being held in an indoor stadium packed with families, food vendors, and the endless array of guru-related trinkets, books, and CDs. Thousands of people throng as sour-faced, middle-aged white women in white attempt to control them — a circuslike atmosphere.

Amma enters, wearing a white sari, surrounded by swamis in orange and saffron robes. There is quite a commotion as she walks down the center aisle, on a red carpet strewn with flowers, to a square platform in the center of the stage. She sits there cross-legged, facing the vast audience. Giant images of her are projected on screens hung from the ceiling. There must be thirty thousand people here. Speeches honoring Amma are made in the local dialect by a variety of dignitaries and then translated into Hindi, all of it broadcast at extremely high volumes. This goes on until eight o'clock, while Amma sits with her eyes closed, in a state of apparent bliss, although I imagine she's probably very tired. Occasionally she opens her eyes and smiles at a thrilled devotee.

Amma speaks for a while, but it is when the bhajans begin that her power is apparent. Most of the bhajans are about her. "Mother Amritananadamayi, You are goddess of immortality and the goddess of the universe . . . Oh Mother, make me mad with Thy love . . ."

The bhajans are beautiful and Amma is absolutely transfixing as she lifts her face up to the sky to sing. She is St. Teresa of Àvila, exuding bliss with a sweet clear voice. Like everything else about her, there's not too much effort — it's natural, like birdsong. She's not beautiful — she's tiny and chubby, and her hair is pulled back in a simple ponytail — but as she sings, she is beautiful to watch. She is in front of thousands, but somehow it still feels intimate. The look on her face is almost obscene — a love swoon.

Toward the end of the bhajans Amma starts rocking back and forth a bit, then lifts her arms skyward in a bowl shape and looks up, swinging her arms energetically as if saying, "Come here! Take me!" It is mesmerizing. Over and over she flings her arms up and drops them back to her sides, all the while staring up toward the sky. At around 10:15 P.M. the last bhajan is sung, a fire is placed in front of Amma, and she tosses rose petals at the people around her.

Then the hugging begins. The crowd surges forward toward either side of the stage, where there are roped-off areas. The left side is for women and the right side is for men. Everyone has gotten a number.

Amma hugs everybody. She never stops hugging. She doesn't eat or go to the bathroom until everyone who wants to receive darshan has been hugged, which is usually by 7 A.M. the next day, but the hugging can go on through the afternoon, depending on how many people show up.

The hugging is handled in a militaristic fashion by the swamis, who first wipe the faces of the seekers, and then shove each one roughly before Amma for an experience that will last all of two seconds. Music blares. The lines are endless.

As devotees we get to sit behind Amma onstage, and watch darshan happening. An old man cries in her arms. Young women approach, frightened but excited. People scream, fall on their knees before her. Then, after she hugs them, they get up and walk away, glowing. It's like watching people being saved on Sunday morning television, except Amma is quiet and gentle throughout.

I watch her do it all night. She has the same enthusiasm for the first person that she has for number 20,000. This incredible ability and energy — not only to sit there without food or a break for eighteen hours in a row, but also to actually seem to love every single person in the exact same, genuine manner — is why her devotees believe she is God. At the very end she hugs the police, who have been standing around all night, making sure everything remains calm.

"I love seeing Amma," says Sri Purna, originally Jennifer Lynch from Oregon. "I love that so many people are being touched by God, I love seeing it. What I think she's really teaching me is to learn to do everything with the same devotion, because Amma is in everything and everyone. I see her as being God, but I see you as being God too."

I go for another hug in Varanasi. I am not transformed by it. I don't start singing or stripping as others do. I'm not the type. But for a moment I feel the heartbreak lift. It's not that I feel free, or over it. It's more the sense that I get riding the subway at rush hour in New York sometimes. The feeling that this might suck, but at least we're all in it together.

In Surat I ask my friend Lakshmi, one of the few Indian devotees who will hang out with the Westerners, to translate Amma's satsang talk for me. That night, Amma spoke about women's rights. She compared women to trained elephants, who from birth are chained to small trees. "Then, when the elephant reaches adulthood, it can be chained to a small sapling, and never escape," she said. "It has been trained, in its mind, that it is not able to break free. But in fact the elephant is very powerful, more powerful than the little sapling," she said.

"She is an enchantress," Lakshmi says. "Every single person who comes here tonight will feel that they have been seen by her. It doesn't matter if there are a hundred thousand. Each one will feel this way."

It's true that even though I know it is impossible, I often do have the unmistakable sensation that she is watching me from the stage. I find myself trying to catch her eye, and then, incredibly, I feel her gaze upon me. It feels wonderful. "Well, that's because she does see you," Lakshmi says. "She sees everything, she knows everything and everyone."

For a moment I understand the devotees. I can feel her love, even among thousands. She's so generous, not requiring anything in return. I even feel forgiven for my by-now-entrenched practice of skipping out on seva to buy scarves.

I had not been generous like that. The last time I told him I loved him, he remained silent and then suggested that we go to the boat show in Annapolis.

I went, but it was a miserable day. I made sure of that.

The tour is nearing its end. I have joined the ranks of the gastro-intestinally distressed. While the devotees pray to Amma, I take Cipro.

I have not reformed. My scarf buying has taken on somewhat pathological proportions. I am obsessed with going into the silk shops, where the Indian method of salesmanship — throwing hundreds of scarves at you as you sit on the floor drinking sweet tea — is a ritual I cannot get enough of. I love being buried in the fabulous colors and textures. I buy hot pinks, greens, and yellows and hide them in my suitcase beneath my dirty white robes.

I have gotten an e-mail from my ex. It is the same bland, remote voice I have grown used to. I don't write back.

The last night of the tour is in Calcutta. I get in line for my final hug. In front of me there is a woman with a horribly disfigured face. It is hard to look at her, and she knows it. When Amma hugs her, the love is so strong that I can feel it from ten feet away.

This time I only have to wait until midnight for my hug. She hugs me like she has missed me for a long time. She whispers "My daughter, my daughter, my daughter" in my ear. For a moment, I love her. It's a physical feeling — a welling up. It feels so good — that wonderful opening up, the expansion. I haven't felt it for a long time.

This is what they're after, I realize, the beating heart of the matter. It's what makes the dysentery, the misery, the staying up all night, the heartbreak, worth it. Even if brief, even if unreturned. Even if they've given up too much. Even if they get nothing back. Even the boat show, even the tears, even waiting too long, has been worth it.

I still wish it had been different. I still wish I had left him, oh, a year earlier. I still regret the trip to Jamaica, that horrible weekend on the Outer Banks, and all those damn dinners. I still wish he'd felt it too.

But I can see why I had hung for so long. I'd been following that same expansive drive, the drive that said open up and give yourself. Probably, it was a mistake, but I had no choice but to try.

I walk back to the accommodations through the quiet streets of Calcutta at 4 A.M. with three other women. Two of them, fanatical devotees, have become my friends. This is the first moment of quiet since joining the tour. As we walk farther from the program, the silence deepens. Our dirty robes pick up some of the moon. This was how I'd imagined it — pilgrims, walking in the quiet night, dogs barking a long way off.

WILFRED M. McCLAY

Idol-Smashing and Immodesty in the Groves of Academe

FROM *In Character*

WE DON'T HEAR the word *modesty* very much these days. And when it is used, it generally has a faintly antique, Victorian sound, a distant rustle of petticoats amid the stillness of overstuffed parlors with lacy tabletops and antimacassars and scrupulously concealed furniture legs. As a consequence, the word *modesty* often carries for us a negative weight of falseness or artifice or timidity. It cannot possibly be both sincere and healthy; it must be either insincere or pathological, or both. That it is seen this way is a sign of how completely modesty has come to embody the very things that modern mores have sought so ardently to defeat.

Even at its very best, modesty for us signifies a restraint or inhibition that one chooses — or more likely, has had drilled into one, so that it is an unconscious reflex — not because it conforms to what is inherently right or appropriate, but because it represents a safe and politic way of handling things, one that protects against public embarrassment, or against the envy or rivalrousness or passions of others. To the extent that the concept still lives, its force has become almost entirely "other-directed" rather than "inner-directed," to use the sociologist David Riesman's famous dichotomy. One is "modest" not because of what one believes but out of concern for how one is seen.

All of which is to say that modesty today is for us a psychological and stylistic category rather than a moral one — a way of presenting oneself rather than a way of grounding or orienting oneself. A woman who habitually chooses to wear "modest" clothing is no longer thought to be doing so on any grounds other than how she presumably "feels" about her body and the public display of it. And that is regarded as entirely a matter of individual choice and taste — although in fact, these days a certain suspicion falls on any reasonably well endowed woman who would not flaunt what she's got. Why not? What possible reason could she have for veiling her beauty?

There used to be a category of something called false modesty, meant to denote that kind of reticence that seems clearly phony or disingenuous. But that category seems superfluous now. We live in an age in which reticence has been discarded as a virtue, and *all* modesty is, in some sense, regarded as equally false, either because it is fake or because it is pathological, or perhaps merely because it is regarded as pathetic. A scholar whose book is praised for making a modest contribution to its field has in truth been tagged with having accomplished next to nothing, though the thought is stated in the most diplomatic of terms. And when the same scholar calls his own contribution modest he is merely trying to preemptively charm, or disarm, his prospective opposition. He does not, in short, mean it. No one, it seems, really wants to be modest.

Largely lost from view is the possibility that there can be a genuine modesty, a trait of character both heartfelt and rational, that stems not merely from socially or parentally inculcated inhibitions and "hang-ups" but from a certain depth of self-knowledge, from an awareness of how far we fall short of what we ought to be. In short, a modesty that arises out of an awareness of precisely who we are, and how much we have to be modest *about.* One recalls that the primordial act of modesty in our civilization was that recounted by the book of Genesis, in the story of Adam and Eve in the Garden of Eden. Having just committed the primal sin of eating from the Tree of the Knowledge of Good and Evil, the pair suddenly become aware of being *naked,* and sew together fig leaves to cover themselves. Their disobedient act had nothing to do with the use or misuse of their genital organs. And yet the first consequence of that act was a generalized sense of shame or ambivalence about the body, the first indication that they had entered a state of at least partial alienation from the true source of their being. The core of the biblical teaching about human nature, particularly as Christianity elaborated it, is that such complexity is part and parcel of the human condition as we experience it. It is thought to color our perceptions of the world's beauties and desires, which we know can shift their moral meanings for us from good to bad in the flicker of an eye.

The loss of modesty, then, is not merely a matter of changing fashions, but also of the larger assumptions behind those fashions, which is precisely why it is always appropriate to conjoin *manners* with *morals*. There is always a philosophy of human nature, however hidden or implicit, lurking behind our manners. And in the optimistic view of the modern world, which has banished such concepts as sin and shame, there is no compelling reason for us to regard modesty as a virtue, or to regard the modest person as anything more than a dissembler or an anxious fool.

It may be helpful at this point to observe that there are, broadly speaking, two meanings we ascribe to the word *modesty*. The first, following the footsteps of Adam and Eve, involves a reticence about the body. This includes preeminently a reticence about sexuality and sexual display, as in the example of women's clothing cited above. This meaning also can extend to the public exposure of anything that is intensely private and personal, and is grounded in a strong sense of discreetness and shame. From this perspective, a modest person is one who exercises discretion and practices hiddenness, eschewing personal display, wanting neither to give offense nor be an occasion of lapses in judgment by others, keeping high walls up around certain aspects of private life.

There is a common belief that such modesty arises out of an unhealthy aversion to physical or emotional intimacy or a poor body image. But that is often little more than a casual slander, or a convenient line used by would-be seducers to flush their quarries. It is a concession to the culture of display, which shows no awareness of an alternative to itself. Indeed, such modesty may well indicate the opposite of unhealthiness, with the construction of those high walls being a sign not of fearful disengagement from the bodily side of life, but rather a testament to how intensely precious the things behind those walls are, and therefore of how important it is to maintain such barriers, letting in only those who are tried and true, and recognizing the dangers entailed in departing from that practice in one's life. Far from being a barrier to intimacy, such modesty may be an indispensable partner to it, precisely because intimacy with many is impossible, a contradiction in terms. In the Song of Solomon, one of the great erotic poems in the Western tradition, which shares canonical status with Genesis — a fact that in itself shows something about the complexity of the biblical testimony regarding bodily beauty and desire — the beloved is vividly described as "a garden enclosed" and "a fountain sealed" (4:12). The image suggests something essential, perhaps, in the relationship between profound sexual intimacy and the protections of enclosure.

Second, *modesty* refers to a sense of tentativeness and humility in one's assessment of one's own accomplishments and status in the ultimate ranking of things. In this view, modesty means having a mature perspective on one's ultimate insignificance and limitations, grounded in a sense of mystery about the vastness and incomprehensibility of the world, and skepticism about the limits of human nature and human capabilities. This is the meaning of the word that ought to attach to the "modest" achievement of even the greatest scholars. Whatever we do is, in the end, pretty puny.

This is also the kind of modesty that remembers the embarrassing contrast between human aspiration and human frailty. It remembers that the legendary King Ozymandias's sole claim on our memory, in the poet Shelley's unforgettable depiction of him, is the bitterly ironic contrast between his boastful claims for himself — "Look upon my works, ye Mighty, and despair!" — and the ruined tomb in the desert that records those words, and in recording them silently reinterprets them as the cruel and empty self-mockery that they are. It remembers the painful contrast between the youthful Cassius Clay's arrogant and scornful cry, "I am the greatest!" and the pathetic figure that the elder Muhammad Ali has cut, his mind and body ravaged by his career in boxing and by the steady advance of Parkinson's disease. It remembers that nearly every human glory and every human boast ends in the same sad and humiliating way.

These two superficially different understandings of modesty — the modesty of exposure and the modesty of pride — actually have a great deal in common. Both are reticent: fond of restraint, slow to disclose, and slow to assert. Both are skeptical, in the sense in which George Santayana meant that word when he proclaimed skepticism to be "the chastity of the intellect," something that it is "shameful" to surrender "too soon or to the first comer." Instead, Santayana observed, warming to the sexual analogy, "there is nobility in preserving it coolly and proudly through a long youth, until at last, in the ripeness of instinct and discretion, it can be safely exchanged for fidelity and happiness."

Both forms of modesty share a suspicion of human desire and human will, a sense of how flawed we are, how frequently we fail to be what we know we can and should be. Both are also inherently conservative, in the sense that they share an awareness of how dangerous it can be to throw off well-established conventions, to disdain the guide rails laid down by previous generations, and instead presume to haul all of previous social reality before the bar of the present, and demand that it prove its worth to us and us only, or be banished in a wink to the ash heap of history.

In that sense, modesty is as countercultural a virtue as one could hope to find in an age of routinized ballyhoo, braggadocio, indulgence, and display — an age that arrogantly fancies itself a time of final truths, in which iconoclasm, the literal or figurative smashing of old revered objects, is the intellectual and moral virtue par excellence.

One would be hard put to think of a more polar opposition than that between modesty and iconoclasm. And, as in all such oppositions, there is a bit of the truth on both sides. Some icons deserve to be retired from time to time, and possibly even smashed for good measure. Modesty, like all virtues, can become a vice when it loses sight of its proper task, and instead becomes, immodestly, an end in itself. But that is hardly our problem in this age. Instead, our obsession with iconoclasm is so one-sided, and so oblivious to the need for balance, as to amount to a cultural pathology. The words of C. S. Lewis in his *Screwtape Letters,* placed in the mouth of that book's devilish protagonist, could not be timelier in this regard:

> The use of Fashions in thought is to distract the attention of men from their real dangers. We direct the fashionable outcry of each generation against those vices of which it is least in danger and fix its approval on the virtue nearest to that vice which we are trying to make endemic. The game is to have them all running about with fire extinguishers whenever there is a flood, and all crowding to that side of the boat which is already nearly gunwale under. Thus we make it fashionable to expose the dangers of enthusiasm at the very moment when they are all really becom-

ing worldly and lukewarm; a century later, when we are really making them all Byronic and drunk with emotion, the fashionable outcry is directed against the dangers of the mere "understanding." Cruel ages are put on their guard against Sentimentality, feckless and idle ones against Respectability, lecherous ones against Puritanism; and whenever all men are really hastening to become either slaves or tyrants we make Liberalism the prime bogey.

Employing the same reverse capability of social fashion, which we will here call the Lewis Reflex — the idea that people are too easily convinced that they should defend the disease and attack the antidote — we might add that the exaltation of iconoclasm has metastasized into an icon that itself is as pernicious as anything it has sought to smash.

This in turn brings us to an additional irony, a twist that I believe to be unique to our own time: that a certain self-consciously countercultural ethos has become, in fact, the dominant one in the ranks of college-educated and culturally aspirant Americans. This observation is at the heart of journalist David Brooks's hilarious but also dead-on depiction of the "bourgeois bohemian" in his book *Bobos in Paradise*. We have "repealed reticence," in Rochelle Gurstein's words, and have made the liberation from social convention into a new social convention all its own. Of course, this ideology rests upon a veiled form of class snobbery, since there must always be those unnamed "others," the suburbanites and functionaries and breeders and Babbitts who are thought to sustain and uphold the conventions from which "we" perpetually need to be liberated. But those "others" are increasingly shadowy and hard to locate. The new convention has been triumphant beyond its wildest dreams, and is now entirely pervasive, suffusing our popular culture and our advertising and assimilated into the mainstream in the most remarkable and incongruous ways.

One can find endless examples of this in just an hour of television viewing or flipping through the *New York Times*. In the latter, for example, one's eyes might light upon the front page of the Arts section for Monday, May 22, 2005, which features two representative articles: one a perfectly serious and sober piece on the birth of skateboarding as a "subculture," and the other a story about the creation of a Museum of the Counterculture in Manhattan's East Village by filmmaker and pizza-chain owner Phil Hartman, a man described as "an entrepreneur whose main form of transportation is his bicycle." Like a good Bobo, Hartman is anxiously aware that "the idea of institutionalizing downtown culture" has "inherent contradictions in it," and the idea has aroused some bitter opposition. But even the opposition has an unmistakably Bobo flavor. There is, for example, the film-archivist neighbor who complained, "We are not counterculture. We in the East Village *are* the culture and everything around us is the opposite of culture." He's so countercultural that he objects to the word itself.

I recently stayed in a meticulously restored Victorian inn in the meticulously restored Victorian town of Cape May. Two ex-artists, refugees from the East Village, run the inn, and throughout the house display their utterly predictable "cutting edge" works (cutting edge circa 1920, that is). They even posted a tasteful little sign "warning" guests that some images might be "disturbing." But this is a silly little conceit on their part — the thought that any of their clientele would even notice let alone be disturbed by the images. And, truth be told, they do not believe it themselves, else they would never have posted the art throughout the house. But it is terribly important to them to *believe* that they are still pushing the envelope and slashing away at bourgeois complacency, even if they run a small business, the quintessential bourgeois enterprise, out of a quintessentially bourgeois structure that is worth millions of dollars, and worry more about real estate taxes and college tuitions than about global warming.

Like the wealthy suburban lapsed Catholic who still fancies himself a radical follower of Dorothy Day, or the hotdog TV journalist who makes a seven-figure salary but still thinks of himself as a "marginal man" who lives off his "shoe leather reporting" and a willingness to "speak truth to power," these inn owners are people in the grip of a personal mythology from which they have no desire to free themselves. There is self-deception at work when people luxuriate in the fruits of worldly success while condemning the cultural forces that sustain them. The flourishing of various forms of "political correctness" shows that the "shame culture," far from being dead, is alive and well, even if it is not acknowledged as such by those who fancy themselves to be living beyond such atavisms.

Yet even the most incongruous social conventions can take hold for a time. And in our era, the conjunction of a certain *gemütlich* neo-Victorian conventionality with a certain countercultural conventionality seems, by now, so entrenched and commonplace as to be almost natural. To be truly countercultural may mean opposing the convention of unconventionalism, bucking the force of the Lewis Reflex — and remembering why the Victorians who built those wonderfully expressive old homes also prized modesty as a personal virtue. It is, in fact, to reestablish an honest link between manners and morals, and recognize that the culturewide repeal of modesty has been halfhearted, self-deceiving, and corrosive.

So what are the ultimate sources of our iconoclastic dogma, which wars against the time-honored ideals of modesty? One might be tempted to look to Madison Avenue, or more generally, to every Bobo's favorite whipping boy, Corporate Capitalism, which is thought to encourage the dissolution of all that is stable to create a constant flow of new desires and new markets for new consumables. There is probably some truth to this. But one should beware of the ease with which the Bobo looks up from his Blackberry to give you that response. In referring to it, might one be succumbing to the Lewis Reflex, and aiming fire extinguishers at the flood — or at any rate, mistaking the symptom for the cause?

To find the originating source of the dogma, one ought also to consider the role played by the world of ideas, since even a materialist has to concede that our ideas are the means by which we map the social landscape and determine what forces are in play. After all, one has to be introduced to the ideas of Marxism, even to the notoriously hazy idea of "class," before one can have any notion of what it would mean to map the world as "nothing but class struggle," and know which icons one should want to bust.

If we consider the role of ideas, then we are led ineluctably to the true Vatican of iconoclasm's cultural authority, the Magisterium wherein its dicta and directives and metaphysics and moral theology are authoritatively formulated and propounded. And that is the vast archipelago of Academia — the very place where, as David Brooks points out, the anticonventional sensibility is most reliably inculcated and most effectively promulgated. There is no stronger correlative to the rise of the Bobo sensibility than the rise in the size and cultural influence of higher education. And that is, as the Marxists used to say, no coincidence.

Iconoclasm is not only de rigueur in popular culture and Hollywood, but is à la mode in high culture and institutionalized in academic life, where Nietzsche, Foucault, and their countless epigones and acolytes call incessantly for the transvaluation of values, the revising of history, the overturning of conventions, the discrediting of tradition, the debunking of pieties, the shocking of the bourgeoisie, the empowering of the powerless, the disempowering of the powerful, the liberation of sexuality, and so on, in an endless cinematic loop of self-congratulatory antimoralistic moralism. Young scholars make their reputations by "overturning conventional wisdom," by publishing "path-breaking" studies, by skewering sacred cows, by "reorienting" and "revisioning" our previous understandings of things.

Even the old coots can get into the act. A retired philosophy professor from Princeton named Harry G. Frankfurt recently published a slim (but not at all modest) book with the title *On* [a common epithet for barnyard excrement]. The book, a reworking of an essay Frankfurt had circulated many years ago that contains no great insights or developed ideas, created a minor sensation and sold many, many copies for Princeton University Press, which used to be above such fraudulence but chose, in this case, to promote the book to the hilt. In the age of immodesty, one shows one's genuineness not only by using a dirty word in print, but by dressing it up in a white tie and tails and parading it before the reviewing stand as a demonstration of how immune one is to the mere social convention of thinking some things not appropriate for public disclosure.

Given that the professors' liberatory rhetoric comports very well with the agenda of most adolescent students who find themselves away from parents and other constraints for the first time in their lives, it's no wonder that it all works together so well, even if the professors sometimes suspect that the students are free riders — more interested in the uses to which the rhetoric can be put than in the ideas behind it. But the effect may have been more lasting than they think. For the post–World War II generation, college was surely the most powerfully formative experience of their lives, which explains the morbid ongoing interest in boomer-sentimental movies like *The Big Chill,* and other such increasingly dated evocations of the halcyon 1960s.

But there is this thing that Max Weber called the "routinization of charisma," and it happens to movements that begin to seriously contemplate creating museums for themselves. Nothing lasts forever, not even Woodstock Nation, without undergoing a sea change, and what has happened in academia, which remains one of the most procedurally conservative areas in American life, is a certain ossification of the liberatory dogma into something both weak and absurd.

I will illustrate this with an example from my own experience as a professor for nearly twenty years. A while back, when I was at an institution different from my present one, I was asked by a departmental search committee to read the files of their three finalists in search of a position in American women's history. I consented, and read the files. They were fairly ordinary examples of their genre, but one of the applicants' letters of recommendation stood out as a document that, precisely because of its ordinariness, illuminated the landscape like a lightning bolt. This letter was written by an uncontested luminary in the field, a very accomplished historian who co-edited an influential book series in women's history and bestrode the field like a colossus. This was also someone whom I had met and knew to be a very pleasant, gracious, agreeable, and well-mannered person. The student's dissertation was a community study, strictly delimited in its coverage of space and time. So I was a bit stunned to read the exact terms of the adviser's praise for this student, our applicant. This sentence, in particular, struck me: "X has written the most transgressive dissertation it has ever been my pleasure to direct."

What on earth could this word *transgressive* mean, I wondered. Did the student pepper the dissertation with offensive slogans, expletives, and racial slurs? Did she jump up on the table at her dissertation defense, strip off her clothes, and shriek like a banshee? Did she make death threats against public officials or disclose the intimate details of their lives? She did none of these things. This was a perfectly conventional, even unusually docile and obedient graduate student, and honoring her work with the title of "transgressive" was, literally, the nicest thing that the adviser could have said about it. It was a conventional piece of work by a conventional graduate student, in an academic order in which the word *transgression* has completely lost its meaning and become equivalent to the "disturbing" art on the innkeepers' walls. A "transgression" rightly understood is a horrifying thing to any civilized person. To transgress is to take the next intensifying step beyond iconoclasm, for a transgressor is not only a person who violates rules but also someone who violates others. There is a gradient toward brutal aggression in the very idea of transgression. What does one make of a moral universe in which there are no words left to describe the things that rightly ought to horrify us, and where there is no justification left for the hiddenness of things that are shameful and embarrassing?

What such a story illustrates, and what the story of Princeton's shameless little book illustrates, is the fact that the iconoclastic narrative that undergirds so much of contemporary academic life is completely exhausted and routinized, seamlessly assimilated into the bureaucracy of academic proceduralism. Those ideas lack any real incendiary power, but they also lack vigorous and principled opposition. The result is a general devaluation of ideas, which for me was epitomized by that strangely uncomprehending use of the word *transgressive*. Academic life suffers, as a result, from an enormous flatness and, to use a favored word of the '60s, irrelevance.

It is perhaps too much to hope for that to change anytime soon. The orthodoxy of iconoclasm may be completely enfeebled and discredited, but it can still summon the force to protect its perquisites. Perhaps what is most needed is something that the academy, at its best, excels in and is (or should be) warmly favorable to: a recovery of the spirit of real skepticism, including a skepticism that is skeptical of itself. Such a comprehensive skepticism will not only call on the carpet the battered pieties of the past, but also the tenured pieties of the present — the general social and cultural wreckage that has been wrought by the ideologies of iconoclasm and personal liberation. It would force the would-be prophets of transgression to answer for themselves, and say what they have to offer that can take the place of the things they have sought to destroy. It would force us to be more honest about the disconnection between the grandiloquent slogans and fantasies by which we claim to live, and the commonplace moral realities that actually order our lives. In short, it would force us to be more honest with ourselves about what flawed and inadequate and needy creatures we are — a recognition that will have to be the foundation of any reassertion of modesty as a cardinal virtue, and a centerpiece of a civilized and morally responsible life.

Such a spirit of skepticism may not be the same thing as modesty. But it is a close relation, and, if conscientiously applied, may be the way back to a recovery of that abandoned virtue. To paraphrase a familiar saying, some are born modest, and some achieve modesty. But there is nothing to prevent others from having it thrust upon them. Indeed, that will surely happen in due course, one way or another, willingly or unwillingly.

ANN McCUTCHAN

Reaching for the End of Time

FROM *Image*

I FIRST encountered Olivier Messiaen's *Quartet for the End of Time* in 1971, in the basement of Florida State University's music library, where I was employed as a work-study student. The folio had languished on a low, dusty shelf for years, never checked out, and I, a scavenger delighting in all things offbeat and obscure, pounced on the composition. The quartet was scored for violin, cello, piano, and clarinet — my instrument. Here, I naively thought, was a piece no one else knew! Leafing through it, I noticed Messiaen's fervent dedication: "in homage to the Angel of the Apocalypse, who raises a hand toward heaven saying: 'There shall be time no longer,'" and saw that the third movement, "Abyss of the Birds," was written for solo clarinet. No matter how it sounded — I was no score reader, then — I had to be part of this ambitious work.

To start, I would perform the solo movement alone in recital, bringing the "lost" quartet to light. I took the music to my clarinet professor, a pedagogue and technician who with one glance pronounced it negligible. I would have to negotiate the odd rhythms, rackety birdcalls, and excruciatingly long-held tones of the "Abyss" (like *om*s that grow louder and louder) by myself. A composer on the faculty helped me find the single available recording of the quartet, and in the music library I listened through enormous headphones to the entire "wondrous strange" piece over and over, moved by its spiritual vigor, a quality no other contemporary music in my experience offered. The severe leaps within its stretching lines were the antithesis of chant, and yet, they *were* chant. The quick turns between dour, weighty statements and bold, flashy warblings might have mocked ritual, and yet, they were as keenly calculated as the pairing of the stern sermon and the joyful hymn that follows. With the intensity of an evangelist, I took up my clarinet and began to practice. But by the time I had rehearsed "Abyss of the Birds" well enough to try it in public, my pride in ferreting out the music had slunk away. The solo required more physical stamina than I'd thought possible, and I was afraid that under pressure I'd crater on it, which I did, in the very last measure, the final flourish. Instead of piping a waterfall of song, I produced one long, desperate squawk.

Thus began a pilgrimage that continues, in all of its uncertainty, today.

At the time I found Messiaen, Florida State's campus was roiling with political demonstrations, a growing drug culture, "free love," and other expressions of rebellion that marked the late sixties and early seventies. Other than a memorial march for the victims of the Kent State shootings and a few experiments with marijuana, I was not part of that scene. I remember well the night of the first "streaking" on Landis Green. A violist friend, her violinist fiancé, and my boyfriend, a pianist, had to concede that watching more adventurous students race naked in front of the library was worth setting aside scale practice for one hour, and the four of us met at the appointed time in the safe shadow of a giant oak at the edge of the green. I could never have torn off my clothes, as one coed did in order to be chased by an entire fraternity, and the lily-white blind boy who galloped into the green's fountain with no accessory but a cane took my breath away: how could he do that if he didn't know what he looked like? Yet the desire for a fresh way of regarding the world lived in us cloistered music students just as surely as it lived in those who engaged in public defiance of "the system." For me, art music, and particularly the *Quartet for the End of Time*, with its deeply spiritual impulse and wild combination of musical materials, satisfied my needs for both a meditative foundation and a radical mode of expression. I may have faltered miserably in the first performance, but "Abyss of the Birds" would help me develop the solo voice I yearned for.

In taking on "Abyss of the Birds," I thought I was breaking ground, and maybe, in the hinterlands of north Florida, I was. Little did I know that everywhere else, other musicians of my generation were unearthing the same work. One year after I struck gold in the music library, the maverick Marlboro Music Festival ensemble Tashi — clarinetist Richard Stoltzman, violinist Ida Kavafian, cellist Fred Sherry, and pianist Peter Serkin, the first nationally known chamber group to perform in hippie garb — made a recording of the quartet that for many listeners remains the standard, though other excellent ensembles have recorded the work since. The spiritual depth and technical challenges of the quartet attracted many musical children of that time who sought strong contemporary statements and performance occasions to which they might rise. The *Quartet for the End of Time* is monumental: with eight movements and a running time of nearly one hour, it is one of the longest pieces of chamber music in the repertoire.

After leaving Florida I vowed to perform the entire quartet, and would not wait for opportunities, but create them. The first took place at the University of Michigan, where I was a graduate student. My compatriots and I were guided by the venerable vocal coach Eugene Bossart, who told me he had always wanted to learn the quartet, and the results, heard in a modest recital hall, were astonishingly lyrical — an argument for the teaching of instrumentalists by experts on the human voice. Two years later, while teaching at Loyola University in New Orleans, I assembled a faculty group to play the quartet in a Catholic church on Saint Charles Avenue. I remember the Sunday afternoon sunlight flickering and flaring through the stained-glass windows and the feeling that Messiaen himself might be listening from a back pew, pondering his creator. The third performance was given in Austin, Texas, in 1983, soon after I moved there, in the opera theater at the University of Texas with faculty from that music department. Of my three performances it was the only one offered on a proscenium stage, and although it went well, we were too far away from the audience, a predicament borne by many chamber musicians obliged to play in large venues. Light, close scoring calls for, and deserves, an intimate space where all communicants can share equally. I reveled in the close-knit ensemble, but missed the intensity I wanted from our listeners.

Each of these performances needed many hours of rehearsal time, because the work demands formidable technique. For example, the swift sixth movement, "Dance of Fury, for the Seven Trumpets," is completely in unison, requiring precise intonation. To adjust pitch, the violinist or cellist must quickly, instinctively roll or slide a finger of the left hand ever so slightly, infinitesimally, up or down the active string. The clarinetist will add or subtract pressure of the lips on the mouthpiece, choose an alternate fingering, or even lower some fingers closer to inactive holes, which dulls the timbre and might not so much flatten the pitch as darken it — an illusion. No matter which instrument one is playing, the finely calibrated ear drives the physical response. The "Dance of Fury" is also unmetered, with varying time values from bar to bar, so players must rapidly and internally count the sixteenth-note subdivisions in diamond-cut accord, even as they achieve a flexible, mellifluous sweep. As with so many beautiful works, both exactness and unpredictability underpin the ethereal.

There are other technical challenges in the quartet. The clarinet and strings are often required to play in the extreme high register, which, even among virtuosos, can be maddeningly precarious. Dynamics run from barely discernible to blazingly loud. And the number of sustained single pitches, like tightly strung, oscillating filaments, also tax the players, even the pianist, who must dedicate her entire upper body and a well-timed pedal in service of the long, tenacious line.

Every generation spawns composers who write music that pushes previously held limits and which traditionalists pronounce unplayable. In postwar Paris, one of those composers was Messiaen.

Olivier Messiaen wrote the *Quartet for the End of Time* during the winter of 1940–41 while incarcerated in Stalag VIII A, near the village of Görlitz in the Silesian mountain region that today is part of Poland. The story goes that the young composer managed to make off with a pencil and some music paper and hid out in the latrines at night, writing secretly, furiously, the piece that would later be regarded as the finest chamber work produced during wartime imprisonment. With special permission from German authorities, he premiered the quartet with three other musicians who had landed in the camp. A crowd of prisoners, many of them badly wounded and borne to the hall on stretchers, made up the audience. This scenario alone might explain why Vietnam-era musicians embraced the work and brought it to the attention of American audiences. However, the *Quartet for the End of Time* did not represent Messiaen's wish for an end to personal incarceration and World War II. It was, he explained, a sustained meditation on the book of Revelation — a hymn to eternity.

Olivier Messiaen is one of the few major twentieth-century composers whose output was openly, uncompromisingly inspired by his religious faith. The only child of the Shakespeare scholar Pierre Messiaen and the poet Cécile Sauvage, who composed a book of poems titled *The Flowering Soul* while pregnant with her son, Messiaen taught himself to play the piano and at age eleven wrote his first piece, a work for piano titled *The Lady of Shalott,* based on the poem by Tennyson. Contact with Debussy's colorful, impressionistic opera *Pelléas and Mélisande* made a lasting impact on the boy — it was a formal model for his own opera — but Messiaen was, from the very start, it seems, dedicated like no other composer of his time to expressing his Catholic faith. Here is an oft-quoted excerpt from his personal manifesto:

> The emotion and sincerity of the work.
> Which shall be at the service of the dogmas of Catholic theology.
> The subject theological? The best, for it comprises all subjects.
> And the abundance of technical means allows the heart to expand freely.

Messiaen's musical language is among the most distinctive of the twentieth century. The composer was intrigued by nature, particularly birds; he was a devoted amateur ornithologist who roamed the French countryside with a tape recorder, collecting the birdsongs he later transcribed and used in his music. Messiaen was also a splendid instrumental colorist, having been blessed with vivid color-sound associations because of a condition called synesthesia — any sound he heard immediately produced a color in his mind's eye, and vice versa. And so the fresh combinations of instruments he employed yielded otherworldly timbres evocative of the stained-glass windows in La Trinité, the Paris church where he served as organist for more than forty years. "During my captivity," he said, "it was colored dreams that gave birth to the chords and rhythms of my quartet." Messiaen was engrossed by rhythm as well. His study of Hindu music led to a lifelong preoccupation with palindrome rhythms, mirror-structures that for him were symbols of eternity because they have no defined beginning or end. Messiaen's life spanned the entire twentieth century, with the exception of exactly eight years each, forward and aft. He was born in 1908 and died in 1992.

After my third performance of the quartet, in 1983, I suspected I might never play the work again. Messiaen's masterpiece, for all its beauty and meaning, had produced carpal tunnel pain in my right wrist and a temporary loss of control in the fourth and fifth fingers. Repetitive motion injuries are common among today's musicians, who rehearse for technical precision to a much higher degree than did our predecessors fifty and more years ago. In the early 1980s, when my problems began, only a few doctors focused on the medical concerns of musicians; today, musician health is a legitimate specialty.

As I gained some relief through cortisone shots and chiropractic adjustments, I gradually accepted the challenge of keeping my hands nimble enough to perform works less taxing than the quartet. That left a lot of repertory; still, the loss of the quartet would foreshadow the eventual loss of my life as a vibrant performer. Any musician will tell you that there is no substitute for music making at physical peak, when the body, mind, and spirit are equally, consummately engaged. Performing is who you are, and where God is. Now I was past peak and had to figure out how to alter the conventional arc, to pitch a tent close to the apex by recapturing and maintaining the passion the quartet engendered. I could do this, I thought, by listening to Messiaen's music. If I entered others' performances passionately as auditor, I might reconnect with what Messiaen must have had when he wrote the quartet: a direct line to a spiritual power. Such intensity would be difficult to achieve by way of recordings. I would have to place myself as close as possible to the music making, listening only to live performances, to which I would travel.

My notion of having to make multiple pilgrimages was realistic, because concerts of Messiaen's music were hard to come by. I would have to leave central Texas to catch the best ones. Two exhilarating evenings stand out in my memory: an organ recital by the late composer-organist William Albright in Dallas and a concert in Boston featuring the *Turangalîla* symphony played by the BSO, led by Seiji Ozawa. In both, Messiaen's interpreters achieved such perfect symbiosis among composer, performers, and listeners that I might as well have been on stage, playing my clarinet. Time stopped.

As my travels proceeded and my knowledge of Messiaen grew, it occurred to me to ingest all of the religious symbols and technical devices behind the music. I should do this, I thought, because it would put me inside the composer's head, surely the source of the intensity I wished to recover. But each time I approached the music this way, I felt stymied by Messiaen's overwhelmingly Catholic "program," and retreated. I couldn't force myself to go this route; mine was a quest of the heart and body, not the intellect. Besides, I was the last person to plunge into what I saw as a theological swamp. My spiritual life hadn't been formally linked to a religion since childhood church attendance, which was mostly benign Methodist (my father's brand), except when my mother, raised Unitarian, switched us over to a Presbyterian church for a time, and then an Episcopal one, because the pastors wrote better sermons. Having a deep-seated aversion to anything resembling a club, I've never as an adult wanted to articulate a faith or join an organized religion. The first activity would devalue an inner experience — to describe it in words would limit it — and the second, which seems to me to be based on fear and tribalism, closes off possibilities.

Still, I have always dabbled in religious matters, which might make me a sort of aspirant, implying upward movement toward some sort of triumph. But I am continually quashing the vertical impulse and reacting against it in others. I want the Shaker hymn "Simple Gifts," not the Protestant battle anthem "Onward Christian Soldiers." There was a time in my thirties, not long after the third quartet performance, when Pope John Paul passed through San Antonio, and the idea of a pope, a king of a religion, struck me as so preposterous that I cultivated a collection of pope memorabilia as a local corrective. Friends aware of my delight in pontiff kitsch made me gifts of pope paper-dolls, pope snow globes, pope soap-on-a-rope. My most prized possession was a signed and numbered pope lawn sprinkler: a three-foot replica of John Paul, painted on plywood, fitted on the back with a hose connector and some plastic tubing. When hooked up to a hose, the pope's hands spouted water. The sprinkler's official name was "Let Us Spray," and it was the envy of my unchurched friends, as well as many of the churched ones. One morning I found it missing from my garden, and though I was angry about the theft, I joked that God was not amused by my irreverence and had seen fit to cast out my graven image. The next time I moved, I carried the rest of my pope trumpery to the Salvation Army. Presumably it was divided into piles headed for the toys and housewares departments, and even women's clothing, where an "I Prayed with the Pope" T-shirt from Denver, featuring the pontiff surrounded by a pestilence of prairie dogs, was snatched up, I hope, by someone with a sense of humor.

While I was traveling to hear Messiaen and chuckling over the pope, the daily newspaper in Austin hired me as music critic, and I began an accidental writing career. Even so, I continued to perform in chamber groups and the city opera orchestra with the help of chiropractors, yoga instructors, and a gifted Rolfer whose manipulations increased my height by half an inch. Working with both music and words was often frustrating. I found that I couldn't practice the clarinet, put down the instrument, and immediately take up the pen. There had to be a transitional hour between the use of each language, during which I would perform a household task such as baking bread or gardening. In shuttling back and forth from one to the other, I experienced a physical sensation, a light-headedness. A neuroscientist could explain exactly why this was so; put simply, verbal and musical language centers reside in different parts of the brain. I felt a slight but real chemical switch.

Eventually, though, words achieved a solid, practical purchase on my life. I returned to school for a degree in writing, and then, sixteen years after my final performance of the quartet, I resigned from my last ongoing chamber group and moved to Ithaca, New York, for a postdoc in writing at Cornell. I embraced a hermetic existence there, retreating to my rented cottage after school, listening not to Messiaen but to recordings of the late Beethoven quartets, as if confirming my musical dotage.

But Messiaen returned to me, upstaging Beethoven, when a Cornell faculty group invited me to take the second clarinet part in a performance of his splashy, fluttery *Oiseaux Exotiques* for piano and small orchestra. By then I played so seldom that it would take two months of rigorous daily practice to execute my part in a professional manner. And, whether or not I was practicing, the carpal-tunnel pain in my right wrist now woke me up at night, spasming up my arm, into my shoulder and neck. One of the doctors I consulted identified mild scoliosis, a structural imbalance that at middle age was affecting more than the wrist; all of my limbs were vulnerable.

Yet I eagerly accepted the invitation to perform *Oiseaux Exotiques.* It was a gift I hadn't expected: a last chance, a coda. And with that commitment in hand, I took on another: a two-month bird-watching course offered by Cornell's renowned ornithology department. My motivation had nothing to do with Messiaen, I thought. I simply wanted to take advantage of a fine program that would force me to get out of the house on Saturday mornings.

The Messiaen concert thrilled me — how could it not, since my job was to plant myself within an ecstatic sound-tapestry, chirping and shrieking the calls of the wood thrush, the lark, and even the prairie chicken? *Oiseaux Exotiques* contains the songs of forty-six birds from India, China, Malaysia, the Canary Islands, South America, and North America, including the Chinese leiothrix, four different vireos, and a vivacious little singer Messiaen calls the Carolina troglodyte, commonly known as the Carolina wren. Within this aviary, the pain in my wrist, arm, shoulder, and back temporarily evaporated, and I walked off the stage and into the night, glowing.

The next morning, in the cold spring rain, I gulped extra-strength Tylenol and drove one-handed with thirty other aspiring bird watchers to the Montezuma National Wildlife Refuge near Seneca Falls, where transient Canada geese, mallards, and dozens of other waterfowl species clogged the marshes, looking to me misplaced and confused. I remember envying the sharp-sighted engineering major who later that day spotted a female ruby-crowned kinglet flitting among the branches of an evergreen thicket. The female bears no red cap; she looks like any number of what our instructor called LBJs, or Little Brown Jobs. How could that young man possibly distinguish her, I wondered? She wasn't even singing.

At the end of that year, I moved to the desolate reach of Wyoming to write, and eventually to teach writing and music history at the state university in Laramie. I was lonely there and resumed my

Messiaen excursions, fixating first on the composer's only American commission, a piece for solo piano, horn, xylorimba, glockenspiel, and orchestra, titled *From the Canyons to the Stars*. For this project, Messiaen was determined to find inspiration in the American landscape, and in 1971, lured by a photograph of Bryce Canyon, he bought a plane ticket to Salt Lake City and spent a month in southern Utah, visiting Bryce Canyon, Cedar Breaks, and Zion national parks. The result was a gloriously excessive work of twelve movements that takes an hour and a half to play.

Knowing I was not likely ever to hear a live performance of *Canyons,* I found the only recording in print, loaded it into my car's CD player, and on one bright weekend in May, the same time of year that Messiaen went west, drove over to Utah to hike Bryce and listen to the same birds Messiaen would have heard exactly thirty years before. I knew my desire to retrace his steps was impure — a greed for someone else's transcendence — but set it aside, for I had come to realize that moving my body through space, by way of motorized vehicles or my two feet, had become a partial substitute for the physical intensity of music. I'd completed my transformation from music maker to witness, relinquishing musical notes, instrument, and stage for words, pens, and geography. I *had* to do this.

I had made a list of Messiaen's Utah birds, whose songs I had learned from a CD of birdcalls acquired at Cornell. I had brought binoculars and a camera, too. But on that morning as I walked the dry red path among the luminous pink spires and hoodoos carved by centuries of wind, rain, and snow, I heard and saw nothing that had anything to do with birds. Had Bryce's environment changed that much in twenty-five years, or had I simply missed the dawn chorus? Once, I spotted a small specimen on a branch of one of the gnarled pines bunched here and there on the canyon floor, but it didn't sing and didn't even fly when I came close. It might as well have been a decoy.

I turned on my booted heel and started up Wall Street, a dark, damp trail that ran between two mammoth bulwarks of stone so high and close together that there was but a slice of light at the top, where the two walls nearly met. The sound of my boots, *heel-toe, heel-toe,* bounced off the rock dryly, like the rhythm of castanets. I stopped to listen to the echo, and in that moment an elderly couple appeared at the other end of the tipped walls and, seeing me, paused. Then they began to speak softly, and their words did not ricochet off the stone edifices, but rather wafted down to me like feathers. They were French.

The woman turned back to rest, but the man continued toward me, to explore the length of the path. As he approached, I greeted him, "Bonjour," and his face brightened as he responded at length in his language.

This was his first visit to the United States, he said. He and his wife had heard of Bryce's beauty and wanted to be sure to see it. I confessed I was there to retrace the steps of his countryman, Olivier Messiaen.

"Why do you want to do this?" he said.

"I want to hear what he heard," I answered.

"And that is . . ."

"Birds," I said. "But all I hear today is the wind."

"Perhaps what you hear is enough," said the Frenchman.

A year later, the San Francisco Opera mounted Messiaen's only stage work, an opera based on the life of St. Francis of Assisi. It would be the first American (and only third ever) production of *Saint-François,* and I flew over for the weekend to witness it — the complicated travel from Laramie taking longer than the time I actually spent in the city. The opera, a series of tableaux dramatizing significant events in St. Francis's life, started at 6:30 P.M. and ended close to midnight, and it required an orchestra so large and varied that wide stage extensions had to be built, eliminating several rows of seats in front. From my perch in the first balcony, I gazed down on what looked like a giant painting of musical hell by Hieronymus Bosch, jammed to the edges with musicians curled around one another, instruments wedged into adjacent armpits or pressed into stomachs. In contrast, when the curtain lifted, I saw a striking, minimal set by Hans Dieter Schaal in shades of gray, with thick movable walls and a raised walkway that curved back to infinity. Hovering over this was an immense round ball: the sun, the moon, an egg, a soul? Together, these represented a monastery, its rooms, its garden, and all that existed within them. With the exception of an angel, who appeared in bluebird blue, all the characters were clad in neutral colors. Messiaen's aural reds and greens, purples and oranges, made up the rest of the spectrum.

The work proceeds with deliberate majesty. A few listeners in my balcony row grew audibly impatient; our seats in the venerable old opera house were tight, and one had the choice of sitting straight up or squinching forward, elbows or forearms on knees: the house-side version of the arrangement in the pit. As much as I loved Messiaen's music, I began to wonder if I'd flown all that way to witness a dud. And then came — at precisely the right place in the opera, in the evening — the scene where St. Francis, after a prolonged, agonizing buildup, reaches out with one hand to touch, and finally embrace, a leper, risking his life to pass the love of God directly to the decaying man, flesh upon flesh. I could not hold back the sudden tears; the impact of the *Quartet for the End of Time* had returned to me.

Yet after I returned to Wyoming I embarked on a head-trip, snatching up the Catholic authors Messiaen revered, as if by reading I could sustain the effect of St. Francis's touch. I found Hans Urs von Balthasar's *Heart of the World* — beautiful, but not as accessible as I'd hoped — and tried to connect with Paul Claudel's poems and his commentary *A Poet Before the Cross*, which I tossed aside after the first chapter — nothing there for me. Finally, I reread the book of Revelation — the inspiration for the quartet — and some recent interpretations of it, and at last realized how wildly mutable and kaleidoscopic that book is. An angel with a rainbow crown and clothing of clouds, one foot in the sea and one on earth? No wonder "godless" musicians of the Vietnam era had latched onto Messiaen's quartet. Revelation was the ultimate trip, complete with symbols one could contemplate long after the drug of the moment — be it chemical, material, or what Karen Armstrong calls a "bad religion" (one that stifles "the individual's search for transcendent meaning and the absolute truth beyond ego") — wears off. Like music, John's vision can be variously perceived, and I began to regard Revelation as a grand, hallucinogenic painting, kin to Messiaen's opera for Saint-François, not holy writ ossified by tradition. Here was a section of the New Testament I could view as more than a historical myth toward living a right life. It was wild, hairy literature; it was, as Messiaen knew, a basis for art.

I put away my books and forgot about Messiaen until a faculty ensemble at the University of Wyoming, planning a performance of the *Quartet for the End of Time* in response to the Iraq war, asked me to speak at the concert. One of them had spotted me marching in an antiwar demonstration in front of Laramie's snow-covered courthouse. The Iraq war was not as unpopular in Laramie as Vietnam had been in Tallahassee; for every passerby who waved in support of our peace march, another gave us the finger. At the performance, I offered a description of the quartet's premiere, stressing Messiaen's heroic feat, his making of art under extreme conditions. Then my colleagues began to play, and I yearned to be the clarinetist, to help sing Messiaen's sorrowful, joyous, mysterious songs. But it could never happen, not now. Although my right wrist had been surgically healed of carpal tunnel syndrome, the pinkie of the same hand resembled a sausage link, bent slightly in the middle. My body had generated a new, more unusual hand ailment, Dupuytren's contracture, a thickening of fascia along the tendons in the palm and fingers. During the "Abyss of the Birds," the crimped finger twitched, a broken wing.

Not long after the concert I happened upon the last book I would ever read about Messiaen. *For the End of Time: The Story of the Messiaen Quartet,* had just been published by Rebecca Rischin, a clarinetist who traveled to France to hunt down the details of the quartet's composition in Stalag VIII A. I was shocked to learn that after the war, the composer developed a simplified story (the one I had known and passed on) of the quartet's genesis, glorifying himself at the expense of others, flattening the fascinating facts, obscuring his compositional process, and magnifying his suffering and the loathsome conditions under which he worked. His wife, Yvonne Loriod, who had been his student and frequently performed his work, tended his musical legacy after his death and further embroidered the tale. Until Rischin made the effort to interview musicians and others who were in the camp, musicologists accepted Messiaen's exaggerations as gospel.

The long-held myth says that Messiaen composed the entire quartet within the walls of Stalag VIII A, when in fact he wrote "Abyss of the Birds" earlier, while stationed as a medical orderly at Verdun. There he met the cellist Étienne Pasquier and clarinetist Henri Akoka, who played together in a military orchestra, and, inspired by Akoka's style and the birds in the area, Messiaen composed the clarinet solo with no thought of a larger work. Then the Germans roared in, and the three musicians were captured. Akoka managed to take his clarinet on the ensuing forty-three-mile march to an encampment near Nancy, and while waiting to be sent to Stalag VIII A, he sight-read "Abyss of the Birds" for Messiaen. Pasquier, who had been obliged to leave his cello in Verdun, held the music for him.

Messiaen also claimed that the fourth movement, "Interlude," was the first he wrote, although it could have been the first he composed in Stalag VIII A, for it is scored only for violin, clarinet, and cello. (Violinist Jean Le Boulaire joined the group in the camp, and Pasquier was given a cello there. The piano was made available later.) Additionally, the fifth movement, "Praise to the Eternity of Jesus," and the eighth, "Praise to the Immortality of Jesus," respectively for cello with piano and violin with piano, were not lightning bolts from the clouds over Görlitz, but refashionings of pieces Messiaen had written before the war. Cannibalizing or building upon previous work is common among composers and other creators — after all, many believe that God cobbled us together from earlier projects, such as clay.

It seemed odd that Messiaen would deny this practice.

More important, there is the tale, kept vividly alive by his wife, of Messiaen sneaking into the camp latrines to compose. Those who were there told it differently. Early on, Messiaen was recognized as a famous composer, relieved of physical labor, and given the materials and privacy to write music. "What I know is that we were not allowed to disturb him," Pasquier told Rischin. Pasquier himself was relieved of work in a granite quarry and assigned a job as camp cook once he was identified as a famous cellist. Le Boulaire and Akoka fared well, too. Anyone familiar with accounts of concentration camp orchestras knows the Reich sometimes protected musicians, providing them instruments, music, rehearsal time, and, in the context of horrible deprivation, relatively easy labor. Many accounts cite one key German — a music lover or secret humanist — who served as intermediary or protector for musicians. In Messiaen's case, it was an officer named Karl-Albert Brüll, who spoke fluent French and whose father was president of the Catholic Youth of Silesia. He was also sympathetic to the Jews. But despite Brüll's extraordinary assistance to Messiaen, the composer failed to acknowledge him publicly until 1991.

A long time ago I must have decided that anyone who creates great art must be an admirable person. It was a naive assumption, or perhaps it was a desire. I wanted the whole package to be perfect, one part a reflection of the other. In wishing this, I succumbed to the vertical impulse, building an exceedingly high pedestal for Olivier Messiaen. Down he crashed, and one day, on a hike in Wyoming's Snowy Range, I found myself, after all those years, talking to him. Why did you lie about the composition of the quartet? Why did you deny Brüll?

Rischin offered possible answers regarding the composing process, politely speculating that Messiaen was motivated by practicality, pedagogy, and kindness. He wanted to make the story simple for students, scholars, and the press, paring down the analytical details of the work, citing the modest fourth movement as the first one composed, even though it meant obliterating the histories of the phenomenal solo movements (the third, fifth, and eighth). "From a compositional standpoint," Rischin wrote, "a less complex and less ambitious movement might serve as a starting point — the prelude to rather than an interlude for — a much greater composition." No matter the sequence of composition, she added, Messiaen might have decided on three solo movements to give his compatriots equal roles in the birth of the work. But however it happened, Rischin concluded the composer wanted to "leave no doubt that he intended a quartet all along."

"His omissions serve[d] to preserve the myths surrounding the piece and the mystery surrounding the man," she wrote.

And Karl-Albert Brüll? Having known a number of image-conscious composers, I began to see how Messiaen and his wife might have wished to impress the public with his brilliance and devotion to art, dramatizing his ability to create heaven-inspired work against the most horrifying odds. Acknowledging Brüll, the real hero of the day, would have blown the couple's miraculous story, revealing an iconoclastic composer to be a mere human being who depended upon, and then selfishly disclaimed, a daring generosity that, like Saint Francis's, transcended doctrine. I will probably never know the full truth — no doubt there are facts and nuances waiting for the next researcher — but the truth Rischin uncovered for me was the image of a gangly fellow in a beret brilliantly working the levers and pulleys of his art and craft, to the glory of something greater than himself, yet not without the pretensions artists attempt and often fail to erase. Messiaen's connection to God came not from something he owned, but something he could only yearn for, and in that sense, he was no different from the rest of us.

My relationship with Messiaen is not over; at the very least, it is teaching me I can't get out of living with contradictions. Last year I consulted a hand specialist who advised surgery for my Dupuytren's. The thickening in the right little finger had increased and dropped down into the palm between the fourth and fifth fingers — the typical starting point for the affliction before it worms its way across the hand. This was the location of my initial carpal-tunnel symptom; the insidious groundwork had been laid since the first performance of the quartet. I put off the surgery, hoping the disease might stall, until one cold day I spilled the contents of my change purse onto the floor of the Laramie Kmart and had to accept the help of a small child to retrieve the coins. How essential is the littlest digit to the most ordinary tasks, such as picking up a dime between the thumb and forefinger. Without their fellows in concert, the big guys are clumsy, inflexible.

To remove Dupuytren's tissue, a surgeon can't simply slice straight down the center of the finger. A to B would deny access to the thickening that has crept into pockets along the sides, and would leave an inflexible scar. The most desirable incision zigzags crazily across the finger and palm. Afterward, the patient embarks on weeks of physical therapy to regain something close to normal functioning. One day I asked my therapist if I could do more at home than repeat my finger exercises and squeeze clay.

"Did you say you were a clarinetist?" she asked.

"Yes," I said.

"The best thing you can do is play your instrument. Practice the piece you love most."

I stared at this strong, ruddy woman, whose clientele consisted mostly of daredevils: bronco-busters, downhill skiers, mountain climbers. What could she possibly know about musicians?

Then I thought of the "Abyss." "I haven't played it in twenty-two years," I said. "My fingers won't work right. I'll sound terrible."

"But you love it. Do it. Trust me," she said.

The Moderate Martyr

FROM *The New Yorker*

IN 1967, A LAW STUDENT at the University of Khartoum named Abdullahi Ahmed an-Naim was looking for a way to spend a summer evening in his hometown, a railway junction on the banks of the Nile in northern Sudan. No good movies were showing at the local cinemas, so he went with a friend to hear a public lecture by Mahmoud Muhammad Taha, an unorthodox Sudanese mystic with a small but ardent following. Taha's subject, "An Islamic Constitution: Yes and No," tantalized Naim. In the years after Sudan became independent, in 1956, the role of Islam in the state was fiercely debated by traditional Sufists, secular Marxists, and the increasingly powerful Islamists of the Muslim Brotherhood, who, at the time, were led in Sudan by Hasan al-Turabi, a legal scholar. Politically, Naim was drifting toward the left, but his upbringing in a conservative Muslim home had formed him. "I was very torn," Naim recently recalled. "I am a Muslim, but I couldn't accept Sharia" — Islamic law. "I studied Sharia and I knew what it said. I couldn't see how Sudan could be viable without women being full citizens and without non-Muslims being full citizens. I'm a Muslim, but I couldn't live with this view of Islam."

Naim's quandary over Islam was an intensely personal conflict — he called it a "deadlock." What he heard at Taha's lecture resolved it. Taha said that the Sudanese constitution needed to be reformed, in order to reconcile "the individual's need for absolute freedom with the community's need for total social justice." This political ideal, he argued, could be best achieved not through Marxism or liberalism but through Islam — that is, Islam in its original, uncorrupted form, in which women and people of other faiths were accorded equal status. As Naim listened, a profound sense of peace washed over him; he joined Taha's movement, which came to be known as the Republican Brothers, and the night that had begun so idly changed his life.

It is a revelation story, and some version of it is surprisingly easy to hear in the Islamic world, especially among educated middle-class Muslims in the generation that came after the failures of nationalism and Socialism. During a recent trip to Sudan, I visited the University of Khartoum, which is housed in a collection of mostly colonial-era, earth-colored brick buildings in the city center, where I met a woman named Suhair Osman, who was doing graduate work in statistics. In 1993, at the age of eighteen, she spent the year between high school and college in her parents' house on the Blue Nile, south of Khartoum, asking herself theological questions. As a schoolgirl, she had been taught that sinners would be eternally tormented after death; she couldn't help feeling sorry for them, but she didn't dare speak about it in class. Would all of creation simply end either in fire or in Paradise? Was her worth as a woman really no more than a quarter that of a man, as she felt Islamic law implied by granting men the right to take four wives? Did believers really have a duty to kill infidels? One day, Osman took a book by Taha off her father's shelf, *The Koran, Mustapha Mahmoud, and Modern Understanding*, published in 1970. By the time she finished it, she was weeping. For the first time, she felt that religion had accorded her fully equal status. "Inside this thinking, I'm a human being," she said. "Outside this thinking, I'm not." It was as if she had been asleep all her life and had suddenly woken up: the air, the taste of water, food, even the smell of things changed. She felt as if she were walking a little off the ground.

The quest for spiritual meaning is typically a personal matter in the West. In the Islamic world, it often leads the seeker into some kind of collective action, informed by utopian aspiration, that admits no distinction between proselytizing, social reform, and politics. The Islamic revival of the past several decades is the history of millions of revelation stories. Far from being idiosyncratic or marginal, they have combined into a tremendous surge that is now a full-time concern of the West. Renewal and reform — in Arabic, *tajdid* and *islah* — have an ambiguous and contested meaning in the Islamic world. They signify a stripping away of accumulated misreadings and wrong or lapsed practices, as in the Protestant Reformation, and a return to the founding texts of the Koran and the Sunna — guidelines based on the recorded words and deeds of the Prophet. But, beyond that, what is the nature of the reform? The father of one modern revelation story is Sayyid Qutb, the Egyptian religious thinker who, after advocating jihad and the overthrow of secular Arab regimes, was hanged by Gamal Abdel Nasser in 1966. Qutb's prison writings reject modernity, with its unholy secularism, and call on adherents of Islam to return to a radically purified version of the religion, which was established in the seventh century. Among the idealistic young believers who found in his books a guide to worldwide Islamization were Ayman al-Zawahiri and Osama bin Laden. With the newest generation of jihadis — Qutb's spiritual grandchildren — the ideas of the master have been construed as a justification for killing just about anyone in the name of reviving the days of the Prophet; earlier this year, several Baghdad falafel vendors were killed by Islamists because falafel did not exist in the seventh century.

Mahmoud Muhammad Taha is the anti-Qutb. Taha, like Qutb, was hanged by an Arab dictatorship; he was executed, in 1985, for sedition and apostasy, after protesting the imposition of Sharia in Sudan by President Jaafar al-Nimeiri. In death, Taha became something rare in contemporary Islam: a moderate martyr. His method of reconciling Muslim belief with twentieth-century values was, in its way, every bit as revolutionary as the contrary vision of Qutb. It is one sign of the current state of the struggle over Islam that, in the five years since September 11, millions of people around the world have learned the name Sayyid Qutb while Mahmoud Muhammad Taha's is virtually unknown. Islamism has taken on the frightening and faceless aspect of the masked jihadi, the full-length veil, the religious militia, the blurred figure in a security video, the messianic head of state, the anti-American mob. At Islam's core, in the countries of the Middle East from Egypt to Iran, *tajdid* and *islah* have helped push societies toward extremes of fervor, repression, and violence. But on the periphery, from Senegal to Indonesia — where the vast majority of Muslims live — Islamic reform comes in more varieties than most Westerners imagine. At the edges, the influence of American policy and the Israeli-Palestinian siege is less overwhelming, and it is easier to see that the real drama in Islam is the essential dilemma addressed by Taha: how to revive ancient sacred texts in a way that allows one to live in the modern world.

Taha was born sometime early in the twentieth century — scholars say 1909 or 1911 — in a town on the eastern bank of the Blue Nile, two hours south of Khartoum, called Rufaa. It is a somnolent, heat-drenched town, one of those silent places — they stretch from one harsh end to the other of the North African region known as the Sahel — where mystical movements often begin. In the years before Sudan's independence, Taha was educated as a civil engineer in a British-run university, and after working briefly for Sudan Railways he started his own engineering business. He absorbed modern political and social ideas by reading widely, if incompletely, in the works of Marx, Lenin, Russell, Shaw, and Wells. In 1945, he founded an anti-monarchical political group, the Republican Party, and was twice imprisoned by the British authorities: first for writing pro-independence pamphlets, and then for leading an uprising in Rufaa against the arrest of a local woman who had subjected her daughter to a particularly severe form of female circumcision. (Taha opposed the practice but believed that the colonial edict banning it would only make it more widespread.) His second imprisonment lasted two years, and when he was released, in 1948, he entered a period of seclusion, prayer, and fasting in a small mud building in the courtyard next to his in-laws' house. By the time I visited Rufaa, in July, the hut had been torn down and replaced, and the house was occupied by a family of southern Sudanese.

While in seclusion, Taha spoke to few people; one man described him as having long, unruly hair and bloodshot eyes. His wife brought him plates of simple food — her family urged her to divorce this formerly successful professional, who some people thought had gone mad, but she refused — and he left the hut only to take swims in the Nile, a short walk away. During this period, which lasted three years, Taha developed his radically new vision of the meaning of the Koran. After emerging from seclusion, in 1951, he dedicated the rest of his life to teaching it.

For any Muslim who believes in universal human rights, tolerance, equality, freedom, and democracy, the Koran presents an apparently insoluble problem. Some of its verses carry commands that violate a modern person's sense of morality. The Koran accepts slavery. The Koran appoints men to be "the protectors and maintainers of women," to whom women owe obedience; if disobeyed, men have the duty first to warn them, then to deny them sex, and finally to "beat them (lightly)." The Koran orders believers to wait until the holy months are finished, and then to "fight and slay the Pagans wherever you find them, and seize them, beleaguer them, and lie in wait for them in every stratagem (of war)." These and other verses present God's purpose in clear, unmistakable terms, and they have become some of the favorite passages in the sermons, fatwas, and Internet postings of present-day fundamentalists to justify violence and jihad. An enormous industry of reform-minded interpreters has arisen in recent years to explain them away, contextualize them, downplay them, or simply ignore them, often quoting the well-known verse that says there is "no compulsion in religion." Not long ago, I received one such lecture from a Shiite cleric in Baghdad, who cited the "no compulsion" verse while sitting under a portrait of Ayatollah Khomeini. In confronting the troublesome verses head on, Taha showed more intellectual honesty than all the Islamic scholars, community leaders, and world statesmen who think that they have solved the problem by flatly declaring Islam to be a religion of peace.

The Koran was revealed to Muhammad in two phases — first in Mecca, where for thirteen years he and his followers were a besieged minority, and then in Medina, where the Prophet established Islamic rule in a city filled with Jews and pagans. The Meccan verses are addressed, through Muhammad, to humanity in general, and are suffused with a spirit of freedom and equality; according to Taha, they present Islam in its perfect form, as the Prophet lived it, through exhortation rather than threat. In Taha's most important book, a slender volume called *The Second Message of Islam* (published in 1967, with the dedication "To humanity!"), he writes that the lives of the "early Muslims" in Mecca "were the supreme expression of their religion and consisted of sincere worship, kindness, and peaceful coexistence with all other people." Abdullahi an-Naim, who is now a law professor at Emory University, translated the book into English; in his introduction, he writes, "Islam, being the final and universal religion according to Muslim belief, was offered first in tolerant and egalitarian terms in Mecca, where the Prophet preached equality and individual responsibility between all men and women without distinction on grounds of race, sex, or social origin. As that message was rejected in practice, and the Prophet and his few followers were persecuted and forced to migrate to Medina, some aspects of the message changed."

As Taha puts it in *The Second Message of Islam,* whereas Muhammad propagated "verses of peaceful persuasion" during his Meccan period, in Medina "the verses of compulsion by the sword prevailed." The Medinan verses are full of rules, coercion, and threats, including the orders for jihad, and in Taha's view they were a historical adaptation to the reality of life in a seventh-century Islamic city-state, in which "there was no law except the sword." At one point, Taha writes that two modest decrees of the Meccan verses — "You are only a reminder, you have no dominion over them" — were appended with a harsh Medinan edict: "Except he who shuns and disbelieves, on whom God shall inflict the greatest suffering." In his distinctive rhetorical style, which combines dense exegesis with humanistic uplift, Taha observed, "It is as if God had said, 'We have granted you, Muhammad, dominion over anyone who shuns and disbelieves, so that God shall subject him to minor suffering at your hands through fighting, then God shall also subject him to the greatest suffering in hell.' . . . Thus the first two verses were abrogated or repealed by the two second verses."

The Medinan verses, directed not to Muhammad alone but to the community of early believers, became the basis for Sharia as it was developed by legal scholars over the next few centuries — what Taha calls the "first message of Islam." In Taha's revisionist reading, the elevation of the Medinan verses was only a historical postponement — the Meccan verses, representing the ideal religion, would be revived when humanity had reached a stage of development capable of accepting them, ushering in a renewed Islam based on freedom and equality. Taha quoted a Hadith, or saying of the Prophet, that declared, "Islam started as a stranger, and it shall return as a stranger in the same way it started." This "second message of Islam" is higher and better than the first, delivered by a messenger who came to seventh-century Arabia, in a sense, from the future. And, in the twentieth century, the time had come for Muslims finally to receive it. Taha offered a hermeneutical way out of the modern crisis of Islam, allowing Muslims to affirm their faith without having to live by an inhumane code.

*

Taha's reputation and importance far exceeded his actual following, which never amounted to more than a few thousand intensely devoted Sudanese: the stories of overwhelming personal transformation that I heard from Naim, Osman, and other Republican Brothers were apparently common among his adherents. (Taha adapted the name of his old political party for his new spiritual movement; he was wary of substituting Islamist slogans for critical thinking.) He received visitors at his house in Omdurman, northwest of Khartoum, at all hours, engaging in a kind of continuous seminar in which he was unmistakably the instructor — Republican Brothers still call him Ustazh, or "revered teacher" — but one who welcomed argument. "He would listen with utmost respect," a follower named Omer el-Garrai told me. "I never saw him frustrated, I never saw him angry, I never heard him shout." Naim recalled, "Taha could not transmit his religious enlightenment to us by talking about it. We would see the fruit of it by his personal lifestyle, in his attitudes. His honesty, his intellectual vigor, his serenity, his charisma — those are the things that we can observe, and from them I understood that this is someone who had a transformative religious experience." Taha lived simply, urging his followers to do the same, and even today Republican Brothers are known for their lack of show in dress and in wedding ceremonies. An aura of saintliness hangs over stories I heard about Taha in Sudan, and, as with Gandhi, to whom he is sometimes compared, there's an unappealingly remote quality to his moral example. A man named Anour Hassan recalled that when Taha's twelve-year-old son vanished in the Blue Nile, in 1954, Taha calmly told people who wanted to continue looking for the boy, "No, he's gone to a kinder father than I am."

Perhaps the twentieth century was too soon for the second message of Islam. Taha was condemned for apostasy by Sudanese and Egyptian clerics, his movement was under constant attack from the fundamentalist Muslim Brotherhood, and his public appearances were banned by the government. Various rumors began to circulate: that Taha and his followers believed him to be a new prophet, or even a divinity; that Taha didn't pray; that he was insane. His legacy became controversial even among liberal-minded Sudanese. One evening in July, I spoke with the moderate politician and intellectual Sadiq al-Mahdi on the terrace overlooking the garden of his palatial home in Omdurman. Mahdi, who twice served as prime minister of Sudan and was twice ousted, in 1967 and 1989, is an imposing man: he was wearing the traditional white djellabah and turban, and his beard was hennaed. He spoke respectfully of Taha but found him theologically unsound. "Amongst the Islamists, there are those who jump into the future and those who jump into the past," Mahdi said, comparing Taha with Qutb. "Taha is amongst those who jump into the future. He definitely is for radical Islamic reform. But he based it on arguments that are not legitimate." Mahdi, like many other modern Muslim thinkers, believes that the Koran already offers the basis for affirming democratic values; there is no need, as he put it, to perform "these somersaults."

What's truly remarkable about Taha is that he existed at all. In the midst of a gathering storm of Islamist extremism, he articulated a message of liberal reform that was rigorous, coherent, and courageous. His vision asked Muslims to abandon fourteen hundred years of accepted dogma in favor of a radical and demanding new methodology that would set them free from the burdens of traditional jurisprudence. Islamic law, with its harsh punishments and its repression of free thought, was, Taha argued, a human interpretation of the Medinan verses and the recorded words and deeds of the Prophet in Medina; developed in the early centuries after Muhammad, it was then closed off to critical revision for a millennium. When Taha spoke of "Sharia," he meant the enlightened message of the Meccan verses, which is universal and eternal. To Muslims like Mahdi, this vision seemed to declare that part of the holy book was a mistake. Taha's message requires of Muslims such an intellectual leap that those who actually made it — as opposed to those who merely admired Taha or were interested in him — took on the quality of cult members, with their white garments, street-corner sermons, and egalitarian marriage contracts. Small wonder that Taha failed to create a durable mass movement. In *Quest for Divinity,* a new and generally sympathetic study of Taha to be published this fall, Professor Mohamed A. Mahmoud, of Tufts University, writes, "The outcome of this culture of guardianship and total intellectual dependency was a movement with impoverished inner intellectual and spiritual resources, intrinsically incapable of surviving Taha's death."

Why did the Sudanese state, the religious establishment, and the

Islamist hardliners consider the leader of such a small movement worth killing? Perhaps because, as Khalid el-Haj, a retired school administrator in Rufaa, who first met Taha in the early sixties, told me, "They are afraid of the ideas, not the numbers. They know that the ideas are from inside Islam and they cannot face it."

Eventually, Taha's teaching collided with Islamist power politics. Sudan's military dictator, Jaafar al-Nimeiri, who had seized control of the country in 1969, was an opportunistic tyrant who had exhausted one model after another to justify his rule: Marxism, Arab nationalism, pro-Americanism. By the early eighties, Nimeiri's hold on power was loosening, and he felt particularly threatened by one of his advisers: Hasan al-Turabi, the legal scholar, who had an increasingly energetic Islamist following. Turabi, a brilliant politician with a British and French education, was an authoritarian ideologue, more in the mold of a Bolshevik than a hidebound cleric. One of Turabi's prime intellectual enemies was Taha, whose interpretation of the Koran he considered illegitimate. Taha, for his part, once dismissed Turabi as "clever but not insightful" — and many Sudanese believe that Turabi never forgot the slight.

In 1983, Nimeiri, aiming to counter Turabi's growing popularity, decided to make his own Islamic claim. He hastily pushed through laws that imposed a severe version of Sharia on Sudan, including its Christian and animist south. Within eighteen months, the hands of more than fifty suspected thieves were chopped off. A Coptic Christian was hanged for possessing foreign currency; poor women were flogged for selling local beer. It was exactly the kind of brutal, divisive, politically motivated Sharia that Taha had long warned against, and southerners intensified a decades-long civil war against Khartoum. Taha and other Republican Brothers, including Naim, had been jailed in advance by Nimeiri to prevent them from leading protests; their imprisonment lasted a year and a half.

Soon after Taha was released, he distributed a leaflet, on Christmas Day, 1984, titled "Either This or the Flood." "It is futile for anyone to claim that a Christian person is not adversely affected by the implementation of Sharia," he wrote. "It is not enough for a citizen today merely to enjoy freedom of worship. He is entitled to the full rights of a citizen in total equality with all other citizens. The rights of southern citizens in their country are not provided for in Sharia but rather in Islam at the level of fundamental Koranic revelation."

Taha, who was now in his midseventies, had been preparing half his life for this moment. It was central to his vision that Islamic law in its historical form, rather than in what he considered its original, authentic meaning, would be a monstrous injustice in modern society. His opposition was brave and absolute, and yet his statement reveals the limits of a philosophy that he hoped to make universal. Taha opposed secularism — he once declared that the secular West "is not a civilization because its values are confused" — and he could not conceive of rights outside the framework of Islam and the Koran. At the very moment that he was defending nonbelievers from the second-class status enshrined in Islamic law, he was extending their equal rights through a higher, better Sharia.

Abdullahi an-Naim defends Taha's approach, saying that in the Islamic world a Turkish-style secularism will always be self-defeating. "It is an illusion to think you can sustain constitutionalism, democratization, without addressing its Islamic foundation," he said. "Because for Muslims you cannot say, 'I'm a Muslim, but —' That 'but' does not work. What unites Muslims is an idea. It is Islam as an idea. And therefore contesting that idea, I think, is going to be permanent." Whenever secular intellectuals in Muslim countries try to bypass the question of Sharia, Naim said, "they leave the high moral ground to the fundamentalists, and they lose." Invoking Islam as the highest authority for universal rights was not simply a matter of belief; it meant that Taha and his movement could stay in the game.

Soon after Taha's Christmas statement was released, he was arrested again. This time, the government pressed charges amounting to apostasy, which carried the death penalty. Taha refused to recognize the legitimacy of the court under Sharia, refused to repent, and in a matter of hours was condemned to death. The hanging was scheduled for the morning of January 18, 1985. Among the hundreds of spectators in the vast courtyard of Kober Prison, in Khartoum North, was Judith Miller, then a *Times* reporter, disguised in a white cloak and head scarf. In the opening of her 1996 book, *God Has Ninety-nine Names,* Miller described the scene:

> Shortly before the appointed time, Mahmoud Muhammad Taha was led into the courtyard. The condemned man, his hands tied behind him, was smaller than I expected him to be, and from where I sat, as his guards hustled him along, he looked younger than his seventy-six years.

He held his head high and stared silently into the crowd. When they saw him, many in the crowd leaped to their feet, jeering and shaking their fists at him. A few waved their Korans in the air.

I managed to catch only a glimpse of Taha's face before the executioner placed an oatmeal-colored sack over his head and body, but I shall never forget his expression: His eyes were defiant; his mouth firm. He showed no hint of fear.

In the instant that the trapdoor opened and Taha's body fell through, the crowd began to scream, *"Allahu Akbar! Allahu Akbar! Islam huwa al-hall!"* — "God is great! Islam is the solution!" — the slogan of the Muslim Brotherhood.

Some of Taha's followers could not accept that he was dead — they had actually come to believe in Taha's divinity — and they spent several days by one of the bridges spanning the Nile, waiting for him to appear. When he didn't (his body was flown by helicopter to an unknown location in the desert for a hasty burial), the Republican Brotherhood essentially died. Some members, including Naim, went abroad; others stayed in Sudan but ceased any public activity. The regime forced a number of imprisoned Republican Brothers to repudiate Taha's ideas in order to avoid his fate. His books were burned in public bonfires.

The execution appalled large numbers of Sudanese, who were unused to political violence, and it helped precipitate the downfall of Nimeiri, four months later, when a popular uprising restored democratic rule. January 18 became Arab Human Rights Day. In 2000, a Sudanese reporter asked Nimeiri about the death of Taha. Nimeiri expressed regret over the killing, then made a startling claim: Taha's execution had been secretly engineered by Hasan al-Turabi.

"I didn't want him killed," Nimeiri said of Taha. "Turabi told me that Mahmoud Muhammad Taha wanted to side with the left against me and that the Republican Brothers are a force not to be underestimated, and that if he united with the left I am definitely doomed. Turabi brought me the order to execute him and asked me to sign off on it . . . I decided to postpone my decision for two days, and on the third day I went to Taha, dressed in civilian clothes. I told him, 'Your death would sadden me. Just back down on your decision.' But he spoke to me in a way that at the time I felt was blustering but now I see it was honorable, considering the situation. He told me, '*You* back down on *your* decision. As for me, I

know that I'm going to be killed. If I'm not killed in court, the Muslim Brotherhood will kill me in secret. So leave and let me be. I
know that I am going to die.'"

I asked a number of people in Khartoum about the role that
Turabi might have played in Taha's death. "Turabi killed him" was
the blunt verdict of Hyder Ibrahim Ali, a sociologist and the director of the Sudanese Studies Center. "I think Turabi was behind all
this. Taha was a real rival for Turabi. At that time, the only people
at the University of Khartoum as strong as the Muslim Brotherhood
were the Republican Brothers." Others echoed this view: even if
Turabi hadn't played a direct role in Taha's death, Taha's reform-
minded movement had offered the most serious theological challenge to Turabi's severe Islamism.

In the decade after Taha's death, Turabi and his hard-line politics flourished. In 1989, he was the prime strategist of the Islamist
revolution that followed the military overthrow of Prime Minister Sadiq al-Mahdi. He became the intellectual architect of the new
regime, led by Omar al-Bashir, and presided over its reign of terror in the nineties. He was the impresario who attracted just about
every leading jihadi terrorist to Sudan; journalists started calling
him "the Khomeini of the Sunnis" and "the pope of terrorism."
In 1999, however, Turabi's fortunes abruptly changed: he lost a
power struggle with Bashir, who fired him.

This spring, Turabi, in a striking return to Sudanese politics, said
some astonishing things about Islam. Though he had always been
more supportive of women's rights than were other hardliners, he
was now declaring that women and men are equal, that women can
lead Islamic prayers, that covering the hair is not obligatory, that
apostasy should not be a crime. He said that Muslim women can
marry Christians or Jews. Quotations in the Arab press made him
sound like a liberal reformer. In Khartoum, people marveled that
he sounded exactly like Taha. Suhair Osman, the young woman I
met at the University of Khartoum, informed me, with a wan smile,
"It is said in the daily papers and in the discussion centers here in
the university that Turabi killed Ustazh Mahmoud and now he's
stealing his ideas."

In the next few decades, several Arab countries — Iraq, Palestine,
perhaps Egypt and Algeria — may well come under some form of

Islamist rule, either by election or by force. If so, they would do well to study the example of Sudan. A whole generation in Sudan has grown up under the hard-line ideology that was imposed by Turabi and his colleagues after 1989. "We are the wounded surgeons, we have had the plague," Sadiq al-Mahdi told me. "We have been the guinea pig of this whole exercise, and you should listen to us."

Islam is as diverse as Muslims themselves, but Islamism, thus far in its short history, tends to look the same wherever it appears. The Sudanese version was not a genuine revolution like the Iranian one; it was more of an elite project that never gained legitimacy outside of student, intellectual, and military circles. Still, Sudan's hard-line party, the National Islamic Front, marched the country through familiar paces. Suliman Baldo, the director of the Africa program at the International Crisis Group, who lived through the years of Islamization in Khartoum and published a report documenting the return of slavery in Sudan, said of the government, "They came with a social-engineering project — they were very open about this." Education became a form of indoctrination: small children learned jihadist chants; school uniforms were replaced with combat fatigues; students engaged in paramilitary drills and memorized the Koran; teachers overhauled the curriculum to focus on the glory of Arab and Islamic culture. Khartoum had been a socially relaxed city that celebrated Christmas, but now the morals police ensured that women were veiled, especially in government offices and universities. The security agencies were taken over by Islamists, and torture chambers known as "ghost houses" proliferated in what had been a tolerant political culture. (Some torturers were reportedly trained by Iranian Revolutionary Guards.) Young men were conscripted into the new People's Defense Force and sent to fight in the jihad against the infidels of the south, thousands of them crying "*Allahu Akbar!*" as they went to their deaths. Turabi declared that the jihadis would ascend directly to Paradise. Actors simulated "weddings" between martyrs and heavenly virgins on state television. Turabi gave asylum and assistance to terrorists, including bin Laden and other Al Qaeda members, and Sudan soon made enemies of every one of its many neighbors, along with the United States. And so an ethnically and religiously mixed African country, with an egalitarian brand of Sufism as its dominant form of Islam, was mobilized by intellectuals and soldiers to create a militaristic, ideologically extreme state whose main achievements were civil war, slavery, famine, and mass death.

Sometime in the late nineties, Turabi realized that his grand enterprise was a failure. Sudan had come under United Nations sanctions for sponsoring a 1995 assassination attempt on President Hosni Mubarak, of Egypt. The country was internationally isolated; the civil war was killing millions. And the Islamist project was bankrupt. As in Iran, it had produced an increasingly wealthy and corrupt ruling class of ideologues and security officers, while young Sudanese, including many of Turabi's followers, left the country or turned inward.

It was at this low point that Omar al-Bashir expelled Turabi from the government. Until last year, Turabi found himself in and out of jail, and he began to rethink his politics. He declared that the war in the south had not been a jihad after all but, rather, a meaningless waste. In prison, he began to write about where the Islamists had gone wrong. The problem, he decided, was a failure to adhere to principles of democracy and human rights. This spring, Turabi began attracting attention with his liberal statements about women and Islam. He welcomed the deployment of a United Nations force to the Darfur region, where the government had launched a campaign of ethnic cleansing, and he mocked bin Laden for threatening to mount a jihad against the peacekeepers. (Some analysts believe that Turabi had a hand in the rebellion that preceded the mass killings in the region, but no one has been able to prove it.) His remarks were so radical that they earned him charges of apostasy by clerics in Sudan and Saudi Arabia. The Saudi edition of the Sudanese newspaper that quoted his proclamations had the offending lines torn out of every copy.

In Khartoum, people used the same phrase over and over: there had been "a hundred-and-eighty-degree turn" in Turabi's views. I heard several explanations. Sadiq al-Mahdi, the former prime minister, believed that Turabi was trying to atone for the damage he had inflicted on Sudan. Others saw old opportunism under new slogans: Turabi realized that, thanks to Islamist misrule, democracy would be the next wave in Sudan, and he wanted to get out in front of it. There was also the possibility that he couldn't bear to be ignored.

One day in late July, during a hard Sahara windstorm that obscured the merciless sun and left sand in my molars, Turabi received me in his office on the outskirts of Khartoum, beyond the airport. I found him sitting behind a vast desk, which was almost bare; so were the bookcases next to it, as if he were waiting for someone to refurnish the trappings of power. Turabi is now seventy-four years old. He has a trim white beard and bright eyes framed by elegant wire-rim glasses; he wore a white djellabah and turban, white patent-leather loafers, and flower-patterned polyester socks. He has a resonant voice, which, when the topic turns serious, often breaks into a disconcerting giggle, accompanied by a bucktoothed grin. Turabi is inexhaustible: before I arrived, he had spoken for three days to members of his breakaway political party, but he required scarcely any prompting to carry on a nearly three-hour monologue with me. It was like trying to follow the flight path of a mosquito: he would leave sentences unfinished, switch subjects in the span of a clause, swallow the point in a laugh, then suddenly alight somewhere — on hidebound Saudi clerics, clueless Algerian Islamists, pigheaded Sudanese soldiers, shortsighted American politicians — and draw blood.

Turabi presented himself as older but wiser, free now to be the one independent thinker in a world of ideologues, an emissary for both sides in the war between Islam and the West, unafraid of uttering any truth, including truths about his own mistakes — but whenever I tried to pin him down on one he blamed someone else and claimed that his role was exaggerated. "Oh, Turabi, he's the 'pope of terrorism,' of fundamentalism, the pope *noir du terrorisme!*" he mocked. The Bush administration's war on terror, he said, was a gigantic misunderstanding based on a failure to communicate. As for the Islamic revival, it held no dangers for the West. "Oh, no, it's positive!" he said. "What is our economic model? It's not the Soviet model. It's not the old capitalist model, or the feudal model. It's your model! What is our political model? It's *your* model! Almost the same model! Okay?"

Toward the end of his discourse, I mentioned that a number of Sudanese had heard echoes of Mahmoud Muhammad Taha in his recent statements. For the first time, Turabi lost his good humor. "Ooh," he groaned. He called Taha "an apostate" who was "not normal," and he insisted that, far from being behind Taha's death, he had argued with Nimeiri for his life: "I said, 'Why do you jail this

man? He won't hurt you, he's not against this regime. He thinks
he's the impersonation of Jesus Christ!'" Turabi laughed dismiss-
ively. "I said, 'Let him go and advocate his message. He will persuade a few people for some time. He's not harmful to you.'" He
said of Taha, "From early days, I don't read his books, I don't mention his name. Even if people ask me questions, I try to evade, because in every society, in America, you have had these cult people
— everyone has to drink the killing material! Jim Jones!"

Turabi giggled and stood up to say goodbye.

When I had asked Abdullahi an-Naim about Turabi's recent statements on women, minorities, and Islam, he had scoffed, "He has
no *methodology*." It was true: Turabi threw out opinions like hand-
fuls of seed. But, as Taha had said, the one constant in his long career has been cleverness. Turabi seemed to recognize that, in the
ruins of his own making in Sudan, his countrymen required a new
notion of Islam and government. Great turns in history seldom
come because someone writes a manifesto or proposes a theory. Instead, concrete experience, usually in the form of catastrophic failure, forces people to search for new ideas, many of which have
been lying around for quite a while. Naim, who had fled the country after the 1989 coup, went back to Sudan in 2003 to find that
"people were totally disillusioned about the Islamist project. They
could see that it was corrupting and corrupt." In reaction, a small
but growing number of Sudanese have come under the influence
of Saudi Wahhabism — turning to an even more extreme theology
as the pure Islam. Others, such as Osman Mirghani, a newspaper
columnist and a former follower of Turabi, have concluded that
the problem in Sudan has less to do with religion than with its civic
culture. Mirghani has formed a new citizens' movement, Sudan Fo-
rum, waging its first campaign against corruption in high places.

Taha's solution to the modern Muslim dilemma hovers over the
conversations of Sudanese who are too young to have any memory
of him. In a dingy office in downtown Khartoum, I met a man
named Hussein and a woman named Buthina, two social activists
who are just the kind of idealists that the Islamists used to attract.
In 1989, as a teenager, Hussein had at first welcomed the new government. He soon realized that its promises of Islamic justice were
false, and he was traumatized by the year he spent as a conscript in
the jihad against the south. "In my view, this regime is a great

shame in the history of Islam," he said. "It's pushed people away from Islam. Their mentality has changed. They are no longer abiding by Islamic regulations." He mentioned prostitution, drinking, and corruption. For all Hussein's disillusionment, he still believed in Sharia — in flogging for fornication, stoning for adultery, and beheading for apostasy — but he wanted it to be applied under a democratic government grounded in human rights. Buthina shook her head; Islamist rule had turned her toward secularism. "This is a very, very sensitive issue," she said. "When you design your regulations and constitution, you have to accept that all the people look at this constitution and see themselves in it. Otherwise, they will not implement it. If we design the constitution and the law of the country on Islam, this will create a problem."

When I described Hussein to Naim, he said, "He sees the corruption of the current regime, and he sees the unworkability of an Islamic state, but he has no alternative. That is the point about Taha. Taha provides an alternative. As the crisis intensifies, the receptivity to something like Taha's ideas will grow." The misrule of Turabi and the Sudanese Islamists, Naim said, had done more to advance the project of reforming Sharia than Taha's followers could ever have achieved. At the same time, he admitted that most people in Sudan today have never heard of Taha. All that is left of his movement is a few hundred followers, some of whom gather in the evenings at a house in Omdurman. I was invited to join them there one night: the men sat in chairs on one side of the courtyard, the women on the other, but they mixed more than the religious Muslims at most gatherings. All dressed in white, they chanted traditional Sufi songs and a mournful hymn about their martyred leader.

The hollowness at the core of Sudan, and the widespread cynicism about Islamist rule, with its enforced ideology and rituals, is reminiscent of Eastern Europe in the years before the fall of the Berlin Wall. But if you spend time in an Islamic country you soon realize that the Communism analogy runs dry. For Islam, unlike Marxism, is deeply rooted and still present in everyday life in profound ways. As such, it is an irresistible mobilizing tool for politicians: an Islamist leader in Morocco, Nadia Yassin, once said, "If I go into the streets and I call people to come with me to a demonstration, and

I talk to them about Che Guevara and Lenin, nobody will go out. But if I start talking about Muhammad and Ali and Aisha and all the prophets of Islam, they will follow me." Islam remains the system of values by which Muslims live; it is strong enough to survive Islamism. Perhaps, in time, the religion's centrality will subside, but, for the foreseeable future, the Islamic enlightenment in which so many Western thinkers have placed their hopes — that is, secularism — will not sweep the Muslim world. The Islamic revival, and its attendant struggles and ills, is less like the eighteenth century in Europe than like the sixteenth, the age of Luther, when the most sensitive and ambitious Englishmen, Frenchmen, and Germans devoted their efforts to finding in the words of the Bible a meaning for which they were prepared to live and die.

On the wall of Naim's office at Emory University, just above a picture of his parents, there is a black-and-white portrait of Taha in old age, seated, with the folds of a white robe draped over his shoulders and the Sudanese turban wrapped around his head; his gaze is both direct and abstracted, taking in something far beyond the camera. Ever since the night Naim attended Taha's lecture as a young law student, he has believed that Muslims must find a way out of the predicament in which their own history has placed them — if not by accepting Taha's vision, then by working toward another.

"I don't really have high hopes for change in the Arab region, because it is too self-absorbed in its own sense of superiority and victimhood," he said. His hope lies in the periphery — West Africa, the Sahel, Central and Southeast Asia: "They are not noticed, but that's where the hope is." The damage done to Muslim lives under the slogan "Islam is the solution," and Islamism's failure to solve their daily problems and answer people's deepest needs, has forced younger Muslims in countries like Indonesia, Turkey, and Morocco to approach religion and politics in a more sophisticated way. Naim's newest project, which he calls a work of advocacy more than of scholarship, is a manuscript called *The Future of Sharia*. Even before its English publication, he has begun to post it on the Web, translated into Persian, Urdu, Bengali, Turkish, Arabic, and Bahasa Indonesia. Its theme is more radical than anything he has written before; although it is based on his long devotion to Taha's ideas, it goes beyond them and, according to some of Taha's followers, leaves them behind. *The Future of Sharia* amounts to a kind of secularism: it proposes not a rigid separation of politics and religion, as in Turkey, but rather a scheme in which Islam informs political life but cannot be introduced into law by an appeal to any religious authority. Otherwise, Muslims would not be free. "I need a secular state to be a Muslim," Naim said. "If I don't have the freedom to disbelieve, I cannot believe."

Two days after we spoke, Naim flew to Nigeria to give a series of lectures, based on the new book, in the northern states that have imposed a particularly harsh form of Sharia. He plans to travel next year to Indonesia and, if possible, to Iran. Two years ago, when he lectured in northern Nigeria, a quarter of his audience of eight hundred people walked out on him, and he had to slip away through a side door. He acknowledged that violence, even murder, might be the response this time. But Naim believes that, despite the evidence of the headlines, Islamic history is moving in his direction.

"In Sudan this simplistic answer failed," Naim said. "In Iran it failed. In northern Nigeria it failed. In Pakistan it failed. As these experiences fail, people are going to realize that there is no shortcut — that you have to confront the hard questions." His message to Muslims on his travels will be this: "I have been that way and I've seen the street is closed and I came back. And I see someone rushing and I tell him, this street is deadlocked, and he will not take my word and go all the way and discover that it is deadlocked and come back." He will tell them, "Listen, you don't have to do this, you don't have to go down this dead-end street. There is an Arabic expression: 'The fortunate ones will learn from the mistakes of others, the unfortunate ones will learn from their own mistakes.'"

By taking his message to the Muslim public and risking his own life, Naim is, perhaps unconsciously, following the example of one of the intellectual heroes of modern Islam. The first years of the twenty-first century hardly seem hospitable to Mahmoud Muhammad Taha's humane vision, but his words are there for young Muslims to discover once they get to the end of the street and need a way to turn around.

SRIDHAR PAPPU

The Preacher

FROM *The Atlantic Monthly*

LAST NOVEMBER 2, in a city that had long ago lost its way and its strength and its ability to rise up, they mourned her. A half-century earlier, on a December evening in 1955, Rosa Parks had refused to give up her seat on a bus to a white man in Montgomery, Alabama, and had become the catalyst for a civil-rights revolution whose iconic moments were captured forever in the grainy footage of black-and-white television. Her refusal to move sparked marches by demonstrators and, in response, violent reprisals by white policemen and others. As a consequence, America was finally moved to begin to address in a serious way the corrosive problems of race at the nation's core. Rosa Parks had been a seamstress before becoming a symbol, and her actions gave powerful emotional impetus to the efforts of leaders like Martin Luther King Jr. and Medgar Evers, John Lewis and Whitney Young Jr. But now, in her ninety-second year, Parks was dead, and an entire era of the civil-rights movement seemed to be going to its grave with her.

Barbara Tuchman, in her book *The Guns of August,* describes the elaborate funeral of England's King Edward VII, in 1910, when the crowned heads of Europe gathered peacefully for one last time before the world was changed utterly by the onset of war. And so it was, in its way, at the Greater Grace Temple, in Detroit, where four thousand people assembled inside for the funeral service, and thousands more held vigil outside. Within the temple you would have seen Louis Farrakhan and Al Sharpton side by side, and you would have seen most of the rest of America's black leadership — people like Congressmen John Conyers and Danny Davis and Senator Barack Obama. There were a lot of white faces there, too — Bill and Hillary Clinton, John Kerry, Michigan governor Jennifer Granholm. You would have heard remarks from the pulpit by Joseph E. Lowery, the former head of the Southern Christian Leadership Conference, and a thundering solo by Aretha Franklin. You would have heard from Bernice King, one of the four children of Martin Luther King. The service lasted for seven hours. Jesse Jackson reminded those in the pews that "some people's lives are worthy of taking the time to say goodbye."

Sitting on the podium with Jackson during the service was a black preacher from Dallas named Thomas Dexter Jakes. T. D. Jakes, as he is popularly called, had visited with Parks a few years before, at her home in Detroit, and now here he was, given a place of honor with Jackson, who for some decades has been the unofficial and presumptive inheritor of King's mantle. And although his own remarks were brief — Jakes spoke of how much he and his generation owed to Parks — make no mistake: this is where Jakes belonged. He, too, is inheriting a mantle, very possibly the same one worn by Jackson.

T. D. Jakes, forty-eight, a child of the civil-rights movement, both epitomizes and stands at the front of a new generation of black leadership. His methods are not those of the 1950s or 1960s, the methods of political organizing or civil disobedience or black power. He has, rather, built a thirty-thousand-member nondenominational church, called the Potter's House, in the Pentecostal tradition, and alongside this church he has built a lucrative multimedia empire, TDJ Enterprises, that produces books and DVDs and a variety of other faith-based products, all of which has made Jakes a multimillionaire. Under the auspices of his church he holds "conferences" that are more like revival meetings — hundreds of thousands of people annually flock to arenas across the country to hear his message about finding the path toward self-healing and economic empowerment, and about how only Jesus can provide the strength to go down that path and to cope with the issues that arise when you do so.

Unlike black leaders such as Jackson and Obama, who are Democrats, or Condoleezza Rice and Alan Keyes, who are Republicans, Jakes is without political affiliation, and thus has the ability to straddle both Left and Right ("I've never seen an eagle that can soar on one wing," he likes to point out). Several hundred prisons in more than half of the states have satellite links tuned to Jakes's inspirational programming. Meanwhile, his international outreach is growing, spearheaded by a television presence in Europe, Australia, and especially Africa, where he has also invested heavily in schools and medical facilities, and in digging wells to provide fresh drinking water. Given his influence and reputation, it is not surprising that he has been sought out and asked to stand with both Bill Clinton (in the aftermath of the Monica Lewinsky scandal) and George W. Bush (in the wake of Hurricane Katrina) when those presidents needed a black man of God at their side.

Jakes is an imposing presence: bald, six feet two inches tall, and with a nineteen-inch neck. He sports a white goatee and custom-made suits. In private conversations his voice drops to a near-whisper. He stretches out his words with a strong country contour, pronouncing, for instance, Kenya as "Keen-ya." He is a man of means: he arrives at church in a Lexus or a Bentley and keeps up with his speaking obligations, which are numerous, by means of a private plane, a Lockheed JetStar II. He is always on the move — "I'm on the clock," you'll hear him say, "I'm on the clock" — because he seems to be the one man who unites the many worlds of America's far-from-monolithic black community, from the well-off professionals in Chicago's Gold Coast to the desperate refugees from New Orleans, fleeing for their lives. T. D. Jakes may be far from a household name in white America, but he was sitting with Jesse Jackson at Rosa Parks's funeral because he is very much a household name among this country's African Americans. Indeed, he is fast becoming what Jackson no longer is: the most powerful black man in America.

Such a statement speaks to the nature of power itself — the will to act, and the ability to make that will a reality. Men like Al Sharpton can walk through New York City streets with bullhorns calling for racial justice. Colin Powell and Vernon Jordan can sit on the executive boards of Fortune 500 companies. What T. D. Jakes possesses is a unique ability to bring affluent white and black Americans to his parishioners, persuading them to sponsor events like the annual MegaFest, a three-day religious extravaganza that attracts more than 150,000 people to Atlanta. Jakes's efforts have elicited historical comparisons, most notably to Billy Graham, whose nonpartisan stance won him the trust of all sectors of the power elite. Thus, when it came time for the Bush-Clinton Katrina Relief Fund to distribute money to religious organizations, it was Jakes (together with former congressman William Gray) whom former presidents Bill Clinton and George Bush Sr. chose to disburse the $20 million in aid.

The African American radio host Tom Joyner, whose show reaches eight million people and is broadcast on 110 stations, may speak to more American blacks on a regular basis than Jakes does, but he bows to Jakes when it comes to actual influence. "If you're an African American anywhere in this country," he says, "the chances are you've been touched by at least one level of his vast ministry."

"I don't know a lot of African American leaders who can go into what used to be called the Superdome and draw fifty thousand people," said longtime Maryland congressman Elijah Cummings when I asked him to rank Jakes with other black power brokers. "I don't know too many African American ministers who can go into a foreign land and draw hundreds of thousands of people, as he did in Kenya.

"When I watch T. D. Jakes," Cummings went on, "it makes me go and work harder in my job, because he is good at what he does, and you know that he has been anointed to preach. You just know it."

You can get a sense of the "it" just by being wherever Jakes is present. You certainly would have gotten a sense of it on a warm October evening in Dallas, when he was unexpectedly maneuvered into speaking to a group in a private home. He and his wife, Serita Ann, had come to a formal dinner party in a large house on the edge of Dallas's old-money bastion, Highland Park. Jakes had come as a favor to one of his publicists, who had wanted him to meet the host, a noted legal scholar, and Jakes had brought a crystal platter from Tiffany's as a gift. For Jakes, a man already of considerable standing in Dallas, this was a chance to make further inroads among people of means and influence in the white community, people who one day might be able to assist the work of the Potter's House. Now, after two hours of eating and sipping Diet Coke (Jakes doesn't drink), he found himself with his back to the door, facing an all-white audience that wanted to hear what this oracle had to say.

Anyone who has seen him preach will have an indelible image of his theatrical sermons, with Jakes hopping around the stage, drenched in sweat, his voice rising to provoke the rapturous thousands around him. But in this Dallas foyer he was a different kind of person, engaging in modulated conversation, listening attentively, nodding, giving quiet, thoughtful replies. He spoke to one man about China and the global economy. He listened as one woman suggested that New Orleans not be rebuilt because "the whole thing's going to happen again," and politely shifted the discussion to the tragedy itself. He went on to talk about Hurricane Katrina relief efforts, about poverty in America and overseas, about the prospects for economic development in nearby Fort Worth (where he himself owns a home worth $5 million). He spoke about his recent meetings with Bill Clinton and global economic leaders, telling them what he had learned.

In a nearby room a number of other guests had been watching the World Series, in which a Texas team (the Houston Astros) was playing, but as Jakes continued to talk, small pockets of these sports fans drifted away from the game and toward the preacher. One of the guests, looking back at the growing knot of people around Jakes, said to me, "When T. D. Jakes came to town, nobody knew what to think of him. In Dallas we do churches big — I belong to one that's six thousand people, and that's nothing compared to him. He's dwarfed them all."

In the process of redefining, and dominating, the religious hierarchy of Dallas, Jakes has won some high-profile followers. In 1996, Carolyn Chambers Sanders, then the wife of Dallas Cowboys defensive back Deion Sanders, decided that her loose-living husband needed a mature male influence. For a decade Deion had run roughshod over the National Football League as the game's most feared kick returner and defensive back, a man who'd danced his way to Super Bowl championships for two different teams. But however successful he was on the field, Deion's skills as a husband — as a man, really — needed help. His lifestyle was out of control. Help could not come from his biological father or his stepfather, who were dead. Carolyn decided that it could come from Jakes, who had just moved to Dallas from West Virginia.

Carolyn and Deion went to Jakes for marriage counseling, at Carolyn's behest, and Deion found in Jakes and his church a father figure and a spiritual home. Deion took in everything that Jakes and the Potter's House had to offer — the Wednesday-night Bible classes; the loud, overgrown services; the one-on-one personal sessions in which Jakes encouraged Sanders to put aside his hedonistic ways for his own sake — and began to spend more and more of his time in the confines of the Dallas church. He embraced the ideals of righteous self-empowerment that Jakes tried to instill in his congregation. In the end, Sanders's marriage did not endure, but his way of life was turned around. "The ministry was like a life raft, and it saved me," Sanders explains. For him, the Jakes connection has remained durable. It would be Jakes who, in 1999, officiated at Sanders's second wedding, to the New York actress and model Pilar Biggers, in the Bahamas.

What is it that has drawn Deion Sanders and millions of others to T. D. Jakes? The place to start looking is probably on the life raft itself: at Jakes's church, a large white structure with all the haunting spiritual resonance of a Maine outlet mall, sprawling across fifty acres in southwest Dallas. On Sunday mornings the Potter's House attracts a long stream of snaking traffic that evokes the triumphant ending of *Field of Dreams*. After parking according to a system designed by the person who helps the NFL with its own traffic problems, a visitor is greeted by men in black fatigues with the word AMEN emblazoned on the chest. The interior of the Potter's House looks less like a sanctuary than like a Broadway theater: seventy-five hundred people can fit into its lower level and balcony. And the pulpit is a stage, really, flanked by two JumboTrons and backed by an imposing two-hundred-person choir that stands above a nine-foot-high re-creation of Jerusalem's Wailing Wall. Every Sunday the sanctuary fills to capacity — twice. The choir warms up the congregation until the arrival of Jakes, who almost always is accompanied by Serita Ann. He begins with mundane announcements of church news (the fitness center is now accepting new members; the upcoming men's retreat will include both spa services and a golf tournament), usually delivered from the pulpit, but he then steps down to the floor like a Vegas showman. He moves into a full-throated sermon, in which he summons the witness of scripture and the testimony of his own life. He voices shortcomings and fears and hopes and doubts, and he calls for self-betterment, sometimes shouting and sometimes speaking softly.

Men and women rise, seized with religious fervor. Some come near
the stage, almost dancing in excitement. Dozens of emotional new
members, cheeks wet with tears, come forward to be received by
Jakes's pastors.

"It is time for the baby to move to the next level," Jakes proclaimed as he looked out at the stream of followers one Sunday
when I was in attendance. "Remember that the womb is supporting
the baby; it's the baby's time to move to the next level. I'm talking
about the power of vision. *The power of vision!*

"If you have not seen God the way you should see Him, right now
you should repent of your small-minded concept of who He is. You
should repent and get an inner vision of your own needs and limitations. Or if you've been so stuck on your own needs and limitations that you fail to see the global, bigger picture of how God can
use you in spite of those limitations, then look out for where you
are. I want you to bow your heads, and whatever level this message
spoke to you on, I want you to respond to God on that level so that
you can say, 'Here am I. Send me.'"

There is, of course, more to the church than this emotional cre-
scendo, much more: ministries for singles and couples, for young
people and prisoners and ex-prisoners and recovering drug addicts
and prostitutes. There are programs and seminars on personal
finance geared to every social class. Although these are open to
anyone, for the burgeoning black middle and upper classes, who
are coping with new social and financial pressures, and also with
the psychological burden of having made it when others in the
black community haven't, the church offers a wide range of programs that seem particularly appropriate. These include a "Doing
Business in Deep Waters" cruise to Alaska and the well-known Atlanta MegaFest, where religious programs are interspersed with appearances by people like the financial guru Suze Orman and the
comedian Steve Harvey.

Like Jakes, the Potter's House is standing on the shoulders of the
1960s-era crusade for civil rights. Its agenda isn't about rights per
se, a battle that has been, if not won, then joined; rather, it represents something new in the black community. Although it continues to serve the needs of the dispossessed, it is just as interested in
the very different concerns of the affluent. It cuts across class lines
and gathers blacks of all socioeconomic strata, functioning in the
black community the way the class-transcending Catholic Church

has always done in America. In the case of the Potter's House, it does this through a common emphasis on personal betterment — moving from one level to the next. The white megachurches that began to spring up in the 1980s, and are now a fixture all over America, have widely been seen as a response to the rootless geographical mobility of the sprawling white suburbs. The Potter's House is a megachurch, too, but it represents a response to something very different — to the challenges presented to the black community by *social* mobility, either when it fails to occur (as among the poor) or when it occurs rapidly and disconcertingly (as among the middle class).

The roots of the Potter's House can be traced back a hundred years to a black Pentecostal movement that arose in America from a church located at 312 Azusa Street, in a multiracial district of Los Angeles, and from the words of its black pastor, William Seymour. Seymour had traveled the country, listening to and learning from white ministers. (One of them — indeed, his mentor — was a racist named Charles F. Parham, a Pentecostal preacher whom he met in Houston and who enforced the conventions of segregation by allowing Seymour to hear his lectures — but only if he listened from outside the door.) Seymour urged his followers to connect with scripture in a deeply intimate way, as the apostles had on the day of the Pentecost, when "a sound came from heaven like the rush of a mighty wind." Seymour offered a spiritual vision embracing all nations and peoples, whose direct connection with the divine would be manifested through speaking in tongues.

Today Pentecostalism is the world's fastest-growing religion within the Christian faith, with an estimated 500 million adherents around the globe. The membership is drawn from all races and from all Christian denominations. Among poor blacks worldwide, who may chafe from the legacy of colonial churches brought by white missionaries, Pentecostalism offers a theology that is more emotionally and experientially based and a liturgy that accommodates local rites, rituals, and traditions. Pentecostalism is by definition a grassroots movement, without an encompassing hierarchical structure. (But there are networks of affiliation: Jakes was named a bishop in 1987 by the Board of Bishops of the Greater Emmanuel Pentecostal Churches.) At the Potter's House, one discovers Baptists and Catholics and Methodists and Episcopalians.

Jakes regards his own conversion, as he explained one morning during a chat in the sanctuary, to have been a matter of providence. It was a Saturday, and Jakes, whom on other occasions I had always seen in an expensive suit, was wearing a windbreaker and jeans and cowboy boots. The previous night he'd come in from Arizona, and the next day he would fly out to Australia. Jakes stretched out his legs and seemed completely at ease.

"At the time I moved from the Baptist Church to the Pentecostal Church I was about sixteen years old," Jakes said. "My father had died, something was missing out of my life, and I was not fulfilled in my spirituality where I was.

"The reason why I say it was destiny is because it was during this time that the charismatic Pentecostal movement was exploding in this country. And with that explosion came a multicultural interdenominational ideology. The megachurch is a place where Baptists and Methodists and Pentecostals intersect. And had I stayed in a mainline denomination, I would have missed that intersection. For the role that I was supposed to play globally, I couldn't be owned by a particular denomination, or be narrow in my perspectives or focus."

That may seem to some like a grandiose interpretation; it calls to mind the observation that the message of Jesus succeeded because it coincided with the fruitful conditions created by the Roman Empire. But there is a large element of simple truth in Jakes's assessment.

The youngest of three children, Thomas Dexter Jakes was born in 1957 to working-class parents in South Charleston, West Virginia. His father, Ernest L. Jakes Sr., a native of Mississippi, owned a janitorial business. His mother, Odith, who studied with Coretta Scott King at Lincoln High School, in Alabama, was a schoolteacher. Odith would help her children get to know the works of African American poets and writers like Langston Hughes and Ralph Ellison, and she raised them to take seriously the prospect of the Kingdom of God.

In 1973, after years of suffering, Ernest Jakes succumbed to a kidney ailment. T. D., a teenager, and for years the only child at home to tend his father, was distraught. He dropped out of high school his senior year to care for his ailing mother, earned a GED, then enrolled at West Virginia State only to drop out after a year or so. He went to work as a processor of oxygen and acetylene at a chemical plant in Charleston, owned by Union Carbide, a job that he assumed would give him the kind of middle-class life that so many of his parents' friends had achieved. But this way of life, which had sustained so many northern black Americans since the end of World War II, was coming to an end, as manufacturing jobs in what was already being called the Rust Belt began to disappear.

Jakes did not see that change coming. But even as he worked his day job he began exploring another path. His religious impulses had never atrophied; indeed, he had begun to preach at nineteen. He did not need reminding that there was more to life than Union Carbide, and he possessed an innate confidence — derived from having had to care for and serve as an advocate for his father — in his ability to talk to older people about things that matter. In 1980 Jakes opened his first storefront church, called the Greater Emmanuel Temple of Faith, in Montgomery, West Virginia, about thirty miles southeast of the state capital, Charleston. At his first service, he spoke to an audience of literally ten, swelled by the presence of his sister and mother. As a Pentecostal minister he did not need a divinity degree, simply a license from the state's Pentecostal Association. He donned long robes when he preached, and he wrapped a towel around his neck to absorb the perspiration.

It didn't take long for Jakes to be noticed; because of his distinctive and fluent sermons, word of mouth began drawing the multitudes. The head of the Pentecostal Association invited him to travel and speak throughout West Virginia, and Jakes honed his message about how to overcome self-loathing and self-doubt. He attracted large crowds — and the attention of Serita Ann Jamison, the daughter of a coal miner who lived in Alpoca, in the northeast part of the state. Before long Jakes was a husband and the father of twins (the couple now have five children, the youngest of whom is eleven). Then, in 1982, Union Carbide sold one of its Charleston plants, and Jakes was out of work.

"We lost everything," Jakes recalls. "And it was a real fight to get back up. I'm glad it happened, from the standpoint that I can relate to extremely poor people. I was literally cutting grass and digging ditches, trying to get diapers for my kids. So when I go into a home of somebody who doesn't have lights on, I've been there. I know what it is to get government milk."

Jakes's sudden financial fall would become a moment of intellectual and religious definition. In practical terms, it also made him realize that he had better start getting more creative about his livelihood and diversifying his income. The ministry would now become, and remain, Jakes's main focus, but he was open as well to business opportunities of various kinds. He did not want to be living off the contributions of his congregation, most of whom were just scraping by.

Our culture expects preachers to be poor, or at least to be of no more than modest means. Scripture itself gives sanction to this idea. And Jakes might have remained that kind of preacher had it not been for a particular Sunday-school class he taught in 1991. Jakes had become increasingly concerned about the issues so many women faced: the drugs, the unreliable husbands, the sexual abuse, the overt misogyny. So on that fateful Sunday he decided to hold a special service to speak just to women. The service — in which he acknowledged and confronted the victimization of women, but also held out a vision of empowerment and personal resurrection — left a deep impression, and word of it spread. Soon women were coming from hundreds of miles away, and Jakes himself was invited to travel long distances — to Kansas, to Oklahoma, to Georgia — and bring his famous sermon with him. Speaking at a televised revival in Oklahoma, Jakes caught the eye of Paul Crouch, the head of the far-flung Trinity Broadcast Network, a Christian organization, and within a year Jakes began appearing regularly on television.

Commercially, though, the real breakthrough came in 1993, when Jakes used the family savings — some $15,000 — to publish a book called *Woman, Thou Art Loosed,* which put into print everything he'd been preaching about. The book combined quotations from scripture (the title itself comes from a passage in the Gospel of Luke, in which Jesus brings the balm of relief to a troubled woman) and large amounts of practical advice. Jakes describes God as "the perfect husband" who "wants to make sweet love to you," adding: "I'm not being carnal. I'm being real." The self-published book, which initially sold for $10, went through printing after printing, and eventually sold more than two million copies, giving Jakes and his family a measure of financial independence. So fundamental is *Woman, Thou Art Loosed* to the Jakes ministry that everyone in his circle now simply uses the shorthand *WTAL.*

Jakes moved his ministry from the original storefront in Montgomery to a theater in Smithers and then, in 1990, to an old bank building in Cross Lanes, which could accommodate hundreds of worshipers. He also began dabbling in real estate, and turned out to be good at it. As his preaching and publishing became more visible, so did certain aspects of his evolving lifestyle. Perhaps inevitably, Jakes found himself the target of the state's largest newspaper, *The Charleston Gazette,* edited by a self-avowed agnostic named James Haught. Haught saw Jakes as a "young guy caught up in the preaching business" who was "cashing in." *The Gazette* ran a front-page story highlighting the seven-bedroom house Jakes had bought in 1994 for $630,000. The property, paid for with the proceeds of *Woman, Thou Art Loosed,* had tennis courts and a swimming pool. The home conveniently symbolized the startlingly rapid expansion of Jakes's preaching enterprise as a whole, with its books and TV shows and conferences around the country that attracted vast throngs. West Virginia is not a racially diverse state — as of the last census only about 3 percent of the population was black — and the emergence of a figure like Jakes caused a certain amount of discomfort and suspicion.

"I never will forget when [members of the press] came to my house with the camera, and I opened up the door and the reporter said, 'Do your members know you live like this?' And I stood there a minute stunned, and I said, 'They should. They were over here last Saturday.' You know? I had had a big open house, and all the deacons were swimming in the pool and were playing on the basketball court. It wasn't like they were discovering a secret. But it was a discovery to *them.*

"I was successful, which was viewed as wrong in a poor state. And I was black? And I was a preacher? Oh, it was like, 'Lunch, boys! Come and eat! Dinner is served!' They were having me for dinner, and I didn't even know I was on the menu."

So there was undeniably a push factor pointing Jakes toward Dallas, where he moved in 1996. There was also a pull factor: Dallas was one of the cities where Jakes had held his conferences — elaborate, multiday gatherings with titles like "ManPower" and "When Shepherds Bleed." During this time he received a call from a colleague in Dallas, drawing his attention to a five-thousand-seat megachurch that was suddenly for sale, tucked into the bucolic hills of southwest Dallas. It had been the property of a televangelist named W. V. Grant, who had a nasty habit of committing fraud and not paying his taxes. That church (which Jakes bought in 1996 for $3.2 million), together with the larger community of Dallas, would provide Jakes with the kind of base he needed. Jakes called his church the Potter's House, a new name for a new place, referring to a passage from the book of Jeremiah ("Like clay in the hand of the potter, so are you in my hand, O house of Israel"). Dallas had a sizable population of African Americans (most recent figures show that they make up about a quarter of the city's more than one million people), and although many of them were poor (blacks in the city have a median household income about half that of whites), the city was also home to a large black middle class, and its members had things on their mind that white Americans scarcely register.

This group, which Jakes hoped in particular to reach with his ministry, has emerged in force largely during the past twenty or thirty years. A year ago roughly 2.3 million African Americans were enrolled in some kind of higher-educational institution, double the number of two decades ago. More than a million held advanced degrees. Between 1990 and 2000, the number of African Americans living in suburban communities grew by some fourteen million. Although today only 1.5 percent of African Americans over twenty-five have annual incomes above $100,000 (the figure for whites is 4.4 percent), the proportion of what Jakes calls this "minority within a minority" is growing.

When Jakes and I spoke about upwardly mobile African Americans, in general, he explained the dilemma facing particular individuals: "He's just arrived, you know? He's the first generation into a suburb, or he's the first generation — or maybe at the most second generation — with a degree. He's upwardly mobile. He's got a community that has people below him who have needs — endless needs. And he wants to respond to those needs. At the same time he's trying to get membership to the country club. He's too black often to fit into the white circles. But he's too successful to be accepted in the traditional black environment. And often they end up stressed out, overworked. A lot of upwardly mobile African Americans use the church as a support base. It is giving a motivational message that says, 'You can make it, everybody.' It says, 'You have issues, too.' It's a place where you're embraced."

What the church does not embrace is politics. To be sure, Jakes forged strong ties with the Dallas political leadership, and with a (Republican) governor who in 2001 would go on to become president of the United States. But politically charged topics like same-sex marriage and abortion are not big issues at the Potter's House. Last November Jakes spurned Louis Farrakhan's call to join in the recent (and tepid) reprise of the Million Man March; his relations with Jesse Jackson are cordial but not politically close. Although the Potter's House has received some federal money through the Bush administration's faith-based initiative, and has participated in voter-registration drives, it has never endorsed candidates or handed down any directive on political issues. Instead, Jakes seems to keep his attention focused on the economic and spiritual development of all people, while encouraging those individuals to make political decisions for themselves. If he has political messages to deliver, he does it behind closed doors.

He talked about this issue of political involvement one day last fall at Princeton University during a public conversation under the rubric "Preachers, Profits, and the Prophetic: The New Face of American Evangelicalism." His conversation partner at the University Chapel, where Martin Luther King once spoke, was the professor/activist/rapper Cornel West, formerly a sharp critic of Jakes — West said on one occasion that Jakes lacked "political courage" — but now a friend, the rapprochement forged over the course of a lengthy dinner one night in Dallas (they spoke for three hours before even ordering salad, the two recalled). On the dais, Jakes and West sat in comfortable black rocking chairs, the pair of them representing physical opposites: the commanding, shiny-domed, easygoing Jakes; the wiry, wild-haired, and tightly wound West. The discussion soon took up politics.

"You get more King-like every minute," West said to Jakes, but then continued. "Let me ask you: what would be the conditions under which you would imagine your ministry to be in a fundamental confrontation with the powers that be — the White House, Wall Street?"

"I guess the question for me really is: is all confrontation public?" Jakes replied. And he went on: "Because I find even in my own leadership style — for me, I respond better when you come to see me than if you just write a [public letter]. You can come and sit down with me and say, 'You know, there might be a better way of doing that. Look at this and look at that.' And bring about the right change in how I do things. Now you won't get the credit, because you don't do it in public."

Jakes's unwillingness to play the political card was evident during the aftermath of Hurricane Katrina, when he was one of the few black leaders who did not come forward with stinging criticism of President Bush. (The rapper Kanye West, for instance, during a telethon to raise money for the hurricane's victims, said bluntly, "George Bush doesn't care about black people.") Instead, Jakes met publicly with the president in Baton Rouge, an encounter that, whatever else it did, allowed Bush to use Jakes as a political fig leaf — though it should be said that the Potter's House's record in Katrina relief efforts has been exemplary. Deploying nearly all of the church's 360 employees and thousands of volunteers, Jakes set up hot lines for refugees, shipped supplies to the needy, and raised nearly $3 million to help settle homeless New Orleans residents in apartments in Dallas. But Jakes raised the hackles even of his own ardent parishioners when he appeared alongside President Bush. Jakes gamely rejects the criticism.

"My grandmother is from Mississippi," he explains. "My father is buried in Mississippi. My mother is in Alabama. And those are my relatives down there on top of the roof, okay? I have a choice between going and getting with a group of African American leaders and screaming into a microphone, 'Mister President! You need to do something about poor people!' Or I get to fly down there and meet with him and say to him, 'Mister President, you need to do something about these poor people. What can be done?'

"Which is more effective? To scream into a mike or whisper in his ear? And to be able to whisper in his ear and say, 'Mister President' — not just, 'You need to do something about poor people' — but I want to say, 'There are thousands of people that you're not being told about, that are not in a shelter, that are living in their houses with their relatives all over Dallas and all over Houston. I've got members, Mister President, all over my church, who are about to lose their apartment because they've got thirty people staying in a two-bedroom apartment. And this girl works for Rite Aid. You know? And she's now trying to feed thirty people every day, because all of her relatives have moved into her house because they're flooded out. And they're not on FEMA's radar screen.'

"I was about trying to find solutions to the problem. Now that's important."

The growth of the Potter's House has been relentless. Some fifteen hundred worshipers turned up for Jakes's first service there. And they kept on coming. The Potter's House eventually spent millions widening the roads to accommodate the traffic. In time, Jakes would spend $45 million to build a new sanctuary. Now even more ambitious plans are afoot. On two hundred acres south of Dallas, Jakes is constructing a red-brick, Harvardesque building to house his Christian prep school called Clay Academy — the "clay" here refers to what "the potter" works with — which in turn will form the nucleus of a planned community of fifteen hundred households, with housing for the low-income as well as the affluent. More than a bedroom community, it will become the hub — albeit a Christian hub, and a predominantly black Christian hub — of southwest Dallas.

The worldly success, as one might put it, of the Potter's House as an organization is resonant with Jakes's emphasis on the worldly self-betterment of its members. This message is not without its critics. Those who still believe in the old guard, including Cornel West before that momentous dinner, have likened Jakes to figures like Tiger Woods and Michael Jordan — people who undeniably induce a level of excitement but who shun controversy because they have too much to lose. Recently Shayne Lee, a sociologist at Tulane University and the author of *T. D. Jakes: America's New Preacher*, told me, "He's turned spirituality into a commodity. Materialism is the car that drives him. His whole message of materialism does not sit well with the gospel, and that's what I find problematic."

Jakes would argue that what is really problematic is the absence of a self-betterment or entrepreneurial ethic among many black Americans. And his ambitions for this message go far beyond Dallas and even America — they extend, for instance, to Africa, where his brand of nondenominational, Pentecostal Christianity is growing as rapidly as it is elsewhere in the world. Jakes's publishing and broadcasting inroads in Africa are deep, and he has a wide personal acquaintance with African religious and political leaders. Jakes's thrust toward Africa has a twofold motivation.

First, he wants to make connections with a population that, according to census data, is finding its way into the United States every year in greater numbers than during the height of the slave trade (some fifty thousand legal African immigrants have been admitted annually since 1990). Many of these hard-driving people share Jakes's bootstrap vision of self-advancement. They have also never shouldered the historical legacy of slavery, and are thus, in Jakes's view, psychologically distinct from the larger black community in America. The difference, which is an increasing source of intramural tension, was brought home to Jakes starkly during a cab ride one day in Baltimore in the mid-nineties. The cabbie was African, and in the course of a conversation the preacher, never one not to speak his mind, told the driver that he had never really connected with African people, that he just didn't understand them, that they came across as arrogant. Turning to Jakes, the man said, "We are not arrogant. We are what you would have been had you not been slaves."

Second, like many African Americans, Jakes feels the pull of ancestry, the pull of identity. "One thing you have to understand is that the African American soul is wounded," Jakes says. "And for us, slavery was like the molestation of a nationality of people. Molestation to me is a good metaphor because it speaks to the person in power taking advantage of the person who had no power. Even though that has passed, there is a scar that remains. And to expect our community to be over it is like molesting somebody from the time they're five years old to when they're fifteen, and then meeting them at eighteen or twenty years old and saying, 'You should be over it!' Well, no. That's part of my life, I can't get over it. And with it comes the loss of your name — inheriting the name of somebody who owned you. At some time you question, 'Who am I?'"

In the past two years alone the Potter's House has invested more than $1 million in development projects in Africa, focusing, for the moment, on Kenya. Jakes does not do things in a small way. He arrived in Nairobi last September for his "Faith for Africa" mission with a party of some four hundred, including other pastors and their spouses, people from various denominations, and those associated with him in Dallas or elsewhere in America (as well as a 140-person choir). Mostly middle aged and middle class, they carried hand sanitizer and bottled water nearly everywhere, traveled in groups, and generally refrained from eating outside their hotel. Jakes's security team — men and women in khaki, with dark glasses and coiled earpieces — was never far away. Jakes intended to show his fellow believers what real poverty looks like when it exists on a systemic national level, and also to foster the development of a network of like-minded indigenous pastors in Kenya. In addition, he hoped to encourage or jump-start more grassroots development projects.

Jakes's progress through Kenya had all the trappings of an American-style evangelical crusade — the gospel choir, the weeping throngs, the insistence that a better day would come — and it had been planned by his own team of advance personnel (the Potter's House staff includes a "Transportation Ministry"). He worked the crusade on both the wholesale and retail level. In Nairobi's Uhuru Park, he held a service and led a rally for nearly a million people — as many as had shown up to see Pope John Paul II in May 1980. But much of his time was spent with small groups. He spoke to a gathering of Kenyan pastors about the pressures, the weight, of trying to carry a congregation. At the Hilton Nairobi one evening he urged business leaders to embrace entrepreneurship, and held up his own vocation as a businessman as an essential complement to his preaching work, because the word of God alone wasn't going to raise people out of poverty. He toured a slum neighborhood where the Potter's House had built a well, and led a group of his fellow visitors down to the sewage-filled stream that had been the previous source of water. "Jesus," Jakes said under his breath.

The trip was filled with talk of brotherhood, of the family coming together, all rendered in a colorful montage of dress and dance and music. But there was a darker undercurrent, a more troubling understanding: when you go looking for your heritage, your roots, sometimes you don't like what you see. At a Masai village, many hours from the capital, Jakes and his wife were given the title of honorary elders. (They were also given a live bull.) At one point we watched as children began to perform a play. In the performance, boys play elders who solve a disagreement by arranging the marriage of a very young girl to a very old man. The girl in the play begins to cry, because she is so young, but that doesn't last very long, because the nuptials apparently solve everything. The play ends with the whole group in a celebratory dance.

"Ask them how old they are when get married," Jakes said aloud to anyone who could provide an answer. When he heard back a number, he shook his head. "Sixteen years? Fifteen years? Oh no, oh no, no. That's terrible."

Later, when we were talking about practices prevalent in Africa such as child marriage and female genital mutilation, Jakes said to me, "When I hear of female genital mutilation, I think of my own children, and it's gut-wrenching for me. My heart goes out to the young girls, and I think, *There's a better way.* And if I'm going to correct something, at least it's not a distortion of who we are culturally. And so it's not that I worship ancestry and that I think that it's flawless or spotless, but at least it is mine. And that's important. It sets the record straight."

Setting the record straight squares with the message Jakes delivers in Dallas. It means filling in the gaps of a person's own history, recognizing the negative aspects of that history as well as its glory. It's a tool that can move one away from always simply looking back to the slave ships and Reconstruction and segregated drinking fountains.

In truth, though, one couldn't get close to Jakes in Kenya, where he'd be surrounded by large groups of children at one event and then retreat into the darkened corners of the Serna Hotel, in Nairobi, and talk for hours to local pastors. To be with him there was to see a man struggle under the weight of the very goals he'd set for himself as a man of God, a promoter of upward mobility, an international evangelist, a husband and father, a simple preacher, a sophisticated businessman. People who set out to change the world are not quite like the rest of us. They can sit in our homes, share our taxis, and attend the birthday parties of our children. But they are never fully detached from the great personal sacrifice that the role entails. For someone like Jakes, everyone from a beleaguered president in the White House to a malnourished Kenyan boy in a shantytown is tugging at his cuffs.

A couple of months after the Africa trip I asked Jakes if he thought of himself as a post-civil-rights-movement leader. The civil-rights issues of the 1950s and 1960s were large, overt, and, in a sense, "simple": it was easy to unite around them. The politics and demographics of today's America, including today's black America, are more complicated. In terms of black leadership, how does Jakes place himself within the paradigm shift that seems to be occurring from the old guard to the new? Laughing, he said, "I struggle with that. My perspectives tend to be pastoral, you know? And I think I'm evolving. And that evolution is still new to me — because though I am pastoral, I also understand that I have an obligation to our people.

"I see myself as a leader, and as a leader I have a responsibility to reflect the views of my faith, and the views of my people — and those are two different things altogether. My thought at this point is, anything that I can do to really help to bring about equality among all people — I'm willing to do that. Even if it stretches my role . . . a little bit. I believe that God created us to be equal, and I believe that we should be treated fairly no matter who we are. Does that make me a civil-rights leader? I don't know. But it does make me an American who would fight to the death for what I believe."

MARILYNNE ROBINSON

Hysterical Scientism

FROM *Harper's Magazine*

RICHARD DAWKINS IS an Oxford professor and the author of
a series of best-selling books that popularize a version of evolutionary theory. According to Dawkins, evolution is driven by "repli-
cators" — genes, and also "memes," viruses of the mind that spread
and persist in human populations. Those genes and memes that
replicate most effectively become dominant, with every consequence for the natural world and for civilization and history. The
usefulness of this notion, which does have the virtue of simplicity, is
a question obscured by the demands Dawkins has placed on it. By
his lights this is the universal etiology, a fully sufficient refutation of
religion in every form and the basis for a new view of humankind.
Under the name of Darwinism it has been thrown into the rhetorical wars that seem, to the combatants, to pit science against religion. As argument it has taken on the character of this environment, getting lost in the miasma of its own supposed implications.

It is never a surprise to find Dawkins full of indignation. In his
new book, *The God Delusion*, he has turned the full force of his intellect against religion, and all his verbal skills as well, and his humane
learning, too, which is capacious enough to include some deeply
minor poetry. Truly this book is a sword which turneth every way,
to judge by the table of contents at least. There is no doubt in
Dawkins's mind that the evils of the world are to be laid at the door-
step of the church, mosque, and synagogue, and that science must
be our salvation. It is the "God delusion," which has afflicted almost
everyone almost anywhere through the whole of recorded time,
that has made us behave so badly. And Science (by which he really

means his version of Darwinism) is our potential rescuer from this vale of tears. We need only to become more Dawkins-like in our thinking. This is a fairly cheery view of things beside others on offer, at least as regards the ongoing life of the planet, which he seems to assume.

Still, it is a difficult thing to set reason aside, and the habit of critical thought, and the sense of the past, not to mention the morning news. While I was reading this book, I noticed an article about a speech the British physicist Stephen Hawking delivered in Hong Kong. In it he said that the early colonization of other planets would be necessary to save humankind from extinction, given the likelihood of disaster that would render Earth uninhabitable. He mentioned nuclear war and biological weapons as probable agents of catastrophe. Another scientist, when asked for his view of Hawking's remarks, noted that Hawking was speaking outside his area of expertise. Much better, said he, to think in the short term about burrowing under Antarctica.

I have never seen the suggestion anywhere that the threat of imminent catastrophe on a "biblical scale" — a phrase favored by journalists — which has hung over the world for more than half a century, might have consequences for the stability of the global public mind. Is it really any wonder so many people turn to mass-market apocalyptics? It is amazing, when the movers and shakers of the so-called postwar have devoted so much effort and rhetoric to policies with names like Mutual Assured Destruction, that anyone could be surprised to find some significant part of the populace reading up on End Times. But here is Richard Dawkins to dispel the clouds of fear and gloom — that is, religion. He is by profession a dedicated promoter of the Public Understanding of Science. In his view, understanding is clearly not to be achieved by looking at history, or at present or potential consequences of science and its practice for that same Public. I note these omissions because Dawkins implicitly defines science as a clear-eyed quest for truth, chaste as an algorithm, while religion is atavistic, mad, and mired in crime.

Since Dawkins's declared intention in this book is to hearten the many atheists who, he is sure, exist, but who conceal their convictions for fear of disapproval or rejection, no doubt his tendentiousness is meant to be enjoyed by the like-minded, as is so much that is called "objectivity" in these fulminating times. Yet Dawkins is in earnest in presenting himself as a man in possession of liberating truth — another characteristic of the genre — and his readership is sure to be much wider than the crypto-atheist community. So it seems fair, if not strictly possible, to take him as seriously as he takes himself.

These are, certainly, troubled times. The tectonics of culture are suddenly active, and all the old rifts and stresses and pressures that seemed to have fallen dormant have awakened at once, with a great deal of portentous rumbling and spouting. *The God Delusion* is another instance of this phenomenon. Like so much of the contemporary clamor, it is out to name and denounce the great Satan, which in this case is religion. This view is commonplace now, in part because the institutions of religion, like the institutions of journalism and government, have done a great deal to trivialize or disgrace themselves lately.

The gravest questions about the institutions of contemporary science seem never to be posed, though we know the terrors of all-out conflict between civilizations would include innovations, notably those dread weapons of mass destruction, being made by scientists for any country with access to their skills. Granting for the purposes of argument that Dawkins is correct in the view that the majority of great scientists are atheists, we may then exclude religion from among the factors that recruit them to this somber work. We are left with nationalism, steady employment, good pay, the chance to do research that is lavishly funded and, by definition, cutting edge — familiar motives of a kind fully capable of disarming moral doubt. In any case, the crankiest imam, the oiliest televangelist, can, at his worst, only urge circumstances a degree or two farther toward the use of those exotic war technologies that are always ready, always waiting. If it is fair to speak globally of religion, it is also fair to speak globally of science.

There is a pervasive exclusion of historical memory in Dawkins's view of science. Consider this sentence from his preface, which occurs in the context of his vision of a religion-free world: "Imagine . . . no persecution of Jews as 'Christ-killers.'" In a later chapter he condemns Jews for discouraging "marrying out" and complains that such "wanton and carefully nurtured divisiveness" is "a significant force for evil." It is of course no criticism to say that he values the tradition of Judaism not at all, since this is only consistent with his view of religion in general. He seems unaware, however, that there was in fact significant intermarriage between Jews and gentiles in Europe as well as secularism and conversion among the Jews, and that this appears only to have fired the anti-Semitic imagination. While it is true that persecution of the Jews has a very long history in Europe, it is also true that science in the twentieth century revived and absolutized persecution by giving it a fresh rationale — Jewishness was not religious or cultural, but genetic. Therefore no appeal could be made against the brute fact of a Jewish grandparent.

Dawkins deals with all this in one sentence. Hitler did his evil "in the name of . . . an insane and unscientific eugenics theory." But eugenics is science as surely as totemism is religion. That either is in error is beside the point. Science quite appropriately acknowledges that error should be assumed, and at best it proceeds by a continuous process of criticism meant to isolate and identify error. So bad science is still science in more or less the same sense that bad religion is still religion. That both of them can do damage on a huge scale is clear. The prestige of both is a great part of the problem, and in the modern period the credibility of anything called science is enormous. As the history of eugenics proves, science at the highest levels is no reliable corrective to the influence of cultural prejudice but is in fact profoundly vulnerable to it.

There is indeed historical precedent in the Spanish Inquisition for the notion of hereditary Judaism. But the fact that the worst religious thought of the sixteenth century can be likened to the worst scientific thought of the twentieth century hardly redounds to the credit of science. To illustrate the point: Dawkins tells the story of Edgardo Mortara, the Italian Jewish child taken from his family by the police in 1858 and reared by priests because he had been secretly baptized by a maid in his parents' house. A terrible story indeed. And how might it have been worse? If the child had fallen, as in the next century so many would, into the hands of those who considered his Jewishness biological rather than religious and cultural. To Dawkins's objection that Nazi science was not authentic science I would reply, first, that neither Nazis nor Germans had any monopoly on these theories, which were influential throughout the Western world, and second, that the research on human subjects carried out by those holding such assumptions was good enough science to appear in medical texts for fully half a century. This is not to single out science as exceptionally inclined to do harm, though its capacity for doing harm is by now unequaled. It is only to note that science, too, is implicated in this bleak human proclivity, and is one major instrument of it.

The nineteenth-century abolitionist, feminist, essayist, and ordained minister Thomas Wentworth Higginson made the always timely point that, in comparing religions, great care must be taken to consider the best elements of one with the best of the other, and the worst with the worst, to avoid the usual practice of comparing, let us say, the fatwa against Salman Rushdie with the Golden Rule. The same principle might be applied in the comparison of religion and science. To set the declared hopes of one against the real-world record of the other is clearly not useful, no matter which of them is flattered by the comparison. What is religion? It is described by Dawkins as a virtually universal feature of human culture. But there is, commingled with it, indisputably and perhaps universally, doubt, hypocrisy, and charlatanism. Dawkins, for his part, considers religion wholly delusional, and he condemns the best of it for enabling all the worst of it. Yet if religion is to be blamed for the fraud done in its name, then what of science? Is it to be blamed for the Piltdown hoax, for the long-credited deceptions having to do with cloning in South Korea? If by "science" is meant authentic science, then "religion" must mean authentic religion, granting the difficulties in arriving at these definitions.

I wish, then, to speak of science in the highest sense of the word, as the astonishingly fruitful human venture into understanding of the world and the universe. The reader may assume a somewhat greater admiration on my part for religion in the highest sense of the word, though I will not go into that here. Science thus defined does not claim to understand gravity, light, or time. This is a very short list of its mystifications, its inquiries, all of which are beautiful to ponder. These three are sufficient to persuade me that conclusions about the ultimate nature of things are, to say the least, premature, and that to suggest otherwise is unscientific. The finer-grained the image of reality physicists achieve, the more alien it appears to every known strategy of comprehension.

The odd thing about Dawkins's work, considering his job description, is that it does not itself seem the product of a mind informed by the physics of the last century or so. A reader might find it instructive to start with his last chapter, in which he does acknowledge the fact of quantum theory and certain of its implications. This chapter is an interesting lens through which to consider the primary argument of the book, especially his use of physicality and materiality as standards for determining the real and objective existence of anything, along with his use of commonplace experience as the standard of reasonableness and — a favorite word — probability. He does this despite his awareness that the physical and the material are artifacts of the scale at which reality is perceived. For us, he says, "matter is a useful construct." Quoting Steve Grand, a computer scientist who specializes in artificial intelligence, he offers these thoughts on the fluidity of matter: "Matter flows from place to place and momentarily comes together to be you. Whatever you are, therefore, you are not the stuff of which you are made. If that doesn't make the hair stand up on the back of your neck, read it again until it does, because it is important." Earlier, Dawkins attributes the origins of the illusion that we have a soul to the persistence of a childish or primitive tendency toward dualism — "Our innate dualism prepares us to believe in a 'soul' which inhabits the body rather than being integrally part of the body. Such a disembodied spirit can easily be imagined to move on somewhere else after the death of the body." Yet the image of deeper reality invoked by him here suggests a basis for the ancient intuition of the persistence of the self despite the transiency of the elements of its physical embodiment.

I do not wish to recruit science to the cause of religion. My point is simply that Dawkins's critique of religion cannot properly be called scientific. His thinking is reminiscent of logical positivism. That school, however, which meant to carry out a purge of language it considered meaningless, specifically metaphysics and theology, by subjecting statements to the "scientific" test of verifiability, plunged into all sorts of interesting difficulty, as rigorous thought tends to do. Dawkins acknowledges no difficulty. He has a simple-as-that, plain-as-day approach to the grandest questions, unencumbered by doubt, consistency, or countervailing information.

The chapter titled "Why There Almost Certainly Is No God" reflects his reasoning at its highest bent. He reasons thus: A creator God must be more complex than his creation, but this is impossible because if he existed he would be at the wrong end of evolutionary history. To be present in the beginning he must have been un-evolved and therefore simple. Dawkins is very proud of this insight. He considers it unanswerable. He asks, "How do they [theists] cope with the argument that any God capable of designing a universe, carefully and foresightfully tuned to lead to our evolution, must be a supremely complex and improbable entity who needs an even bigger explanation than the one he is supposed to provide?" And "if he [God] has the powers attributed to him he must have some-thing far more elaborately and non-randomly constructed than the largest brain or the largest computer we know," and "a first cause of everything . . . must have been simple and therefore, whatever else we call it, God is not an appropriate name (unless we very explicitly divest it of all the baggage that the word 'God' carries in the minds of most religious believers)." At Cambridge, says Dawkins, "I chal-lenged the theologians to answer the point that a God capable of designing a universe, or anything else, would have to be complex and statistically improbable. The strongest response I heard was that I was brutally foisting a scientific epistemology upon an unwill-ing theology." Dawkins is clearly innocent of this charge against him. Whatever is being foisted here, it is not a scientific episte-mology.

Evolution is the creature of time. And, as Dawkins notes, mod-ern cosmologies generally suggest that time and the universe as a whole came into being together. So a creator cannot very well be thought of as having attained complexity through a process of evo-lution. That is to say, theists need find no anomaly in a divine "com-plexity" over against the "simplicity" that is presumed to character-ize the universe at its origin. (I use these terms not because I find them appropriate to the question but because Dawkins uses them, and my point is to demonstrate the flaws in his reasoning.) In this context, Dawkins cannot concede, even hypothetically, a reality that is not time-bound, that does not conform to Darwinism as he understands it. Yet in an earlier book, *Unweaving the Rainbow,* Dawkins remarks that "further developments of the [big bang] the-ory, supported by all available evidence, suggest that time itself be-gan in this mother of all cataclysms. You probably don't under-

stand, and I certainly don't, what it can possibly mean to say that
time itself began at a particular moment. But once again that is a
limitation of our minds." That God exists outside time as its creator
is an ancient given of theology. The faithful are accustomed to expressions like "from everlasting to everlasting" in reference to God,
language that the positivists would surely have considered non-
sense but that does indeed express the intuition that time is an aspect of the created order. Again, I do not wish to abuse either theology or scientific theory by implying that either can be used as
evidence in support of the other; I mean only that the big bang in
fact provides a metaphor that might help Dawkins understand why
his grand assault on the "God Hypothesis" has failed to impress the
theists.

The God Delusion has human history and civilization as its subjects,
inevitably, considering the pervasiveness of religion. Dawkins dwells
particularly on Christianity, since he is most familiar with it, and because its influence is and has been very great. On the one hand, he
professes a lingering fondness for the Church of England and re-
grets that familiarity with the Bible, a great literature, is in decline.
On the other hand, he finds the Old Testament barbarous and abhorrent and the New Testament mawkish and fairly abhorrent as
well. His treatment of these texts depends to a striking degree on a
"remarkable paper" by John Hartung, an associate professor of an-
esthesiology and an anthropologist. The paper, titled "Love Thy
Neighbor: The Evolution of In-Group Morality," originally published in 1995, is available on the Web. Dawkins and his wife are
thanked in the acknowledgments. Curious readers can form their
own impression of its character. A sympathetic review by Hartung
of Kevin MacDonald's *A People That Shall Dwell Alone: Judaism as a
Group Evolutionary Strategy, with Diaspora Peoples* is also of interest.
These are murky waters, the kind toward which Darwinism has often tended to migrate.

Dawkins says, "I need to call attention to one particularly unpal-
atable aspect of its [the Bible's] ethical teaching. Christians seldom
realize that much of the moral consideration for others which is apparently promoted by both the Old and New Testaments was originally intended to apply only to a narrowly defined in-group. 'Love
thy neighbor' didn't mean what we now think it means. It meant

only 'Love another Jew.'" As for the New Testament interpretation of the text, "Hartung puts it more bluntly than I dare: 'Jesus would have turned over in his grave if he had known that Paul would be taking his plan to the pigs.'" Pigs being, of course, gentiles.

There are two major objections to be made to this reading. First, the verse quoted here, Leviticus 19:18, does indeed begin, "You shall not take vengeance or bear a grudge against any of your people," language that allows a narrow interpretation of the commandment. But Leviticus 19:33 – 34 says, "When an alien resides with you in your land, you shall not oppress the alien . . . You shall love the alien as yourself." In light of these verses, it is wrong by Dawkins's own standards to argue that the ethos of the law does not imply moral consideration for others. (It would be interesting to see the response to a proposal to display this Mosaic law in our courthouses.) Second, Jesus provided a gloss on 19:18, the famous Parable of the Good Samaritan. With specific reference to this verse, a lawyer asks Jesus, "And who is my neighbor?" Jesus tells a story that moves the lawyer to answer that the merciful Samaritan — a non-Jew — embodies the word *neighbor.* That the question would be posed to Jesus, or by Luke, is evidence that the meaning of the law was not obvious or settled in antiquity. In general, Dawkins's air of genteel familiarity with scripture, though becoming in one aware as he is of its contributions to the arts, dissipates under the slightest scrutiny.

Nor is Dawkins's argument from history impressive. He cheerfully posits a *"Zeitgeist"* that wafts us to ever higher states of ethical sensitivity, granting lapses, specifically those associated with Hitler and Stalin: "We are forced to realize that Hitler, appalling though he was, was not quite as far outside the *Zeitgeist* of his time as he seems from our vantage-point today. How swiftly the *Zeitgeist* changes — and it moves in parallel, on a broad front, throughout the educated world." Dawkins fails to note that the racial anti-Semitism that arose in Germany in the later nineteenth century had appeared to recede, until Hitler and others revived it. The article on anti-Semitism in the 11th Edition of the *Encyclopaedia Britannica,* published in 1911. describes the movement as a German "craze" that had "shown little activity since 1893." According to the article, "While it remained a theory of nationality and a fad of the metaphysicians, it made considerable noise in the world without exercising much practical influence." So, although Dawkins's *Zeitgeist* might seem a harmless fudge, a *spiritus ex machina* meant to rescue his Darwinian atheism from the charges of bleakness and emptiness, it excuses his consistent inattentiveness to history. It is precisely the swiftness with which the *Zeitgeist* can change that makes it profoundly unworthy of confidence.

If the only bad effect of the notion to yield a highly selective reading of the past by dismissing the modern horrors as anomaly, that in itself would be grounds for objection. But it enables a misreading of the history it chooses to acknowledge. For example, Dawkins quotes a passage from an essay by T. H. Huxley, Darwin's contemporary and champion, in which Huxley says the black man will not "be able to compete successfully with his bigger-brained and smaller-jawed rival [that is, the white man], in a contest which is to be carried on by thoughts and not by bites." Dawkins cringes at this, but, he says, "good historians don't judge statements from past times by the standards of their own." He finds evidence for his advancing moral *Zeitgeist* in the crudeness of Huxley's racism: "The whole wave keeps moving, and even the vanguard of an earlier century (T. H. Huxley is the obvious example) would find itself way behind the laggers of a later century."

But *was* Huxley in the vanguard? The essay from which Dawkins quotes, "Emancipation — Black and White," published in 1865, is an explicit rejection of the belief in racial equality active in America before and for some time after the Civil War. Huxley dismisses "standards" that had long been salient among his contemporaries. He is saying that emancipation may well prove to have very mingled consequences — "emancipation may convert the slave from a well-fed animal into a pauperised man" — and that the egalitarian hopes the movement inspired should be rejected. This was the crucial period of Reconstruction and of the ratification of the Fourteenth Amendment to the Constitution, which established the full rights of citizenship to everyone born or naturalized in this country. Its passage was the work of emancipationists, and it was meant to create meaningful political equality for African Americans, among others. The vanguard in the period in which Huxley wrote were those Christian abolitionists whose intentions he dismissed as, of course, at odds with science. Huxley's racism, like Hitler's, is not a standard from which ineluctable progress can be inferred but instead a proof of the power of atavism.

Dawkins allows that our upward moral drift is a "meandering

sawtooth" — he is admired for his prose — but he seems not to be alert to historical specifics. The United States never suffered a more grievous moral setback than when it allowed thinking like Huxley's to make a dead letter of the Fourteenth Amendment. As for the lesser issues of justice that arose in the wake of slavery, Huxley had this to say: "whatever the position of stable equilibrium into which the laws of social gravitation may bring the negro, all responsibility for the result will henceforward lie between Nature and him. The white man may wash his hands of it, and the Caucasian conscience be void of reproach for evermore. And this, if we look to the bottom of the matter, is the real justification for the abolition policy." No, he wasn't joking.

Finally, there is the matter of atheism itself. Dawkins finds it incapable of belligerent intent — "why would anyone go to war for the sake of an absence of belief?" It is a peculiarity of our language that by war we generally mean a conflict between nations, or at least one in which both sides are armed. There has been persistent violence against religion — in the French Revolution, in the Spanish Civil War, in the Soviet Union, in China. In three of these instances the extirpation of religion was part of a program to reshape society by excluding certain forms of thought, by creating an absence of belief. Neither sanity nor happiness appears to have been served by these efforts. The kindest conclusion one can draw is that Dawkins has not acquainted himself with the history of modern authoritarianism.

Indeed, Dawkins makes a bold attack on tolerance as it is manifested in society's permitting people to rear their children in their own religious traditions. He turns an especially cold eye on the Amish:

> There is something breathtakingly condescending, as well as inhumane, about the sacrificing of anyone, especially children, on the altar of "diversity" and the virtue of preserving a variety of religious traditions. The rest of us are happy with our cars and computers, our vaccines and antibiotics. But you quaint little people with your bonnets and breeches, your horse buggies, your archaic dialect and your earth-closet privies, you enrich our lives. Of course you must be allowed to trap your children with you in your seventeenth-century time warp, otherwise something irretrievable would be lost to us: a part of the wonderful diversity of human culture.

The fact that the Amish are pacifists whose way of life burdens this beleaguered planet as little as any to be found in the Western world merits not even a mention.

Yet Dawkins himself has posited not only memes but, since these mind viruses are highly analogous to genes, a meme pool as well. This would imply that there are more than sentimental reasons for valuing the diversity that he derides. Would not the attempt to narrow it only repeat the worst errors of eugenics at the cultural and intellectual level? When the *Zeitgeist* turns Gorgon, the impulses toward cultural and biological eugenics have proved to be one and the same. It is diversity that makes any natural system robust, and diversity that stabilizes culture against the eccentricity and arrogance that have so often called themselves reason and science.

HUSTON SMITH

The Universal Grammar
of Religion

FROM *Sophia*

NOAM CHOMSKY HAS described a universal grammar that is built into the human mind and structures every human language. What follows is my attempt to do the same with religion.

The Chandogya Upanishad provides a nice entry into the project.

> . . . as by knowing one lump of clay, all things made of clay are known, the difference being only in name and arising from speech, and the truth being that all are clay; as by knowing one nugget of gold, all things made of gold are known, the difference being only in name and arising from speech, and the truth being that all are gold — exactly so is that knowledge, by knowing which we know all.

I have broken the "clay/gold" into fourteen different pieces as follows:

1. Reality is Infinite. The Infinite is the one inescapable metaphysical idea, for if you stop with finitude you face a door with only one side, an absurdity.

2. The Infinite includes the finite or we would be left with infinite-plus-finite and the Infinite would not be what it claims to be. The natural image to token the Infinite's inclusiveness is a circle. The Infinite is that out of which we cannot fall.

3. The contents of finitude are hierarchically ordered. Arthur Lovejoy titled his important study in the history of philosophy *The Great Chain of Being* and argued that its underlying idea was accepted by most educated people throughout the world until mo-

dernity mistakenly abandoned it in the late eighteenth century. The Great Chain of Being is the idea of a universe composed of an infinite number of links ranging in hierarchical order from the most meager kind of existence through every possible grade, up to the boundless Infinite. The ascent may be a smooth continuum, but for practical purposes it helps to divide it into categories — steps on a ladder, so to speak. Aristotle's categories of mineral, vegetable, animal, and rational remain useful but stop too soon. *Homo sapiens* are only midway up the chain.

4. Causation is from the top down, from the Infinite down through the descending degrees of reality.

5. In descending to finitude, the singularity of the Infinite splays into multiplicity — the One becomes the many.

The parts of the many are virtues, for they retain in lesser degree the signature of the One's perfection. The foundational virtue is existence; to be more than figments of the imagination, virtues must exist. In scholastic dictum, *esse que esse bonum est,* "being as being is good." It is good simply to exist. As for what the virtues other than existence are, India begins with *Sat, Chit, Ananda* (being, consciousness, and bliss). The West's ternary is the good, the true, and the beautiful, and these beginnings open out into creativity, compassion, and love until we arrive at Islam's Ninety-nine Beautiful Names of God. Above these lies the hundredth name which — symbolically absent from the Islamic rosary — is unutterable.

6. Reversing the drift of downward causation, as we look upward from our position on the causal chain, we find that as the virtues ascend the causal ladder, their distinctions fade and they begin to merge.

This requires that the images of ladder and chain be replaced with a pyramid. Flannery O'Connor titled one of her short stories *Everything That Rises Must Converge,* and this is so. God knows lovingly and loves knowingly, and so on until the Infinite differences (which token separation) completely disappear in the divine "simplicity" or "singularity," a technical term that can be likened to a mathematical point that has no extension. To refer to that point, any virtue will serve as long as the word is capitalized, whereupon they become synonyms. God is the conventional English name for the Infinite, but Good, True, Real, Almighty, One, etc., are equally accurate.

7. When the virtues converge at the top of the pyramid, the religious worldview makes its most staggering claim. Absolute perfec-

tion reigns. In Hegel's dictum, despite the fact that the world is in about the worst shape imaginable, in the eye of the cyclone all is well. This brings us face to face with the problem of evil. Human beings are mixed bags, capable of great nobility and horrendous evil. Our primary mistake is to put ourselves ahead of others. We cannot get rid of that error, but we can and must work to restrain it.

8. The Great Chain of Being, with its links of increasing worth, needs to be extended by the Hermetic Principle, "As above, so below." Everything that is outside is also inside us — "the Kingdom of God is within you." We intersect, inhabit all the echelons of the chain of being, as Sir Thomas Browne recorded in his *Religio Medici:* "Man is a multiple amphibian, disposed to live, not only like other creatures in diverse elements, but in divided and distinguishable worlds." When we look outward it is natural to visualize the good as up — angels invariably sing on high and gods live on mountaintops. But when we look inward the imagery flips and the best things lie deepest within us. The complete picture shows the ineffable, unutterable, *apophatic* Godhead at the top, descending through the personal, describable, *kataphatic* God, to angels, and from there on down to the physical universe. But as our eyes continue down to the lower half of the page, value inverts and the divisions increase in worth. Mind is more important than body, our multiple souls more important than our minds, and Spirit (which is identical in us all) is more important than souls. Animation proceeds upward on the lower half of the page, not downward as in the top half.

9. Human beings cannot fully know the Infinite. Intimations of it will seep into us occasionally, but more than this we cannot manage on our own. If we are to know it confidently, the Infinite must take the initiative and show itself to us in the way nature takes the initiative in instilling the universal grammar of languages in the human mind.

10. Intimations of the Infinite have to be interpreted, hence the science of exegesis (the critical interpretation of the religious experiences and texts to discover their intended meaning).

These intimations progress through four steps of ascending importance: literal, ethical, allegorical, and anagogic, the text's capacity to inspire us. What does the text explicitly assert, what does it tell us we should and should not do, what allegorical meaning does it suggest, and how does it inspire us?

11. All these factors were taken for granted until the rise of twen-

tieth-century fundamentalism and the literalism it fixes on. It has generated so much confusion that it justifies an excursus to indicate its mistake.

Science has shown us that there are three domains of size — the micro-world of quantum mechanics where distance is measured in picometers; the macro-world that we inhabit where distance is measured in millimeters, meters, and kilometers; and the mega-world of the astronomers and relativity theory where distance is measured in light-years. Neither of the worlds that flanks ours can be consistently and accurately described in ordinary language — try to do so and you run into the contradictions that plague cartographers when they try to portray our three-dimensional planet on the two-dimensional pages of a geography book. Scientists can, however, describe the micro- and mega-worlds consistently in their technical language, which is mathematics.

The Infinite is at least as different from our human world as are the micro- and mega-worlds because it includes them. It follows that if we stick to the Bible's literal assertions we find ourselves in a tangle of contradictions analogous to those that quantum scientists encounter when they try to draw verbal pictures of their subjects. We can almost hear the despair in Robert Oppenheimer's voice when he tells us, "If we ask whether the electron's position changes with time, we must say, 'No'; if we ask whether the position of the electron remains the same, we must say, 'No'; if we ask whether the electron is at rest, we must say, 'No'; if we ask whether it is in motion, we must say, 'No.'" We too are driven to the brink of despair if we stay with the contradictions that the Bible's actual words confront us with if they are taken literally.

Religion's technical language is symbolism, the science of the relations between the multiple levels of reality. More fully, it is myth, metaphor, parable, figures of speech, and story. Plato calls stories that deflect our attention upward "likely tales," thus indicating that it is the nonliteral denotations of their words that are important. By extension, the technical language is also sacred art. Prosaic language is useful as a medium of exchange, which like money ordinarily serves us well, but in times of crisis we look for bread — in this context, the bread of life. The bread of life transports us to a higher plane of reality.

12. There are two distinct and complementing ways of knowing: the rational and the intuitive.

The life and career of Blaise Pascal throw the two into exceptionally sharp relief. When he exclaimed in what was to become his famous aphorism, "The heart has reason the mind knows not of," the
"mind" he was thinking of was his scientific mind through which he
achieved fame for his theory of probability in mathematics and his
work on hydrodynamics in physics, and "heart" was his word for the
organ through which burst the epiphany that turned his concern
from science to religion: "FIRE. God of Abraham . . . Isaac . . . Ja-
cob. Not the philosophers and the learned . . . Tears of Joy . . . May
God . . . let me not be separated from Thee forever." But that he
never intended to dismiss philosophy and learning in total is amply
evidenced by his eighteen closely reasoned *Lettres Provincales,* in
which he examined the fundamental problems of human existence, and the fact that he titles the entries in his notebook *Pensées*
(thoughts), in which he spells out his conviction that the true func-
tion of reason is to attain the truth or supreme good.

All the religions of the world spell this out carefully. In the West,
intellect *(intellectus, gnosis, sapientia)* is not reason *(ratio);* in San-
skrit, *buddhi* is not *manas,* in Islam *ma'rifah,* situated in the heart, is
not *aql,* situated in the brain. In Hinduism the knowledge that effects union with God is not discursive; it has the immediacy of
direct vision, or sight. In Greece, *theoria* referred to the kind of
knowledge that one derived from watching the great Greek dramas. Our word *theater,* which derives from it, is closer to its meaning
than our word *theory,* which has degenerated from *theoria* in much
the same way *belief* has degenerated from something more than
knowledge (conviction and the determination to act on it) to something less than knowledge.

13. Walnuts have shells that house kernels, and religions likewise
have outsides and insides; outer, exoteric forms that house inner,
esoteric cores.

People differ in the way they relate to the two. The difference
comes down to how adept they are with abstractions. Esoterics are
comfortable with abstractions while exoterics need for ideas to be
concrete and representational to be clear.

It follows that exoterics like (one might almost say need) to think
of the Infinite in personal terms, whereas esoterics, while subscrib-
ing to the Infinite-clothed-in-human-attributes, are at the same time
aware of the danger that this can easily turn into anthropomor-
phism — making God too human — so it needs to be supplemented

by esoterism. We need for God to be both like and unlike us — like us so we can connect to him/her/it, and different from us because we cannot worship our own kind. Absolute imminence and absolute transcendence in absolute tension is what gives maximum tonus to our spiritual lives.

14. What we know is ringed about with darkness. It is a numinous darkness that lures, for we know that God sees it as light and at times we sense a kind of twilight zone around its edges. But to cognition the darkness remains — we are born in ignorance, we live in ignorance, and we die in ignorance. In relation to the Infinite we stand as less than a simple protein in a single cell on a human finger. Though living, that protein cannot know the cell in which it lives. How then can it conceive of the skin, the knuckle, or the finger's articulating joints, the intricacies of the ligaments, nerves, and muscles, the electro/biochemical processes of that finger of which it is a negligible part? And even if it could contain all that understanding, it could never conceive of the whole hand of which it is a part that can find expression in the fingering of a guitar, the fist clenched in anger, the delicate touch needed for surgical repair of a heart. It is only a simple protein, an amino acid building block. So much less are we in this mass of the universe and beyond it, the Infinite. We are born in mystery, and we die in mystery.

Compressed into a single paragraph consisting of topic sentences, religion's Universal Grammar causes the religions it structures to affirm that existence is Infinite and includes the finite and its value-laden degrees, hierarchically ordered. As virtues ascend in the hierarchy, they meld into one another until their differences disappear in Singularity. Evil features in the finitude but not in the Absolute, and as the Absolute is all-powerful, in the end, absolute perfection reigns. Human beings intersect the degrees of reality, but in them they are inverted in the way the image on the surface of a glassy lake inverts the mountain it reflects. We cannot comprehend the fullness of Reality on our own, but its outlines are given to us in the Universal Grammar and the languages that stem from it. The key to unlocking the truths of religion is symbolism. Knowing is both rational and intuitive, both concrete and abstract. After we have done our best to understand the world, it remains mysterious.

In a single sentence: The world is perfect, and the human opportunity is to see that and conform to that fact.

MARK STRAND

Storm

FROM *The New Yorker*

On the last night of our house arrest
a howling wind tore through the streets,
ripping down shutters, scattering roof tiles,
leaving behind a river of refuse. When the sun
rose over the marble gate, I could see the guards,
sluggish in the morning heat, desert their posts
and stagger toward the woods just out of town.
"Darling," I said, "let's go, the guards have left,
the place is a ruin." But she was oblivious.
"You go," she said, and she pulled up the sheet
to cover her eyes. I ran downstairs and called
for my horse. "To the sea," I whispered, and off
we went and how quick we were, my horse and I,
riding over the fresh green fields, as if to our freedom.

JOHN UPDIKE

Half Moon, Small Cloud

FROM *The Atlantic Monthly*

Caught out in daylight, a rabbit's
transparent pallor, the moon
is paired with a cloud of equal weight:
the heavenly congruence startles.

For what is the moon, that it haunts us,
this impudent companion immigrated
from the system's less fortunate margins,
the realm of dust collected in orbs?

We grow up as children with it, a nursemaid
of a bonneted sort, round-faced and kind,
not burning too close like parents, or too far
to spare even a glance, like movie stars.

No star but in the zodiac of stars,
a stranger there, too big, it begs for love
(the man in it) and yet is diaphanous,
its thereness as mysterious as ours.

ROBERT LOUIS WILKEN

Jaroslav Pelikan, Doctor Ecclesiae

FROM *First Things*

WHEN I WALKED INTO the chapel at St. Vladimir's Seminary on a bright spring morning for the funeral of Jaroslav Pelikan, I saw an open casket in the center of the church. Next to it was a young woman standing at a reading desk chanting a psalm with tears running down her cheeks. As she turned the pages of the psalm book, her other arm held a young girl standing on a chair to her left. Members of the seminary community had been taking turns through the night reciting psalms as they kept vigil over Jaroslav's still body.

As I listened to the recitation of the psalms, the eyes of the saints painted on the walls of the chapel looked down on the simple ritual unfolding before them. Soon the building would be filled with mourners, but it seemed that the church was already present to commend Jaroslav to the care of the angels. When people began to take their places, I sensed that on this occasion there would be few reminders of the university world in which Pelikan had lived for so many decades. Besides the Pelikan family, most in attendance were from the local community: students and faculty garbed in the Orthodox inner cassock, called a *podryasnik;* mothers and wives; women and men carrying infants in arms; two little girls playing quietly on the wood floor close to the casket. The company that gathered that morning was more like a family, the family of the Church, a fellowship united by much deeper bonds than those of the academy. Their words and music and gestures were the solemn liturgy of God's people who had come to offer praise to the holy, mighty, and immortal God and to celebrate, in the language of the

Orthodox Church, a "Divine Service for the Funeral of a Layman During the Forty Days of Pascha."

It was fitting that Professor Pelikan's funeral should take place at St. Vladimir's. He and his wife, Sylvia, had been regular communicants in this chapel, and his final book, a theological commentary on the Acts of the Apostles, was dedicated to "my liturgical family at Saint Vladimir's," with the inscription "And they continued steadfastly in the apostles' doctrine and fellowship, and in the breaking of bread, and in prayers" (Acts 2:42). But there was another reason a theological seminary was the right place. Though Jaroslav Pelikan had a distinguished career in the university, he was a graduate of Concordia Seminary in St. Louis, where he taught for several years. He always felt at home in a theological community and saw himself, and was revered by others, first and foremost as a doctor ecclesiae, a teacher of the Church.

The first volume of his history of Christian thought, *The Christian Tradition,* begins: "What the church of Jesus Christ believes, teaches, and confesses on the basis of the Word of God: This is Christian doctrine." His life was devoted to the exposition and teaching of that Christian doctrine, but he knew that doctrine is not the only activity of the Church. The Church worships God and serves the poor and needy, the sick and dying, and is always more than a school. And yet it cannot be less than a school, for without doctrine, without teaching, it would not be the Church of Jesus Christ.

By doctrine Pelikan did not mean just any teaching. He meant the central truths of Christianity: that God is triune, that Christ is fully God and fully man — those teachings that were solemnly declared in the ancient councils and are confessed in the ecumenical creeds. His historical study had convinced him that the most faithful bearer of the apostolic faith was the great tradition of thought and practice as expounded by the orthodox church fathers.

In the past generation, it has become fashionable among historians of Christian thought not only to seek to understand the Gnostics or the Arians but also to become their advocates and to suggest, sometimes obliquely, sometimes straightforwardly, that orthodox Christianity made its way not by argument and truth but by power and coercion. The real heroes in Christian history are the dissidents, the heretics, whose insights and thinking were suppressed by the imperious bishops of the great Church.

Pelikan never succumbed to this temptation. In the classroom, in public lectures, and in his many books, he was an advocate of creedal Christianity, of the classical formulations of Christian doctrine. In one of his last books, *Credo,* he cited such writers as Edward Gibbon, Adolf von Harnack, and Matthew Arnold, who believed that "creeds pass" and "no altar standeth whole." But he answered them with John Henry Newman, who said that dogma is the principle of religion, and Lionel Trilling, who wrote that "when the dogmatic principle in religion is slighted, religion goes along for a while on generalized emotion and ethical intention . . . and then loses the force of its impulse, even the essence of its being."

Pelikan knew, and his scholarship demonstrated, what many Christian theologians and Church leaders have forgotten, that over the Church's long history, the orthodox and catholic form of Christian faith, what the Church "believes, teaches, and confesses on the basis of the Word of God," has been the most biblical, the most coherent, the most enduring, the most adaptable, and yes, the most true.

Long before the study of the biblical commentaries of the church fathers and medievals had become fashionable, Pelikan turned his attention to the role of the scriptures in the formation of Christian thought. He suggested, for example, that I write my doctoral dissertation on the commentaries of St. Cyril of Alexandria. He was not alone in urging study of the classical Christian biblical commentators. In the 1950s the French Jesuit Henri de Lubac was publishing his four-volume *Exégèse Médiévale,* where he showed that theological science and the interpretation of the scriptures are one.

What de Lubac did for the patristic and medieval period Pelikan did for Martin Luther. Helping prepare the American edition of Luther's works, he insisted that fully half of the volumes be devoted to Luther's exegetical writings. Luther had been known and interpreted primarily through his polemical and catechetical works, and the history of Christian thought was being taught as largely an affair of ideas and concepts, theological terms and philosophical distinctions, that floated free of the exegetical scaffolding supporting them. In a companion volume to the edition *Luther the Expositor,* Pelikan challenged his fellow scholars to open their eyes to the scriptural foundations of Christian thought. "Historians have sought to assess the influence of everything from the theologian's vanity to the theologian's viscera upon the formulation of theological doctrines, meanwhile regarding as naive and misinformed the suggestion that the Bible may be a source of these doctrines."

Pelikan's scholarship helped put classical Christian thought at the center of the theological enterprise. The great figures of the past were not disqualified because of the accident of death. He taught us that Christian thinking takes place in conversation with a great company of thinkers whose writings span the centuries: Justin Martyr, Origen, Tertullian, Athanasius, Gregory of Nyssa, Ambrose, Augustine, Cyril of Alexandria, Maximus the Confessor, John of Damascus, Symeon the New Theologian, Anselm of Canterbury, Bernard of Clairvaux, Thomas Aquinas, Martin Luther, and John Calvin, even Friedrich Schleiermacher, Albrecht Ritschl, and Adolf von Harnack (whose picture hung on his study wall across from one of Alexander Schmemann). More than any other scholar, he gave the history of Christian thought a public face in the United States.

And he had the largest vision. Most other scholars were specialists in a particular historical period, but Pelikan roamed freely and confidently over the whole history of Christian thought — and that history was never simply history for him. He had a certain diffidence about the merits of modernity. The great thinkers of the past were living interlocutors whose ideas, way of reasoning, and imagination commended them to Christian thinkers today.

When Pelikan began to teach in the 1940s, it was assumed, at least among most Protestant thinkers (and it must not be forgotten that for most of his life Pelikan was Lutheran), that the chief points of reference for theology were the Bible (as filtered through the historical critics), the Reformers, and the nineteenth-century thinkers. There would be an occasional genuflection in the direction of Augustine or Anselm of Canterbury, but the Greek church fathers, the Byzantines, and the medievals were seldom part of the conversation. Today it is unthinkable that one can do serious theological work without reference to the full sweep of the classical Christian tradition. This has brought a new confidence, a new assertiveness, a new willingness, to present the truth of the faith on its own terms and to interpret the scriptures within the Church's theological and liturgical tradition.

I saw Jaroslav Pelikan for the last time a few weeks before his death. I knew that he was gravely ill, and I wanted to have one last conversation with him. On that day he was bright and alert, and I enjoyed a simple Lenten luncheon with him and Sylvia at their home in Hamden, Connecticut. We talked about many things: about his scholarship and writing, about the church fathers, about his joy in the Orthodox Church, about friends and colleagues, about books and music, and about the strange ways of God. He learned that he had terminal lung cancer two days after he had received the prestigious Kluge Prize from the Library of Congress.

He said he had been reading again Dostoevsky's *Crime and Punishment,* Milton's *Paradise Lost* (even though Milton was an Arian and probably a Pelagian, quipped Pelikan), and Goethe's *Dichtung und Wahrheit.* But it was when we came to music that his eyes shone and he spoke from the heart. He said that he was listening mostly to Bach and in particular to the B-minor Mass. As we talked about Bach, he told me a story about the conductor Robert Shaw. On several occasions Shaw had invited Pelikan to give a theological lecture in connection with the performance of a great religious choral work at Carnegie Hall in New York. On the evening Shaw conducted Bach's St. Matthew Passion, before he lifted his baton to begin the performance, he addressed the audience. He said that for some in the audience this evening, this will be the first time you will hear the St. Matthew Passion; for others, it will be the last time. Then he turned to the orchestra and choir to begin the opening chorus.

Jaroslav Pelikan will not hear again the serene boys' voices high above the full chorus in the opening strains of the majestic chorale "O Lamm Gottes unschuldig." Now he joins the "great number, which no man can number, from every nation, from all tribes, standing before the throne and before the Lamb, clothed in white robes, with palm branches in their hands, and crying out with a loud voice, 'Salvation belongs to our God who sits upon the throne and to the Lamb.'"

GARRY WILLS

What Jesus Did

FROM *The American Scholar*

IN CERTAIN RELIGIOUS CIRCLES, the letters WWJD serve as a password or shibboleth. Web sites sell bracelets and T-shirts with the cryptic motto. Some politicians tell us this watchword guides them in making decisions. The letters stand for "What Would Jesus Do?" We are assured that doing the same thing is the goal of real Christians.

But can we really aspire to do what Jesus did? Would we praise a twelve-year-old who slips away from his parents in a big city and lets them leave without telling them he is staying behind? The reaction of any parent would be that of Jesus' parents in Luke: "How could you treat us this way?" Or if relatives seek access to a Christian, should he say that he has no relatives but his followers? We might try to change water into wine; but if we did, would we take six huge water vats, used for purification purposes, and fill them with over a hundred gallons of wine, more than any party could drink? If we could cast out devils, would we send them into a herd of pigs, destroying two thousand animals? Some Christians place a very high value on the rights of property, yet this was a massive invasion of another person's property and livelihood.

Other Christians lay great emphasis on family values — should they, like Jesus, forbid a man from attending his own father's funeral or tell others to hate their parents? Or should they go into a rich new church in some American suburb, a place taking pride it its success, and whip the persons holding out the collection plates, crying, "Make not my Father's house a traders' mart" or "a thieves' lair"? Would it be wise of them to call national religious leaders "whitewashed tombs, pleasant enough to outer appearance, but inside full of dead bones and every rottenness"? Are they justified in telling others, "I come not imposing peace, I impose not peace but the sword"? Or "I am come to throw fire on the earth"? Should they imitate Jesus when he says, "Heaven and earth will pass away, but never will my words pass away?" Or when he says, "I am the resurrection" or "I am the truth," or "I have the authority to lay down those my life and I have the authority to take it up again"? None of those who want to imitate Jesus should proclaim that "I am the light of the world" or that "I am the path" to the Father.

These are just a few samples of the way Jesus acts in the Gospels. They were acts meant to show that he is *not* just like us, that he has higher rights and powers, that he has an authority as arbitrary as God's in the book of Job. He is a divine mystery walking among men. The only way we can directly imitate him is to act as if we were gods ourselves — yet that is the very thing he forbids. He tells us to act as the last, not the first, as the least, not the greatest. And this accords with the common sense of mankind. Christians cannot really be "Christlike." As Chesterton said, "A great man knows he is not God, and the greater he is the better he knows it." The thing we have to realize is that Christ, whoever or whatever he was, was certainly not a Christian. Romano Guardini put it this way in *The Humanity of Christ:*

> If Jesus is a mere man, then he must be measured by the message which he brought to men. He must himself do what he expects of others; he must himself think according to the way he demanded that men think. He must himself be a Christian. Very well, then; the more he is like that, the less he will speak, act, or think as he did; and the more he will be appalled by the blasphemy of the way he did behave. If Jesus is a mere man as we are, even though a very profound one, very devout, very pure — no, let us put it another way: the measure of his depth, devotion, purity, reverence, will be the measure in which it will be impossible for him to say what he says . . . The following clear-cut alternative emerges: either he is — not just evil, for that would not adequately describe the case — either he is deranged, as Nietzsche became in Turin in 1888, or he is quite different, deeply and essentially different, from what we are.

To read the Gospels in the spirit with which they were written, it is not enough to ask what Jesus did or said. We must ask what Jesus *meant* by his strange deeds and words. He intended to reveal the Father to us, and to show that he is the only-begotten Son of that Father. What he signified is always more challenging than we expect, more outrageous, more egregious. That is why the Catholic novelist François Mauriac calls him "of all the great characters history places before us, the least logical." Dostoevsky's Grand Inquisitor knew this when he reproached Christ for puzzling men by being "exceptional, vague, and enigmatic."

It is true that St. Paul tells us to "put [our] mind in Christ's when dealing with one another." But looking to the mind of Christ is a way of learning what he *meant,* on many levels. We can learn what he valued in the human drama as he moved among his fellows. According to the Gospels, he preferred the company of the lonely and despised to that of the rich and powerful. He crossed lines of ritual purity to deal with the unclean — with lepers, the possessed, the insane, with prostitutes and adulterers and collaborators with Rome. (Was he subtly mocking ritual purification when he filled the water vessels with wine?) He was called a bastard and was rejected by his own brothers and the rest of his family. He was an outcast among outcasts, sharing the lot of the destitute, the defiled, the despised. "He was counted among the outlaws," according to Luke.

He had a lower-class upbringing, as a cabinetmaker's son. That was a trade usually marginal and itinerant in his time. He chose his followers from the lower class, from fishermen, dependent on the season's catch, or from a despised trade (tax collection for the Romans). There were no scribes or scholars of the law in his following. Jesus not only favored the homeless. He was himself homeless, born homeless and living homeless during his public life: "Foxes have lairs, and birds have nests in the air, but the Son of Man has nowhere to put down his head," as Jesus says in Matthew. He depended on others to shelter him. He especially depended on women, who were "second-class citizens" in his culture. He was not a philosopher. He wrote nothing for his followers in a later age. He depended on his uneducated disciples to express what he meant. First Corinthians says he knew that the Spirit moving them had no need of men with Ph.D.'s or with grants from learned foundations.

His very presence was subversive. He was born on the run, fleeing Herod. As the Anglican bishop N. T. Wright puts it, he "came into the world with a death sentence already hanging over him, as

the paranoid old tyrant up the road got wind of a young royal pre-
tender." Jesus would later move through teams of men setting traps
for him, trying to assassinate him, to crush his following, to give
him the same treatment given the beheaded John the Baptist. As
the Gospels tell it, he had to "go into hiding." He was in constant
danger — of being kidnapped, of being arrested, of being assassi-
nated, of being stoned for his irreligion, of being thrown off a cliff.
Herod Antipas, who killed John the Baptist openly, plotted to kill
Jesus secretly.

Jesus was called an agent of the devil, or the devil himself. He was
unclean, a consorter with Samaritans and loose women. He was a
promoter of immorality, a glutton and a drunkard, a mocker of the
Jewish Law, a schismatic. He was never respectable. In fact, he
shocked the elders and priests of the Temple when he said, "In
truth, I tell you, tax collectors and whores are entering God's reign
before you." Even when a Pharisee was well disposed to Jesus, he
was afraid to be seen with the radical by daylight. Jesus seemed to
prefer the company of the less-than-respectable, since he said that
his father "favors ingrates and scoundrels." I am reminded of the
journalist Murray Kempton, who relished the company of rogues.
A political leader once said that Murray would have liked him if
only he had a criminal record — though I am sure Murray liked
him anyway, from the way he used to tell me goodbye by saying
"God bless you," as if we would never meet again.

For two years, Jesus slipped through all the traps set for him.
He moved like a fish in the sea of his lower-class fellows. He kept on
the move, in the countryside. If I think of a music to be heard in
the background of his restless mission, it is the scurrying *agitato*
that opens Khachaturian's violin concerto. He went into cities as
into alien territory. He was a man of the margins, never quite
fitting in, always "out of context." He sought the wilderness, the
mountaintop. He gave the slip even to his followers. The puzzled
disciples trotted behind, trying to make sense of what seemed to
them inexplicable, squabbling among themselves about what he
was up to. It would never have occurred to them to wear a WWJD
bracelet.

Jesus ghosted in and out of people's lives, blessing and cursing,
cursing and condemning. If he was not God, he was a standing blas-
phemy against God. The last thing he can be considered is, in

Charles Wesley's words, a "gentle Jesus meek and mild." To quote Chesterton again:

> We have all heard people say a hundred times over, for they seem never tired of saying it, that the Jesus of the New Testament is indeed a most merciful and humane lover of humanity, but that the Church has hidden this human character in repellent dogmas and stiffened it with ecclesiastical terrors till it has taken on an inhuman character. This is, I venture to repeat, very nearly the reverse of the truth. The truth is that it is the image of Christ in the churches that is almost entirely mild and merciful. It is the image of Christ in the Gospels that is a good many other things as well. The figure in the Gospels does indeed utter in words of almost heartbreaking beauty his pity for our broken hearts. But they are very far from being the only sort of words that he utters . . . There is something appalling, something that makes the blood run cold, in the idea of having a statue of Christ in wrath. There is something insupportable even to the imagination in the idea of turning the corner of a street or coming out into the spaces of a marketplace, to meet the petrifying petrification of that figure as it turned upon a generation of vipers, or that face as it looked at the face of a hypocrite . . . [The gospel story] is full of sudden gestures evidently significant except that we hardly know what they signify; of enigmatic silences; of ironical replies. The outbreaks of wrath, like storms above our atmosphere, do not seem to break out exactly where we should expect them, but to follow some higher weather chart of their own. The Peter whom popular Church teaching presents is very rightly the Peter to whom Christ said in forgiveness, "Feed my lambs." He is not the Peter upon whom Christ turned as if he were the devil, crying in that obscure wrath, "Get thee behind me, Satan." Christ lamented with nothing but love and pity over Jerusalem, which was to murder him. We do not know what strange spiritual atmosphere or spiritual insight led him to sink Bethsaida lower in the pit than Sodom.

The Jesus of the Gospels is scandalous, and one of those scandalized was Thomas Jefferson. He was so offended by the miracles and the curses, by the devils assailing and defeated, that he created his own more acceptable Jesus, excising all those parts of the Gospels that he considered unworthy of a wise man's story. The result, cleansed of all the supernatural hocus-pocus, is the tale of a good man, a very good man, perhaps the best of good men — therefore a man who would not pretend to work miracles, to wrestle with demons, or to have unique access to God the Father. Jefferson's re-

vised New Testament is not only much shorter than the real one
but much duller. Nothing unexpected occurs in it. There is, for instance, no Resurrection. Jefferson's Jesus is shorn of his paradoxes
and left with platitudes. He is a man of his time, or even ahead of
his time, but not outside of time, whereas the Jesus of the Gospels is
both temporal and above time. As Chesterton concludes:

> There is more of the wisdom that is one with surprise in any simple per-
> son, full of the sensitiveness of simplicity, who should expect the grass to
> wither and the birds to drop dead out of the air, when a strolling carpen-
> ter's apprentice said calmly and almost carelessly, like one looking over
> his shoulder: "Before Abraham was, I am."

Needless to say, that verse (John 8:58) is excised by Jefferson. His
mild humanitarian moralizer is not allowed to say anything shocking, challenging, or obscure. Devils and miracles are not the only
things to go. So are passages like this:

> "Think not that I come imposing peace on earth. I impose not peace,
> but a sword. I bring conflict between a man and his father, a daughter
> and her mother, a wife and her mother-in-law — a man's foes will be
> found in his own home. One who loves father or mother before me does
> not deserve me. One who loves son or daughter before me does not de-
> serve me. And anyone who does not take up a cross and tread in my foot-
> steps does not deserve me. The man protective of his life will lose it, but
> the one casting life away on my account will preserve it." (Matthew
> 10:34–39)

Jefferson's extraction of the "real" gospel from the traditional
one — a task he called as easy as "finding diamonds in dunghills"
— has been taken up in recent years by a team that finds the task
more difficult, but productive of much the same result. This team
of scholars calls itself the Jesus Seminar, and it prints a Bible that
sets apart by different colors the "authentic" sayings or deeds of Jesus and the sayings invented by the evangelists or their sources.
Though these experts use linguistic and historical tests for qualify-
ing the diamonds in their dunghill, they work from a Jeffersonian
assumption that anything odd or dangerous or supernatural is
prima facie suspect. That disqualifies the Resurrection from the
outset. The Seminar's founder, Robert Funk, agreed with Jefferson
that Jesus was "a secular sage," and the team trims the Gospels even
more thoroughly than Jefferson did. One whole Gospel, John, has

no authentic saying (Jefferson liked quite a lot of John). Most of Mark (usually counted the most authentic Gospel, since it is the earliest) also falls by the wayside, along with the last three and a half chapters of Matthew. Luke, as the most "humanist Gospel," comes off best, but overall the Seminar retains fewer than a fifth of the gospel acts of Jesus and fewer than a fifth of his words.

This is the new fundamentalism. It believes in the literal sense of the Bible — it just reduces the Bible to what it can take as literal quotation from Jesus. Though some people have called the Jesus Seminarists radical, they are actually very conservative. They tame the real radical, Jesus, cutting him down to their own size. Robert Funk called Jesus "the first Jewish stand-up comic" — which is not as far as it might at first glance seem from Jefferson's view of him as the last sit-down Stoic sage.

Of course, the sayings that meet with the Seminar's approval were preserved by the Christian communities whose contribution is discounted. Jesus as a person does not exist outside the Gospels, and the only reason he exists there is because of their authors' faith in the Resurrection. Trying to find a construct, "the historical Jesus," is not like finding diamonds in a dunghill, but like finding New York City at the bottom of the Pacific Ocean. It is a mixing of categories, or rather wholly different worlds of discourse. The only Jesus we have is the Jesus of faith. If you reject the faith, there is no reason to trust anything the Gospels say. The Jesus of the Gospels is the Jesus preached, who is the Jesus resurrected. Belief in his continuing activity in the members of his mystical body is the basis of Christian belief in the Gospels. If that is unbelievable to anyone, then why should that person bother with him? The flat cutout figure they are left with is not a more profound philosopher than Plato, a better storyteller than Mark Twain, or a more bitingly ascetical figure than Epictetus (the only ancient philosopher Jefferson admired). If his claims are no higher than theirs, then those claims amount to nothing.

With certain religious figures, the original story that reaches us does not begin with literal facts that are later "embellished," as the Seminarists put it. The first reports spreading from such figures are all a blaze of holiness and miracle. That is as true of St. Francis as of the Baal Shem Tov. It is their impact on the faith of others that makes these men noticeable in the first place. Miracles, as it were,

work themselves around such men. Jesus is the preeminent example
of this. The fact that he seems like other wonder-working holy men
(Apollonius of Tyana, for instance) does not mean that he is an im-
itation of them. Rather, they are a reaching out toward him. They
are a hunger and he the food. They are an ache, he the easement.
As Chesterton said, his story resembles the great myths of mankind
because he is the fulfillment of the myths. When someone said that
other stories tell of God's voice coming down from heaven, and so
does the scene of Christ's baptism, therefore his story must be just
like the other ones, Chesterton asked, "From what place could a
voice of God come, from the coal cellar?"

   In the case of Jesus, the first blaze of wonder and miracle is regis-
tered in the letters of Paul, which preceded the Gospels by a quarter to half of a century. The Seminarists treat the Gospels as if they
were just a distortion of the "real" sayings of Jesus that preceded
them. But what preceded them in fact was the testimony of Paul,
who already preached the divinity of Christ, his descent from the
Father, his saving death and Resurrection. Nor can we say that he
invented something different from the Gospels, as if they were already in existence. He is passing on what was given to him in the
Christian community. We know this is the case because he quotes
hymns of the community that preceded his letters, including this
one:

> He, having the divine nature from the outset,
>   thinking it no usurpation to be held God's equal,
> emptied himself out into the nature of a slave,
>   becoming like to man.
> And in man's shape he lowered himself,
>   so obedient as to die, by a death on the cross.
> For this God has exalted him,
>   favored his name over all names,
> that at the name of Jesus all knees shall bend
>   above the earth, upon the earth, and below the earth,
> and every tongue shall acknowledge
>   that Jesus is the Lord Christ, to the glory of God the Father.
>   (Philippians 2:6–11)

   The proclamation of divinity is not something "added on" later.
It is the very thing to which all later explanations are added. The
Gospels, following on this profession of an active and shared faith,

trace the theological implications of that faith, and cite Jesus' words only in the context of that belief, the only context that exists for them. What Jesus meant is conveyed to us by what the Gospels mean. There is no other Jesus but the Jesus of faith. The "historical Jesus" does not exist for us. Romano Guardini put the matter well in his book on the psychology of Jesus:

> Were we in a position to disregard all [later] accounts and gain an immediate impression of Jesus Christ as he was on earth, we would not be confronted by a "simple" historical Jesus, but by a figure of devastating greatness and incomprehensibility. Progress in the representation of the portrait of Christ does not mean that something was being added to what was proclaimed; it means that we are witnessing the unfolding step by step of that which "was from the beginning" . . . If we could get back to the "original," that is, if we could work our way back to the picture of Christ as it existed before it had been turned over in the apostles' minds or elaborated by their preaching, before it had been assimilated by the corporate life of the faithful, we could find a figure of Christ even more colossal and incomprehensible than any conveyed by even the most daring statements of St. Paul or St. John . . . The statements of the apostles are guides to him which never quite do justice to the fullness of his divine-human natures. The apostles never state more about the historical Jesus than he actually was; it is always less.

To accept the Gospels as an authentic account of what Jesus meant should not make us revert from the new fundamentalism to the old one, treating everything in the Gospels as literally true in a later sense of historical truth. The Gospels express the ineffable in the language appropriate for the task, a language inherited from the Jewish scriptures. Luke's Gospel, for instance, spells out the meaning of Christ's Incarnation in the poetic forms of divine birth, because he and his fellows knew that this is what the Christ event *meant*. To believe in the Gospels is to take everything in them as meant, though at various levels of symbolization. This is a task for faith, a reasoning faith, one hopes, and reasonable — what St. Anselm called "faith out on quest to know" (*fides quaerens intellectum*) — but faith all the same. There is no other way of knowing Jesus.

FRANZ WRIGHT

Music Heard in Illness

FROM *Ploughshares*

"Everything changes but the avant-garde." — Paul Valéry

A few words are left us from the beginning.
Thank you, God, for allowing me a little to think again this
    morning.

Touch my face, touch this scarred heart.

Here, touch this upturned face as wind as light.

So they labored for three or four decades
to turn the perfectly harmless word quietude
into a pejorative sneer.

Call no man happy until he has passed,
beyond pain,
the boundary of this life.

We were standing alone at the window when it started
to rain and Schumann quietly.

The imbecilic plastic hive of evil.

When it started to

night, and you
turned

and said,
although you were not there, Night.

What do we know but this world.

And although I could not speak, I answered.

Contributors' Notes

Other Notable Spiritual Writing
of 2006

Contributors' Notes

Dick Allen's many books of poetry include *The Day Before: New Poems* and *Ode to the Cold War: Poems New and Selected.*

Dore Ashton is a professor of art history at The Cooper Union and the author of numerous books on the arts.

Fred Bahnson's essays and poems have appeared most recently in *Christian Century, Orion, Rock & Sling,* and *Fugue.* He farms with his wife and son in Orange County, North Carolina.

Robert Bly is the author of many books including the best-selling *Iron John: A Book About Men, My Sentence Was a Thousand Years of Joy, The Night Abraham Called to the Stars,* and *The Light Around the Body* (National Book Award for poetry, 1968).

Joseph Bottum is the editor of *First Things.* His books include *The Fall and Other Poems* and *The Pius War.*

Eric Cohen is the editor of *The New Atlantis.*

Robert Cording's fifth volume of poems, *Common Life,* was published in 2006. He is the Barrett Professor of Creative Writing at the College of the Holy Cross in Worcester, Massachusetts.

Harvey Cox is the Hollis Professor of Divinity at Harvard University and the author of many books, most recently *When Jesus Came to Harvard: Making Moral Decisions Today.*

Madeline DeFrees has published eight collections of poetry, most recently *Spectral Waves*. *Blue Dusk*, a volume of new and selected poems, won the Lenore Marshall Prize in 2002.

Deborah Digges is the author of several books of poetry, including *Trapeze* and *Rough Music* (Kingsley Tufts Poetry Prize, 1996), as well as two memoirs, *Fugitive Spring* and *The Stardust Lounge*.

Gretel Ehrlich is the author of *The Solace of Open Spaces*, *The Future of Ice*, and ten other books of fiction and nonfiction. She is the recipient of a Guggenheim Fellowship, a Whiting Award, and the Harold B. Vurcell Award from the American Academy of Arts and Letters. Currently she is traveling around the circumpolar north to write a book about the effects of climate change on indigenous Arctic peoples.

Joseph Epstein's most recent books are *Alexis de Tocqueville: Democracy's Guide* and *Friendship: An Exposé*.

Kate Farrell is the author of seven books, including *Sleeping on the Wing: An Anthology of Modern Poetry with Essays on Reading and Writing* (with Kenneth Koch) and *Art and Wonder: An Illustrated Anthology of Visionary Poetry*.

Natalie Goldberg is the author of ten books, including *Writing Down the Bones* and, most recently, *The Great Failure*. Her next book is *Old Friend from Far Away: How to Write a Memoir*. With filmmaker Mary Feidt, she has recently completed a documentary, *Tangled Up in Bob: Search for Bob Dylan*.

Adam Gopnik is a staff writer for *The New Yorker* and the author, most recently, of *Through the Children's Gate: A Home in New York*.

Mary Gordon is the author of seven books of fiction, among them the novels *Final Payments*, *The Company of Women*, and, most recently, *Pearl*.

Vicki Hearne, who died in 2001, was known for her poetry and prose on the relationship between domestic animals and humans. She was the author of three volumes of poetry, several works of nonfiction, and one novel. A volume of her unpublished poems is forthcoming.

Carol Huang is a magazine writer and formerly a reporter for Reuters. She met Nebiy Mekonnen in November 2004, during her third trip to Africa.

Pico Iyer is the author of several books about trying to find stillness in a fast-moving world, including *The Lady and the Monk*, *The Global Soul*, and a novel, *Abandon*. His next book, *The Open Road*, is a story of his encounters, over thirty years, with the XIVth Dalai Lama.

Michael D. Jackson is Distinguished Visiting Professor in World Religions at Harvard Divinity School and the author of numerous books, including works of anthropology, fiction, and poetry.

Philip Jenkins is Distinguished Professor of History at Pennsylvania State University and the author of many books, including *The New Faces of Christianity: Believing the Bible in the Global South*.

Galway Kinnell's many books of poetry include *Strong Is Your Hold* and *Selected Poems* (National Book Award for poetry, 1983; Pulitzer Prize for poetry, 1983).

Patrick Madden is an assistant professor of English at Brigham Young University and the editor of an anthology of classical essays at http://quotidiana.org. His essays have been published in *Northwest Review, Fourth Genre, River Teeth*, and other journals.

Frederica Mathewes-Green is a columnist for Beliefnet and the author of numerous books, most recently *First Fruits of Prayer*.

Dara Mayers is a writer and editor living in New York City. Her work has been published in the *New York Times, U.S. News and World Report, Glamour,* and other periodicals.

Wilfred M. McClay teaches history and humanities at the University of Tennessee at Chattanooga. He is the author of *Figures in the Carpet: Finding the Human Person in the American Past* and *The Masterless: Self and Society in Modern America*.

Ann McCutchan is the author of *The Muse That Sings: Composers Speak About the Creative Process* and *Marcel Moyse: Voice of the Flute*. She teaches at the University of North Texas and is prose editor of the *American Literary Review*.

George Packer is a staff writer for *The New Yorker* and the author, most recently, of *The Assassins' Gate: American in Iraq,* which won the Overseas Press Club's 2005 Cornelius Ryan Award and the Helen Bernstein Book Award of the New York Public Library. His other works of nonfiction include *Blood of the Liberals* and *The Village of Waiting*. He is also the author of two novels, *Central Square* and *The Half Man*.

Sridhar Pappu covers politics for the Style Section of the *Washington Post.* He has been a media columnist for the *New York Observer* and a correspondent for the *Atlantic Monthly.*

Marilynne Robinson is the author of many books of fiction and nonfiction, most recently *Gilead: A Novel* (Pulitzer Prize for fiction, 2005).

Huston Smith is the Thomas J. Watson Professor of Religion and Distinguished Adjunct Professor of Philosophy, Emeritus, at Syracuse University. He is the author of many books, including *The Soul of Christianity* and *The World's Religions.*

Mark Strand's numerous books of poetry include *Man and Camel, Blizzard of One* (Pulitzer Prize for poetry, 1999), *Dark Harbor,* and *The Continuous Life.* He has served as poet laureate of the United States.

John Updike's books have won the Pulitzer Prize, the National Book Award, and the National Book Critics Circle Award. His volumes include *Due Considerations: Essays and Criticism, Terrorist,* and *Americana and Other Poems.*

Robert Louis Wilken is the William R. Kenan Jr. Professor of the History of Christianity at the University of Virginia and the author of *The Spirit of Early Christian Thought* and other books.

Garry Wills is the author of many books, including *What Paul Meant, What Jesus Meant, The Rosary,* and *Lincoln at Gettysburg: The Words That Remade America* (Pulitzer Prize for general nonfiction, 1993).

Franz Wright is the author of *Earlier Poems, God's Silence, Walking to Martha's Vineyard* (Pulitzer Prize for poetry, 2004), and other books.

Philip Zaleski is the editor of The Best American Spiritual Writing series and the author of many books, most recently *Prayer: A History* (with Carol Zaleski).

Other Notable Spiritual Writing of 2006

LORENZO ALBACETE
"For the Love of God," *New York Times,* February 3

LEORA BATNITSKY
"Jewish Vengeance, Christian Compassion?" *In Character,* Fall
WENDELL BERRY
"The Great Subject," *Hudson Review,* Summer
WALLACE BEST
"Gospel According to . . . ," *Harvard Divinity Bulletin,* Spring

MAURO JAVIER CARDENAS
"Our Baby Christ: Ecuador, 1987," *Antioch Review,* Fall
ROBERT CORDING
"The Art of Devotion," *Image,* Spring

DAVE DENISON
"Balance Due," *New York Times Magazine,* June 11
BRIAN DOYLE
"What Would Jesus Drink?" *Commonweal,* April 7

PAUL FARMER
"If We Fail to Act," *Notre Dame,* Autumn
RACHEL FULTON
"Praying with Anselm at Admont: A Meditation on Practice," *Speculum,* July

ADAM GOPNIK
"Judas Laughed," *The New Yorker,* April 17

PAUL J. GRIFFITHS
"Allah Is My Lord and Yours," *Christian Century*, October 17
ALLEN C. GUELZO
"The Prudence of Abraham Lincoln," *First Things*, January

PETER S. HAWKINS
"Surprise Ending," *Christian Century*, November 14

ROGER LIPSEY
"'How I Pray Is Breathe': Thomas Merton in the Hermitage Years," *Parabola*, Spring
THOMAS LYNCH
"One of a Kind and All the Same," *Portland*, Summer

SUSAN STEWART
"Dante and the Poetry of Meeting," *American Poetry Review*, July/August

ALGIS VALIUNAS
"Spirit in the Abstract," *First Things*, January

MIROSLAV WOLF
"Memory, Salvation, and Perdition," *Harvard Divinity Bulletin*, Winter
WENDY M. WRIGHT
"Seeking Stillness," *Weavings*, January/February

THE BEST AMERICAN SHORT STORIES® 2007. STEPHEN KING, editor, HEIDI PITLOR, series editor. This year's most beloved short fiction anthology is edited by Stephen King, author of sixty books, including *Misery, The Green Mile, Cell,* and *Lisey's Story,* as well as about four hundred short stories, including "The Man in the Black Suit," which won the O. Henry Prize in 1996. The collection features stories by Richard Russo, Alice Munro, William Gay, T. C. Boyle, Ann Beattie, and others.

ISBN-13: 978-0-618-71347-9 • ISBN-10: 0-618-71347-6 $28.00 CL
ISBN-13: 978-0-618-71348-6 • ISBN-10: 0-618-71348-4 $14.00 PA

THE BEST AMERICAN NONREQUIRED READING™ 2007. DAVE EGGERS, editor, introduction by SUFJAN STEVENS. This collection boasts the best in fiction, nonfiction, alternative comics, screenplays, blogs, and "anything else that defies categorization" (*USA Today*). With an introduction by singer-songwriter Sufjan Stevens, this volume features writing from Alison Bechdel, Scott Carrier, Miranda July, Lee Klein, Matthew Klam, and others.

ISBN-13: 978-0-618-90276-7 • ISBN-10: 0-618-90276-7 $28.00 CL
ISBN-13: 978-0-618-90281-1 • ISBN-10: 0-618-90281-3 $14.00 PA

THE BEST AMERICAN COMICS™ 2007. CHRIS WARE, editor, ANNE ELIZABETH MOORE, series editor. The newest addition to the Best American series — "A genuine salute to comics" (*Houston Chronicle*) — returns with a set of both established and up-and-coming contributors. Edited by Chris Ware, author of *Jimmy Corrigan: The Smartest Kid on Earth,* this volume features pieces by Lynda Barry, R. and Aline Crumb, David Heatley, Gilbert Hernandez, Adrian Tomine, Lauren Weinstein, and others.

ISBN-13: 978-0-618-71876-4 • ISBN-10: 0-618-71876-1 $22.00 CL

THE BEST AMERICAN ESSAYS® 2007. DAVID FOSTER WALLACE, editor, ROBERT ATWAN, series editor. Since 1986, *The Best American Essays* has gathered outstanding nonfiction writing, establishing itself as the premier anthology of its kind. Edited by the acclaimed writer David Foster Wallace, this year's collection brings together "witty, diverse" (*San Antonio Express-News*) essays from such contributors as Jo Ann Beard, Malcolm Gladwell, Louis Menand, and Molly Peacock.

ISBN-13: 978-0-618-70926-7 • ISBN-10: 0-618-70926-6 $28.00 CL
ISBN-13: 978-0-618-70927-4 • ISBN-10: 0-618-70927-4 $14.00 PA

THE BEST AMERICAN MYSTERY STORIES™ 2007. CARL HIAASEN, editor, OTTO PENZLER, series editor. This perennially popular anthology is sure to appeal to mystery fans of every variety. The 2007 volume, edited by best-selling novelist Carl Hiaasen, features both mystery veterans and new talents. Contributors include Lawrence Block, James Lee Burke, Louise Erdrich, David Means, and John Sandford.

ISBN-13: 978-0-618-81263-9 • ISBN-10: 0-618-81263-6 $28.00 CL
ISBN-13: 978-0-618-81265-3 • ISBN-10: 0-618-81265-2 $14.00 PA

THE B·E·S·T AMERICAN SERIES®

THE BEST AMERICAN SPORTS WRITING™ 2007. DAVID MARANISS, editor, GLENN STOUT, series editor. "An ongoing centerpiece for all sports collections" (*Booklist*), this series stands in high regard for its extraordinary sports writing and topnotch editors. This year David Maraniss, author of the critically acclaimed biography *Clemente*, brings together pieces by, among others, Michael Lewis, Ian Frazier, Bill Buford, Daniel Coyle, and Mimi Swartz.

ISBN-13: 978-0-618-75115-0 • ISBN-10: 0-618-75115-7 $28.00 CL
ISBN-13: 978-0-618-75116-7 • ISBN-10: 0-618-75116-5 $14.00 PA

THE BEST AMERICAN TRAVEL WRITING™ 2007. SUSAN ORLEAN, editor, JASON WILSON, series editor. Edited by Susan Orlean, staff writer for *The New Yorker* and author of *The Orchid Thief,* this year's collection, like its predecessors, is "a perfect mix of exotic locale and elegant prose" (*Publishers Weekly*) and includes pieces by Elizabeth Gilbert, Ann Patchett, David Halberstam, Peter Hessler, and others.

ISBN-13: 978-0-618-58217-4 • ISBN-10: 0-618-58217-7 $28.00 CL
ISBN-13: 978-0-618-58218-1 • ISBN-10: 0-618-58218-5 $14.00 PA

THE BEST AMERICAN SCIENCE AND NATURE WRITING™ 2007. RICHARD PRESTON, editor, TIM FOLGER, series editor. This year's collection of the finest science and nature writing is edited by Richard Preston, a leading science writer and author of *The Hot Zone* and *The Wild Trees.* The 2007 edition features a mix of new voices and prize-winning writers, including James Gleick, Neil deGrasse Tyson, John Horgan, William Langewiesche, Heather Pringle, and others.

ISBN-13: 978-0-618-72224-2 • ISBN-10: 0-618-72224-6 $28.00 CL
ISBN-13: 978-0-618-72231-0 • ISBN-10: 0-618-72231-9 $14.00 PA

THE BEST AMERICAN SPIRITUAL WRITING™ 2007. PHILIP ZALESKI, editor, introduction by HARVEY COX. Featuring an introduction by Harvey Cox, author of the groundbreaking *Secular City,* this year's edition of this "excellent annual" (*America*) contains selections that gracefully probe the role of faith in modern life. Contributors include Robert Bly, Adam Gopnik, George Packer, Marilynne Robinson, John Updike, and others.

ISBN-13: 978-0-618-83333-7 • ISBN-10: 0-618-83333-1 $28.00 CL
ISBN-13: 978-0-618-83346-7 • ISBN-10: 0-618-83346-3 $14.00 PA

HOUGHTON MIFFLIN COMPANY www.houghtonmifflinbooks.com